Homer's
Odyssey

Homer's
Odyssey

John H. Finley, Jr.

HARVARD UNIVERSITY PRESS
CAMBRIDGE, MASSACHUSETTS
LONDON, ENGLAND

Publication of this book has been aided by a grant
from the Loeb Classical Library Foundation.

Library of Congress Cataloging in Publication Data

Finley, John Huston, Jr., 1904–
    Homer's Odyssey.
    Includes bibliographical references and index.
    1. Homerus.   Odyssea.   I. Title.
PZ4167.F5   883'.01   78-9308
ISBN 0-674-40614-1

Preface

The detail with which these pages retrace the story of the *Odyssey* attests once more to its spell. It is the timeless poem of the journey of middle life, of the enforced privilege of the instruction, and of the harbor that may await. But there is another reason for following the story in detail, to try to enter the poet's mind. Post-Socratic ages have mountingly assumed conceptual schemes behind human narratives. Philosophy, theology, history, political and social structures and much else have given backgrounds against which characters live their inner lives. Chief writers, needless to say, partly subsume these mental settings in the thoughts and acts of their characters. But people's uniquely felt experience is uppermost; their lone consciousness has appeared the basic human fact. Homer did not share this assumption. His preconceptual age and tradition gave his characters the double role at once of living their lives and showing the nature of the world. The two spheres intermingle; immortal agents and settings surround and help define the characters. The outspread brilliance lures and ennobles but does not finally include the mortals.

The poetic tradition that descends in Hesiod, of the so-called succession myths of the generations of the world-establishing gods, was familiar in some form to Homer. Phoenix in the *Iliad,* before trying to persuade Achilles by the heroic tale of Meleager, describes the spirit Madness, *Ate,* and the Prayers, daughters of Zeus. Achilles in his supreme onset fights the river Scamander and is joined by the fire-god Hephaestus. Odysseus on his journeys meets elemental figures. Hesiod gives his structural divinities human feelings, and Homer blends the agents of experience with the heroes' response. To follow Homer is to enter a world in which characters are at once themselves and more than themselves, diagnostic figures in a scheme of earthly reality. The history of the Greek mind, which over centuries moved from life seen through persons to life seen through ideas and which at its best joined the two means, is foreshadowed in him, but preconceptually, directly.

Many consequences for the nature of the Homeric poems follow, two of which may be mentioned here. First, the characters' double function of living their own lives and describing mortals' position on earth makes them change as their positions change. Their responses accompany rather than dominate their circumstances. The guiding themes of the poems give the chief characters a final unity but only after the many turns that the nature of things imposes. Second, because the themes of the poems are traditional, the poet inherited for his characters motifs and attitudes which he bent to his own ends but did not reject, with further resulting complication. The Delphic and Socratic precept "know thyself" would one day commend a mental consistency that to Homer emerged only in a hero's final self-understanding. The spare purity of Sophocles' dramatic structures and the lucid antitheses of his characters' stated positions show an intellectuality that Homer lacked. Sophocles still saw reality in the legendary figures, but ideas rise beneath them, almost but not quite breaking the human surface. With Euripides, ideas surround and enter into the characters, and a new subjectivity begins.

Detail is fundamental to the Homeric poems, which nevertheless pursue single themes. Their unity is part of their mysterious greatness. That unity in turn draws from more than the chief characters' ultimate self-recognition, rather from their simultaneous understanding of their mortal stance toward the world-revealing gods. The two steps become one. To follow the *Odyssey* is to wander not only with the hero's travels but with the many attitudes that he, his wife, his son, and even minor characters exhibit, yet to reach a clarifying goal. That goal at once describes them and yields a possible understanding of humans' positions on earth.

Contents

Homer's
Odyssey

1. *Penelope*

The hero of the *Odyssey* joins his end with his beginnings. He regains Ithaca after the dangers of Troy and the near-obliteration of his travels. In spirit the poem at once follows and precedes the *Iliad*. Achilles and Hector both conceived themselves by their secure thoughts of home but failed to recover it in peaceful later years. Achilles' immense fighting powers do not make him the full hero of the *Iliad;* he becomes such by consciously choosing his death at Troy. He had imagined his future open, but on withdrawing from the war after his quarrel with Agamemnon and thereby letting Patroclus die without him, he accepts his prophesied early death by returning to battle. In killing Hector he portends the fall of Troy and in his mercy to Priam asserts a humanity beyond war. His greatness did not come as he foresaw; it was his brief maturity's bleak demand, and his response begot his glory. His, and only to less degree Hector's, was the incompleteness, yet the completeness of brilliant years cut short. Odysseus wins another kind of fame but at as unforeseen a price. The bond between the two parts of the *Odyssey*, the travels and the homecoming, is his lone self, not his self as Trojan victor. On his farthest, most reducing journey to the Underworld, he sees both his start and end of life.

The ghostly prophet Teiresias tells him what he must do to reach home and win a bright old age and gentle death; his dead mother Anticleia declares his birth. The shades of his former companions at Troy convey the evanescence of the great victory. Though he will live longer than they, he too beholds his mortal lot, himself. On reaching Ithaca as a beggar, he regains Penelope by the test of the bow that she sets for her necessary remarriage. Their son Telemachus' maturity compels her to the long-postponed step, which to her harbors memories of Odysseus. Twenty years ago he would string and shoot the great bow, but he had not taken it to Troy. To her it still conveys him. As the meetings in the Underworld declare his birth and death, the bow declares his marriage. Beneath the wise Odysseus and as precondition of his fame, is Odysseus the son, husband, and father, the mortal Ithacan. Like the *Iliad,* the *Odyssey* traces a fame got from loneness.

Because Penelope's decision for the test of the bow makes possible Odysseus' homecoming, she is a key to the unity of the poem. It starts with her and her son, and they remain the natural starting-place. Each of the three main characters dominates a part of the *Odyssey,* and each makes a journey, son and father outward journeys on sea and land, Penelope an inner journey from the sad fixity of her twenty-year isolation. It is not in the epic manner to explain connections; on the contrary, its detail can obscure. That is notably true of the so-called Telemacheia, the first four Books describing Telemachus' plight in Ithaca and travels abroad. In the opening divine council that determines Odysseus' return, Athene states her plan for Telemachus: "I shall send him to Sparta and sandy Pylos to inquire of his father's homecoming, if he may perhaps hear, and that good fame among men may possess him" (1.93–95). In Ithaca he sits dejectedly apart from the boisterous suitors when the goddess enters as Mentes, a purported former friend of his father from overseas. Her encouragement, his new confidence, his journeys to famous survivors of Troy, and Menelaus' account of having heard from the sea-god Proteus that Odysseus was alive but held on Calypso's island, all may seem ends in themselves as description of the youth's maturing. By fit performance among eminent people he in fact begins to show himself his father's son, and the disorder in Ithaca grows more evident in the example of heroic manners and memories abroad. But these and other purposes are secondary. The reason why the narrative must start with his maturing is that only his new independence will bring Penelope to the question that she could evade until then, the bitter question of her remarriage.

Her decision becomes the more urgent because Telemachus' independence prompts the suitors to plot to intercept and kill him on his way home. Only her choice of a new husband, she must believe, will save not merely her son's property but his life. This is the start. When, after the account of Odysseus' wanderings, the hero appears in Ithaca as an unknown beggar, he initially has no scheme for killing the 108 suitors but only Athene's first help in his transformation as beggar and her promise of future help when it will be needed. That help becomes Penelope's decision to face remarriage. In Book 17, at the start of the crucial day that ends in Book 19 with her still unknowing conversation with the beggar by firelight, signs and prophecies declare that Odysseus is already in Ithaca or soon will be. But both her actions and what is said of her make clear that, though she has always intensely welcomed such reports, she does not let herself believe them. Yet such are these assurances and such especially is her new anxiety for Telemachus, that by desperate instinct she sets the test of the bow for the morrow, the first day of the new month, the archer-god Apollo's day. Duty to her son and crowding prophecies that she neither accepts nor wholly rejects create in her the painful agitation from which the decision rises. But her instinctual choice of the bow gives Odysseus a means of victory that he had not seen until then. In sum, the order of the poem is a causal order. Telemachus' independence inspires Penelope to a choice that uniquely offers Odysseus his success. Athene acts in all three events, which at the same time issue from the three human agents and reveal their natures. The interweaving makes of the poem a half-divine comedy.

Penelope's part in these events is at once the most necessary and the most mysterious. In Book 24 as climax to the Second Nekyia, the second scene in the Underworld, the ghost of Agamemnon asks the dead suitor Amphimedon how so great a company died and, on learning, exclaims at Odysseus' fortune in his wife: well did she remember her wedded husband; therefore the fame of her excellence will never fade, but immortals will create for men on earth a fair song of prudent Penelope (24.192–202). That comes near making our *Odysseia* a *Penelopeia*. The song of her that immortals will inspire contrasts to the lament described just earlier that the Muses sang at Achilles' pyre at Troy (24.60–61). The two songs contain the themes of the *Iliad* and the *Odyssey:* early death far from home, therefore consigned only to the Muses, and life brought home, therefore finally shared. Penelope is the central figure of home; she both kept it in existence and makes it recoverable.

When in Book 2, inspired by Athene-Mentes, Telemachus has convened the Ithacans and protested the suitors' usurping his house and wasting his property, the most violent of them, Antinous, confutes him with the tale of the web. Penelope, he says, declared that she would be disgraced among Achaean women if she should remarry before finishing a shroud for Odysseus' father Laertes, but for three years she unwove by night what she had woven by day, until at the present start of the fourth year she was betrayed by a servant and made to finish (2.89–110). The story is told twice again, by Penelope to the beggar to explain how her last expedient has been taken from her (19.141–158), and in the Second Nekyia by the dead Amphimedon to fix the time of Odysseus' arrival in the house (24.131–187). He naturally but mistakenly assumes collusion between husband and wife in the test of the bow, which he thinks was Odysseus' idea as the web was Penelope's. He adds that she had just washed the finished cloth and displayed it shining like the sun or moon when an evil god brought Odysseus from the swineherd's hut. It has been called characteristic of oral poetry that incidents take on a different emphasis at different singings but are not wholly left out.[1] The coincidence of the finished web with Odysseus' return is a case in point. It marks his timeliness; her weaving had been her protection for three years, but she has just turned defenseless or nearly so. She will prove to have one device left in the trial of the bow which, Amphimedon notwithstanding, is her last desperate gamble. In plan it describes her, as in execution it describes Odysseus.

Antinous adds, "she holds out hope to all and gives each encouragement sending messages, but her mind intends other things" (2.91–92). This same comment on her mind is made by Athene to Odysseus on his arrival at the Bay of Phorkys (13.380–381) and, on the crucial day of signs and prophecies, is repeated by the poet of Penelope's inspired appearance before the suitors to ask marriage-gifts (18.283). Not only the web but hope and encourage-

---

1. A. B. Lord, *The Singer of Tales* 98–123.

ment to the suitors have been her defense. Antinous sees that she has a secret purpose, but such trust as he has in the proffered hope is as mistaken as Amphimedon's notion about the bow; both only imagine that they understand her. Encouragement and messages were her means of keeping some control over the suitors. If she gained nothing final, she lost nothing final and meanwhile, though at loss of property, maintained a kind of order and kept the future open for Telemachus and for herself. Yet it is clear that she has ceased to imagine Odysseus' return with any exactitude. In the firelit scene with the beggar she reminds the nurse Eurycleia that he would now be old—"mortals age fast in hardship" (19.360)—but in dreaming of him later that night sees him as he was when he left for Troy (20.88–89). She keeps that youthful image but, while knowing that it can no longer exist, can seriously credit no other. Delay has been her sole recourse, for Telemachus' sake in any practical sense, and it was this instinct that the device of the shroud, itself looking to a long postponed death, and her enchantment of the suitors for three years let her keep intact.

With Athene-Mentes' encouragement of Telemachus this imperfect, yet half-viable state of affairs collapses for her. According to the story of the web it has already collapsed and her son's independence is a second blow, but the start of the poem does not make this connection, which is simply in the myth. From his point of view his self-assertion is fitting: he is more than twenty years old and his mother has just been shown unable to avert remarriage much longer. Now, if ever, he must in her interest seek conceivable news of his father and in his own interest try to save the remnant of his property. The gods make actual what is already implicit; they assert reality, welcome or unwelcome. Thus Athene-Mentes does not need to tell Telemachus of his plight; he tells her: his mother neither accepts hateful marriage nor can be rid of the suitors (1.249–250). His acting on the knowledge is what the goddess makes real. The theme of the initiation or apprenticeship of the son of a long-absent hero has been traced in Jugoslav oral poetry: his initial state of sorrow and neglect among the grown warriors, hard words, the quest that is set before him, guidance by a mentor, recognition as his father's son, his meeting a girl but, interestingly, his failure in fact to retrieve his father, who returns by his own efforts.[2] In the repertory of themes, he seems fixed in youth, never

2. David E. Bynum, "Themes of the Young Hero in Serbocroatian Oral Epic Tradition."

his father's achieved replacement. In the *Odyssey* Telemachus' god-prompted emergence fittingly first looks to his mother. The first sight of her is as she stands by a pillar with a veil before her face and a servant on either side bidding the singer Phemius stop his song of the heroes' bitter return from Troy under Athene's anger. She is a figure of ceaseless sorrow, and it is this unchanging state that he interrupts. Other heroes also, he says, died at Troy; let her return to her weaving; talk will be men's business (1.346–359). He less gently repeats Hector's rebuke to Andromache about war as men's business (*Il.*6.492–493), and near the climax, just before the shooting, will thus refer to the bow (21.352–353). This seems his first act of authority. She is of course astonished but returns to her upper room to lament Odysseus among her women until Athene casts sleep on her lids.

Her repeated sleep—before the recognition she sleeps six times and dreams three times—has been thought a mark of interpolaters,[3] but sleep and dreams, like the iteration of her weaving, describe her state. She is not seen again until, in secret from her and from the suitors, Telemachus has reached Pylos and then Sparta, when his absence is suddenly grasped and the plot is laid to inter-

3. This assumption that repeated accounts of Penelope's tears and sleep show imitative expansion (P. Von der Mühll, "Odyssee" 704) may illustrate in small a once-dominant method. Adolf Kirchhoff (*Die Homerische Odyssee*, Zweiter Teil, Excursus a, 571) expounds it of two like passages—at Eumaeus' hut and at the palace, 16.284–296, 19.4–13—in which Odysseus bids Telemachus take the arms from the walls. One of the passages, he thinks, must be original, the other imitated; the problem is to identify the prior, which will be the more necessary. Again—in this case from Eduard Schwartz, *Die Odyssee* 100—Penelope twice says, to the suitors at 18.251–256 and to the beggar at 19.124–129, that her beauty faded when Odysseus left. Schwartz thinks the lines fitting in her first words to the beggar; therefore judges their previous use and the episode of her soliciting marriage-gifts, of which they are part, imitative and added. Possibilities for such speculation are boundless. The two divine councils of Books 1 and 5, huge Cyclopes and Laestrygonians, captivating Circe and Calypso, the hero's testing of his wife and of his father, are only a few of the near-repetitions that could raise the question which is prior. From Kirchhoff, through Wilamowitz (who made two such schemes), to Schwartz, Von der Mühll, Theiler, Merkelbach, and others, the additive designs changed radically. Gifted scholars, needless to say, made many acute judgments, which however are hard to disentangle from their arguments in favor of layers. But the fact remains that repetition is Homeric. Repeated passages never have the same effect because contexts change. The fact (further discussed below, pp. 75–76) is assumed in this book, but with apology for virtual neglect of well-known writings.

cept his return. When the herald Medon comes to tell her of the plot, she at first will hardly let him talk. Like Achilles in *Iliad* 16 (7–19) on Patroclus' return from the Achaean chiefs, she is so full of past troubles as not to see the trouble impending. She is devastated by the news; sits on the floor lamenting; speaks of Telemachus as a boy and clearly thinks of him as such, though Athene-Mentes had told him that he was a boy no longer and he himself had so claimed to the suitors. She is at last somewhat comforted by Eurycleia's confession to have been sworn to silence and by the old woman's faith that the gods will not let the line of Arcesius perish (4.716–757). She prays to Athene and without food or drink ponders her son's death or safety—such thoughts as a huntsmen-encircled lion would ponder—then sleeps her second sleep and in dream is addressed by Athene in the guise of her sister, wife of Eumelus of Pherae. How can her sister bid her not weep, Penelope asks (4.810–823), when she has first lost her noble husband, foremost in varied merits among the Danaans, and has now lost her young son, a child, still ignorant of labors and councils? But the dream repeats assurance: Pallas Athene accompanies him, she for whose protection many pray; for she can give it. Penelope then asks the dream about Odysseus: is he alive and does he still see the sun, or dead and in Hades' house? But without answer the dream turns away along the door-bolt into the wind (4.838–839). Her state of mind is evident. Telemachus is vivid in her thought, her more pressing concern because she thinks him young and incapable. But Odysseus has become almost legendary, her title to fame as her former husband, a man of every merit, of wide glory throughout Hellas and middle Argos (4.814–816), but as object of inquiry second to her son. He has become to her almost his description, which will not at all fit the beggar and suitor-killer whom she will soon see. A dream can say nothing tangible of such an image.

In Book 17 with Telemachus' safe return to Ithaca and the beggar's appearance at the palace, two severe forces beat on Penelope: the new urgency of her remarriage and hopeful signs of Odysseus' return. These signs are five in number. First, Telemachus confidently (he has just met his father at the swineherd's hut) and somewhat officiously (in the prophet Theoclymenus he has a guest to attend to) tells his tearful mother nothing about his journey but bids her vow hecatombs if Zeus will bring to pass acts of vengeance (17.46–51). Though the curt command conveys hope and she does as he says, his greater interest in Theoclymenus than in herself offends her. It is still early in the day when they next meet but she threatens to go to bed again if he will not tell her what he has learned abroad about his father. Then—second sign—he repeats the assurance that Menelaus heard from Proteus that Odysseus was alive but held on Calypso's island (17.140–146). Third, Theoclymenus at once goes much further, swearing by Zeus the god of hospitality and by Odysseus' hearth that the hero sitting or walking is already in Ithaca surveying the suitors' godless acts (17.152–161). The beggar's approach to town, entrance into the palace, begging at the tables, and maltreatment by Antinous follow, which last event prompts Penelope's question to Eumaeus about him and —fourth sign—the latter's account of how the beggar talked like a bard and claimed to be a Cretan, of the family of Minos and a guest-friend of Odysseus whom he had just heard about in Thesprotia preparing to return with riches (17.513–527). When she wishes that that might be so, Telemachus—fifth sign—propitiously sneezes and she laughs aloud (17.541–542).

The collision of these signs with Telemachus' mounting danger (Medon has reported a second council of the suitors to discuss killing him) explains the intense oscillation of feeling that, in Book 18, produces the first of her two drastic and enigmatic acts; the other will be her decision for the test of the bow. It should be added that she thinks that Telemachus wants her to remarry. Their relationship is uneasy, he resenting her tears and protectiveness, she his lack of consideration and effort to act mature. He in fact has not said in her presence that he wants her to remarry and after his recognition of his father obviously has no such thoughts, but in Sparta Athene roused him to go home by the particularly young and unworthy dream that his mother planned to marry the richest suitor Eurymachus and, in the way of wives, would impoverish the house to benefit her new husband (15.10–23). The theme of tension between mother and son continues more operative with her than with him. But though on the surface resentful of him, she is profoundly moved by his interest and especially for his safety. The poet's concern not for explained motives but for actions is evident now. She gives an aimless laugh—with that after Telemachus' sneeze, her second laugh in the poem (18.163). The odd adjective "aimless" recurs only in *Iliad* 2 (269) in Thersites' glance after

Odysseus has struck him. It here suggests somewhat helpless surprise, but whether the surprise is to the servant Eurynome or to herself in what she is about to say is unclear, perhaps to both. She has the impulse to appear before the suitors in order to flutter their hearts and to seem more admirable than before to her husband and son (18.161–162). The poet, not she, knows the beggar to be her husband, but he has been roughly treated and she takes the disorder in the house as an offense to herself also. The show of decorum that she has kept for three years is frayed. More superficially, she surprises Eurynome by proposing to appear before men whom by her own admission she detests. Hence the inexplicable character of her laugh, explicable only as prompted by Athene.

Eurynome advises that, if such be her wish, she had best wash and anoint herself. The servant expects her to announce her choice of husband from among the suitors. "Your son is now of age," she says, "whom you have most besought the gods to see bearded" (18.170–176). But when the queen refuses on the ground that her beauty faded when Odysseus left, Athene again casts sleep on her eyelids. "She slept leaning back, and all her joints were loosed. Then the divine of goddesses gave her immortal gifts in order that the Achaeans might marvel at her. With beauty first she washed her fair face, with ambrosial beauty wherewith the Cytherean anoints herself when she joins the Graces' lovely dance. She made her taller and fuller to behold, whiter she made her than sawn ivory. Having done so the divine of goddesses left, and white-armed servants entered with chatter, and sweet sleep left her. She passed her hands over her face and said, 'In my wretched sorrow soft sleep swathed me. Would only that chaste Artemis might send so soft a death now, at once, that weeping no more in heart I might not waste my life away desiring my husband's manifold merit, since he was supreme of Achaeans'" (18.189–205). Her gesture of passing her hands over her face shares with her aimless laugh the surprise of the inspired moment.

The goddess is working in her—which is not to say that she herself is not acting. She knows that she must act for Telemachus' sake, but the day's signs further agitate her. She is voyaging from her fixed past almost as did Odysseus from Calypso's island. Her sudden laughs and consciousness of her beauty are almost girl-like. Yet in another mood she wishes that she were dead; in still another, she flies out at Telemachus. She has cut her moorings, yet—

in her final self-command—not quite. Here a point about Homeric method is worth repeating. The beggar told Eumaeus and will this evening tell her that Odysseus will return "as one moon sets and another rises" (14.161–162, 19.306–307): namely, on the first day of the month which, as several passages make clear, will be tomorrow. Everything converges toward the bowman-god's day, and the queen acts as if she had already heard the beggar's prophecy, though, like her son's expectation that she will remarry, it has yet to be said in her presence. As in the movement whereby Telemachus' new independence follows on the failure of her stratagem of the shroud, the poet follows a sequence postulated by the myth without fully explaining it. For three years her defense has in fact lain less in the web than in her beauty, which is now her sole recourse. This passage is its revelation. The watching beggar rejoices to see her bewitchment of the men, but, as Athene told him at the Bay of Phorkys and as Antinous said, "her mind intended other things" (18.283). What is in her mind is, in one mood, desire to test the exceptional recent prophecies but, in another mood, sheer inability for Telemachus' sake to postpone marriage much longer. Her beauty is in either event her remaining weapon. Her gesture of passing her hands over her face, like the surprise of her laugh, expresses a spiritedness and pride of self that have survived the long years. Her resilience matches her husband's.

Her beauty, her covert purpose, her agitation, Athene's prompting, expectation that she will announce her choice, in her own mind the connection of her beauty with Odysseus, and her mingled concern and resentment toward Telemachus all complexly work in the scene. As before, she stands veiled beside a pillar with a servant at either side; the suitors limbs are loosed; they melt with desire and all pray to lie with her. But she first addresses Telemachus rather than them, and although she had told Eurynome that she wished to warn him against the suitors' company, she in fact says nothing of the sort but criticizes his failure to protect the stranger in the house. He looks mature, she says, but does not act so (18.215–225). He protests his helplessness against the many suitors; besides, he goes on, the beggar came off well against the local bully Irus; would that the suitors' heads might droop as does Irus' now. The conversation has been excised as interrupting her appearance before the suitors and, if kept, has been thought secret from them, but her beauty evidently exerts the greater spell as against her express dislike.[4] The politic but treacherous Euryma-chus in any case observes that, if all Achaeans could see her, still more would be present. The mood of expectation is strong.

She replies: "Eurymachus, truly the immortals destroyed my merit, beauty, and form when the Argives took ship for Ilium and among them went my husband Odysseus. If returning he might tend my life, my fame would be greater and fairer. As it is, I sor-row, so many evils has a god roused against me. When he was about to embark leaving his fatherland, he took my right hand at the wrist and said, 'Lady, the well-greaved Achaeans I do not think will all return happily from Troy unscathed. They say that the Tro-jans are warriors, spearsmen, drawers of arrows, and mounters of quick-footed horses, who would fastest have decided the great ar-gument of equal war. Therefore I do not know whether a god will restore me or I shall be taken in Troyland. Let all things here be your concern. Be mindful of my father and mother in the house, as now or yet more, I being absent. Then when you see our son bearded, marry whom you wish forsaking your house.' So he spoke, and all is now coming to pass. A night will come when hated marriage will meet me, wretched that I am, from whom Zeus has taken joy" (18.251–273). She ends by rebuking the suit-ors' slackness, saying that others who woo noble ladies bring bride-gifts but they despoil her house. Antinous grants her point, and as in the *Iliad* (7.436–441) the vast Greek wall rises in a day when it is needed, splendid gifts at once appear for her though most suitors live on other islands. The beggar smiles to see her ex-tracting gifts when her mind has other intentions. As for herself, she has committed herself to remarriage, but with a slight delay. She has been faithful to Odysseus' old command that she remarry when Telemachus will have grown. His maturity is what Eury-nome hailed as happy fortune; she expected her to name her future husband but Penelope does not do so. Her delay is her retrenched but still existent defense after the failure of her stratagem of the shroud. Her thin hope is in the prophecies, but nothing is yet said of the test of the bow, which occurs to her only on that evening by reason of the beggar's still firmer prophecy and his stories that vi-vidly evoke Odysseus. As Athene roused Telemachus, so the god-

4. The scene is well interpreted in this sense by Siegfried Besslich, *Schweigen-Verschweigen-Übergehen* 138–143.

dess inspires this final effort, which at the same time describes the queen's tenacity.

Before the supreme scene in the firelight, it will be well to go back. In the Underworld Odysseus' mother Anticleia spoke of Penelope's unappeased sorrow and Teiresias described the suitors (11.117–118, 181–183); on his landing Athene repeated both points with, as noted, "her mind intends other things" (13.381). But before his entrance as beggar two new points are made that prove of first importance. First, he will return unknown to test his wife together with all the household. The first statement of the theme again shows the divine and human interworking. Athene gives as reason for her attachment to him the fact that any other man returning from long absence would rush home to see children and wife, but not he, who would first test his wife (13.330–336). Testing is thus already in his mind, yet it is just this plan that the goddess sets forth as reason for his disguise and for which he heartily thanks her; he might otherwise, he thinks, have died like Agamemnon. Admittedly the theme is wider as she presents it, being a device for revenge also, yet the goddess makes real only what is in his mind. Thus at the start of Book 19, in dismissing Telemachus just before the firelit conversation, he says that he will rouse Penelope in order that in sorrow she may tell all things (19.44–46). His rousing of her emotions will be his means of test. As was evident in her appearance before the suitors, she has already moved from the semilethargy of her habitual sorrow but is now to move still further.

The second point, though passingly mentioned early in the poem, emerges most clearly in the conversation at the swineherd's hut. The queen, Eumaeus says, used to receive him and send him home with some welcome gift but has not done so since the suitors came. Yet she receives false and mercenary strangers who get gifts from her and make her weep by tales of having seen Odysseus but whom she does not believe (14.122–130). Eumaeus shares her feelings since an Aetolian came to the hut claiming to have seen Odysseus in Crete repairing his ships and about to return; since then he believes no one (14.378–387). The point is important because it is this distrust that the beggar, the teller of lies like to truth, must dispel in Penelope. One way by which he carries conviction is his refusal of luxuries; he will not accept her offer of a warm bed, nor of being washed by young servants. In his effort to stand clear of venality he suddenly goes too far: no servant, he says, shall wash his feet unless it be some old woman of sage mind who had endured in her heart as much as he (19.336–348). But that statement invites Eurycleia, who recognizes him by the scar. As impetuosity had made him wait to see the Cyclops and oppose Scylla, he has now thought only of convincing. He has not, as critics allege, foreseen Eurycleia;[5] on the contrary, has failed to foresee the danger of her recognizing him. Divisionists have had him precisely inviting recognition, therefore have had the poet aware of a tradition whereby husband and wife become united before the test of the bow. But no sign of such a version exists in the poem. Rather, Odysseus as tester only too successfully overcomes his wife's suspicion of venal taletellers. Indeed he does not convince her that Odysseus is surely in Ithaca or about to be, yet carries sufficient conviction that in one mood she is willing to trust the test of the bow, though in another mood she simply resigns herself to remarriage. Most important, the idea of the bow is evoked to her by the painfully present memory of Odysseus that the beggar's stories awaken.

That morning after Telemachus' sneeze she had had Eumaeus summon the beggar, but he—prudently, as she herself agreed (17.586–588)—postponed the conversation until the evening when they might be alone. The swineherd's earlier statement makes clear that others who came with tales of Odysseus did not show such restraint; his praise of the beggar also enhances him, and the queen's excited mood heightens her expectation. In the actuality the beggar, interesting before, becomes more impressive to her at each stage, by two means chiefly: his superficially false but tonally true stories of Odysseus and by a theme that suffuses the poem, the contrast between confident youth and thinned age. Sense of age nearly undoes him when his refusal of a soft bed and of being washed by young maid-servants (the scene began with scorn of him by one such) unexpectedly brings Eurycleia's recognition, from which Athene turns the queen's gaze. But with that exception his effect is consciously sought, and the already agitated Penelope is still more deeply roused. But one of the marvels of the scene, as of the later scene of recognition, is her final control even under intense strain. As the theme of the *Iliad,* which presumably

5. So, among others, Wilamowitz, *Homerische Untersuchungen* 55, and Eduard Schwartz, *Die Odyssee* 109.

once extolled a fast, invincible killer, verges in Homer's treatment toward the inward heroism of lone people willing to face death, so Penelope's decision and Odysseus' desire for home draw finally from silent states of mind. For all the poet's objectivity of manner and tradition, his great moments show secret exigencies of character. Her unexplained final decision for the test of the bow surprises Odysseus, who suddenly sees his means of victory.[6] But in her the decision emerges, in one sense, with the mystery of her previous sleep; it is surrounded by her accounts of sleep and dreams and

6. As the scholiast says (Dindorf II 725.15), dead Amphimedon's statement in the Second Nekyia, 24.167–169, that Odysseus craftily had Penelope set the test of the bow, is his own inference. All that Amphimedon knew was that Odysseus appeared. The poem keeps showing people's wrong ideas: Penelope's that Telemachus was still a child, 4.818, then that he wished her to remarry, 19.532–534, Antinous' idea that she was enticing the suitors, 2.90–92, Eurymachus' that the omen at the Ithacan assembly meant nothing, 2.181–182, Alcinous' that the stranger might be a god, 7.199–206, Eumaeus' that the beggar would tell Penelope simply another false tale, 14.131, the suitors' that Theoclymenus was raving, 20.358–362.

But on the gratuitous assumption that some earlier version had Odysseus and Penelope jointly plan the test of the bow, the actual version shows the poet's mind the more clearly. He traces his characters' exigencies by what they do. The brilliant Lydia Allione is the queen's best interpreter. "Dolore e speranza non appaiono in lotta nell' anima della donna, non cercano soverchiarsi l'un l'altra," she writes (*Telemaco e Penelope* 78) of Penelope's decision in Book 18 to face remarriage. That is: the queen's quandary as between the day's good signs and her suddenly pressing need for Telemachus' sake to name a husband dictates her actions. "In verità, i personaggi dell' *Odissea* non si trovano mai in preda a simili conflitti interiori. La valutazione, piu o meno esatto, di una determinato situazione, valutazione da cui strettamento dipendono sentimenti ed emozioni, avviene sempre mediante un rapido e sicuro ragionamento. Rapida e sicura è quindi la decisione di agire in un determinato modo." Decisions are Penelope's mirror.

The point has a further consequence. In the following firelit scene of Book 19, she does not, as moderns can imagine, subconsciously recognize her husband in the beggar. His stories heighten her sense that Odysseus will have aged, though later that night she dreams of him as still young, 19.353–360, 20.88–90. Her response to the beggar chiefly heightens her sense of the morrow. As Lydia Allione goes on to say (p. 93), her decision for the test of the bow "consiste nell' aver intuito l'avvicianarsi dell' giorno decisivo." By his exact prediction of Odysseus' return at the new month, the beggar has brought her to her inspired plan. The tantalizing power of the myth may suggest subconscious recognition, but Homer does not note it. (Like a mother silencing quarrelsome boys, Sophocles' Jocasta tells Oedipus and Creon to go indoors, *O.T.*634–637, but ignorantly and by the myth.) Like Amphimedon but from deeper sources, Penelope simply decides.

carries their tone. In another sense, it is forcibly chosen; she consciously resists belief that what she wants can happen. One other point is important. In *Iliad* 9, 10, the start of 23, and 24 night carries a tone of inwardness: in the first and last two of those Books the inwardness of lone emotion, in *Iliad* 10 the frenetic desperateness of the disturbed chiefs. As poetic setting, this tone is the opposite of daylit frontality, and to the poet it evidently evokes the mystery of the inner self for which neither his tradition nor his characters have full language. Dreams are the intensification of night, and it is from their mood that Penelope finally draws her choice.

The scene starts with her rebuke to the young and pretty Melantho, antithesis of Eurycleia, for insulting the beggar and with a demonstration of her own kindness. In the running contrast between youth and age she, though beautiful, is on the side of age. The beggar replies with an extraordinary comparison of her to a just king under whom earth blooms, flocks teem, the sea abounds, and the people flourishes (19.107–114). It echoes Teiresias' prophecy to Odysseus in the Underworld that, on return from final travels and labors, he would achieve death at home in shining old age among a flourishing people (11.134–137). The two passages are at the heart of the optimism of the poem, but husband and wife have still to reach that harbor. She repeats the story of the web, concluding, "I cannot now escape marriage nor any longer find another device" (19.157–158). He retells a version of his tale to Eumaeus of himself as a once rich and admired, now traveled and battered Cretan. He claims twenty years ago to have entertained Troy-bound Odysseus (it is here that the poet notes his ability to tell lies resembling truth, 19.203) and though she weeps like snow on the mountains when Eurus melts it, she does not believe him before asking what Odysseus wore. Eumaeus had described her impressionability and her scepticism, and her husband shares both traits; he hides his tears making his eyes like horn or iron. At moments one smiles at, rather than with Odysseus, but it is hard to know whether the poet, for all his obvious liking for him (a subject to be pursued later) shares amusement at his cleverness. Excess fits characters of some dimension. So the beggar now claims to have trouble remembering what Odysseus wore, the clothes that she herself had made, but in fact describes them (19.221–248), also the appearance of Eurybates, his herald in the *Iliad*. The poet's view of his cleverness may show in its now, as did once his extreme curiosity about the Cyclops, nearly undoing him in the scene with Eurycleia. Suddenly aware of danger, he moves into the shadow, and Athene distracts Penelope from seeing the old woman's emotion or hearing the clatter as she lets his leg fall into the basin. Yet Penelope had said that, wherever he might be, Odysseus would be old now, and the nurse replied that she had never seen a man in form, voice, and legs so like Odysseus—which, the beggar quickly rejoined, others too had noticed (19.380–385). Time and age penetrate the scene, the more from the long, far-off account of his youthful boar-hunt on Parnassus with his grandfather and uncles when he got the scar. In offering him bed and bath, Penelope explains her kindness by calling life brief and a reputation for hardness detestable. The cruel man, she says, is cursed in life and scorned in death, but "of one who is himself blameless and knows blameless acts, guests carry the broad fame to all people, and many call him good" (19.332–334). Her kindness, here in the context of age and time, belongs among her complex traits.

The language of night and dreams mounts in the roughly two-hundred lines surrounding her mysterious decision for the test of the bow. After winning credibility by describing Odysseus' clothes, the beggar repeats in full detail the prophecy of the king's return that he had made to Eumaeus and that the latter had more briefly told to the queen: "in this self-same light-passing Odysseus will reach here as one moon wastes and the next rises" (19.306–307). The obscure word "light-passing" my have sounded oracular even to the poet, but its import to the queen is clear: the beggar says that Odysseus will come tomorrow. Trusting rather him than the prophecy, she says: "Stranger, I myself shall still ask a small question. A season of glad rest will be his whom sweet sleep touches, even though he grieve. But fate has given me quite measureless woe, in that my joy by day is weeping and lament as I look to my and my women's tasks in the house, but when night has come and rest holds all men, I lie in bed and thick about my thronging heart sharp cares rouse me lamenting. As when Pandareus' daughter, the nightingale, creature of the green, sings her fair song as spring newly rises, abiding among the trees' thick leaves, and with frequent change pours out her many-toned voice, mourning for her son Itylus whom with bronze she once in folly killed, son of king Zethus, so in me too my heart diversely turns this way and that, whether I am to stay with my son and guard all things firmly, my wealth, my servants, and my high-roofed great house, revering my husband's bed and the people's talk, or now shall accompany the best of the Achaeans who woos me in the hall offering measureless bride-gifts. While my son was childish and heedless, he would not permit my leaving my husband's house and marrying. But now that he is grown and has reached youth's estate, he prays that I may quit the house, chafing for his property which the Achaeans devour" (19.509–534).

Like all else surrounding Penelope, the nightingale's voice describes her sad beauty, but its alternating phrases chiefly speak her dilemma whether to stay or to leave. From the time of her husband's parting command she had foreseen the bitter possibility, but it has become pressing and immediate. From common nights she goes on to one night and dream. "Come, interpret me and hear this dream. Twenty geese in the house eat wheat from water and I am warmed watching them. But come from a mountain, a great curve-clawed eagle broke all their necks and killed them. They lay strewn together in the hall, but he lifted aloft into the bright air. Then I wept and lamented in the dream, and fair-tressed Achaean ladies were gathered by me mourning because the eagle killed my geese. But he returning sat on the jutting roof and with human voice checked me and said, 'Take heart, daughter of far-famed Icarius. It is not a dream but waking good that will come to pass for you. The geese are the suitors, and I was then an eagle but now have returned your husband who to all the suitors will bring unlovely death.' So he spoke, then honey-sweet sleep released me. I looked and saw the geese still feeding on the wheat at the basin where they were before" (19.535–553).

Like the nightingale's alternating song, the dream has two sides. But the song spoke a more mental dilemma, to stay or to leave. The dream is more violent: the imperious eagle destroys her small daily comfort. She clearly would not have dreamed it if she had lacked hope of Odysseus, but the tone of violence is strong. If false, the dream imports the ruin of her long-kept balance. The beggar assures her that the eagle's words are true; Odysseus himself as eagle spoke them. But she goes on in the famous lines on the gates of dreams. "Stranger, dreams are intractable and confused of utterance, nor are all things in any way fulfilled for mortals. Double are the gates of bodiless dreams. The one gates are made of horn, the others of ivory. Such dreams as fare through the sawn ivory deceive, bearing speech unfulfilled. Such as go abroad through the carved horns, these bring to pass truth when a mortal sees them. But I do not believe that this dire dream came to me thence. Truly it would be welcome to me and to my son. I will tell you another thing and do you ponder it in your heart. That ill-named day is coming which will take me from Odysseus' house. For now I will set a contest, the axes that he would plant in a line in the hall like oaken props, twelve in all, and standing far off would shoot an arrow through them. I will now set the suitors this feat. Who most lightly stretches the bow in his hands and shoots through all twelve axes, him I will accompany, parted from this house, the house of my marriage, beautiful, full of substance, which I think I shall remember even in dream" (19.560–581).

In a brief speech the beggar accedes. Though the poet does not dwell on the fact—surely an accepted, central part of the story—he has seen his means of victory. It is late, she concludes, and the gods set times for all things; she must return to bed to her ceaseless lament. She does so, and toward dawn Odysseus hears her outcry to Artemis: might she resemble Pandareus' daughters who received beauty and discretion from Hera, stature from Artemis, and beautiful works from Athene but whom, when Aphrodite approached Olympus to ask for their wedding, Zeus gave to storm-winds to snatch away. So might the Olympians snatch her from sight or Artemis strike her with her shafts, "that I might go even beneath bitter earth with Odysseus before my gaze and not at all delight the mind of a lesser man . . . A god has sent me bad dreams. In this very night one like to him slept by me again, as he was when he went with the army. Then my heart was glad, because I said it was not a dream but at last waking truth" (20.80–90).

The crucial words are, of the dream of the eagle, "dire dream" and, of that of Odysseus as young man sleeping with her, "bad dreams." They are obviously not bad as signifying what she does not want. "But for me," she says of true dreams from the gates of horn, "I think the dread dream did not come to me thence. Truly it would be welcome to me and to my son." Rather she resents vision of a happiness that her judgment will not let her believe. The dreams are dire because they evoke the impossible—yet the not quite impossible, since she would otherwise have named a husband at once and not have postponed the choice until the propitious morrow, nor as test would have chosen Odysseus' old feat. Yet she seems not to acknowledge the hope even to herself; in spite of interpretations that make her subconsciously see Odysseus in the beggar, her sole hope is in the recent signs, now intensified by the beggar's testing her by rousing her emotions. Later, on waking after the slaughter, she thinks that only a god might have accomplished it (23.63). Her firm rejection of unreal hope shows in her sorrow for the dead geese, who do not signify the suitors, in the sense of a flattering companionship, but the state of half-orderliness that had been her comfort.[7] She liked to watch them taking grain from the water-trough; even after the eagle told who he was, she waked to see in them familiar reality. Antinous had seen in her messages and kind words the sign of her secret purpose; the state of semicalm that she had maintained until lately had been her satisfaction. The vision of dead geese heaped on the floor signified the

7. George Devereux ("Penelope's Character," 382) writes of Penelope's dreamed tears. "Obviously the chaste Penelope could be expected to rejoice over the destruction of the geese—specifically stated to represent the suitors—by the eagle, which is specifically equated with Odysseus; therefore her tears cannot represent an inversion of affect, but must represent real affect. In fact, it is hard to understand how literary critics could have overlooked the fact that a rapidly aging woman, denied for some twenty years the pleasures of sex and the company and support of a husband, would inevitably be unconsciously flattered by the attentions of young and highly eligible suitors, which is precisely what the chief suitor accuses her of in public. We therefore believe that Penelope cried over the geese for the simple reason that unconsciously she enjoyed being courted though the suitors were probably more interested in inheriting Odysseus' kingdom by marrying his widow, than in her fading charms."

This subtle but un-Homeric explanation carries a step further the modern notion, discussed above in note 6, that Penelope subconsciously recognized Odysseus in the beggar. As was quoted there, Lydia Allione is clearly right in discovering Penelope's mind quite simply in her decisions. On waking from her dream, she saw the geese still familiarly feeding at the basin. The unchanged reality of the house had been her twenty-years comfort. Carnage befits warriors, not ladies; she sleeps during the suitor-slaying. Her dream of dead geese heaped on the floor is to her shockingly violent. Moreover, she has continually resisted easy hope. The eagle's assurance that he is Odysseus is no more surely credible to her than were the day's five good signs. Yet it enhances them, therefore produces her decision for the test of the bow. The lines 19.552–553, on her waking to see the familiar geese, are the key. In the poem the suitors never give her pleasure; her vision of dead geese does not convey that kind of loss. It rather conveys her shudder, which in her plan for the test of the bow becomes also her courage, before tomorrow's drastic change.

end of that compromise. It could mean, as the eagle said, brightest gain but could also mean harsh loss. In the dream, fair-tressed Achaean women join her as she laments the geese; they perform a formal dirge of the sort that, Nestor said, would not have been granted Aegisthus had Menelaus killed him (3.258–261). The geese express what a well-bred lady wants as least denominator, not as happiness but as minimal order. It is part of the characterization of Penelope that she has achieved and made do with that much. But the state of change that the poem traces for all the chief figures means for her something much worse or—what she will not seriously credit—much better. Her reluctance to believe is the measure of her long resistance.

The future solution is now clear, achieved by the independent but interlocking actions of son, wife, and husband. They have been characteristic actions, yet characteristic of fortunes and natures at their most fulfilled—which emergence into full and right reality is the god-given element. It took a god's intervention to rouse father and son from the lethargy of their long inaction, and the beauty-giving sleep that Athene shed on Penelope similarly attended her will for final risk. She too discovers gain by acceptance of danger, by a greater acceptance to the degree that her sign-nourished hope is more intangible; her sole tangible motive is duty to Telemachus. Yet that duty would have been met simply by the choice of an important suitor; her choosing the test of the bow contains unexpressed expectation of Odysseus' return, as the beggar prophesied, on the first day of the month, tomorrow. When, prompted by Athene, she in the morning gets the bow from the storechamber, she sets it on her lap and weeps; how he got it from Iphitus son of Eurytus is related; he did not take the bow to Troy but carried it at home (21.11–41); to her it signifies him in his house. With the earlier theme of the web and the later theme of the bed, that of the bow is surely deeply lodged in the legend; as test of the true bridegroom or husband, it has wide mythic parallels.[8] But to Penelope now it carries, together with the possibility of a new husband and the chimerical hope that he be Odysseus' equal, the thin hope that the true owner and user of the bow might appear. In this sense her choice of it describes her long desire as, in legitimacy and mastery, its stringing and use describe Odysseus. Its identification with her

8. Gabriel Germain, *Genèse de l'Odyssée* 11–129.

memory of him, now that in a way different from past storytellers the beggar has recalled him to her and has further prophesied his return tomorrow, makes possible the actual return. The inward tone of night and dreams from which her choice issues shows her secret instinct fashioning its own reality.

The scene of recognition after the suitors' death comes nearest to explaining her because it ends with her self-explanation. When at Odysseus' command Eurycleia in intense excitement, her legs trembling, wakes her with the glad news of his return and victory, she first leaps up and kisses the old woman but then disbelieves. Told about the sign of the scar, she asserts that gods can trick even the clever; even so consents to join her son "in order to see the dead suitors and whoever it was who killed them" (23.84). She takes her seat near the fire at the wall away from Odysseus, who leans against a pillar looking down and waiting to see whether she will address him. She is long silent, at one time recognizing him as she glances, then not knowing him in his foul clothes. Telemachus, true to old irritations, bitterly upbraids her; no other wife, he says, would stand off from a husband thus returned in the twentieth year; her heart is harder than stone (23.97–103). Among Odysseus' many gifts is a sudden way of speaking gently, as he now does by bidding the youth let his mother test him in her own way. Then, practical again, he notes the continuing danger from the dead suitors' kinsmen. He has neither injured his son nor forgotten the situation, yet has shown his wife in still greater degree the consideration that he once showed Calypso and Nausicaa.

Penelope had said nothing overt about his foul clothes, but—as before in her assumption that Telemachus wanted her to remarry or that she might expect something on Apollo's day—the unexpressed fact is assumed. Odysseus is bathed, meanwhile having ordered music in the house in order that passersby might assume the queen's marriage in preparation; their talk had been one element in her delay. Her silence is not vacant. As she had habitually questioned strangers but without credence and as last evening had heard the beggar's assurance that Odysseus would return at the new month, yet to that and to his interpretation of the dream of the eagle and geese had sceptically replied with the test of the bow, so now she has her own plan. For all his usual fullness the poet can produce basic acts abruptly. When Odysseus returns transformed by Athene as by a goldsmith shedding gold on silver—his fourth such enhanced resumption of his old form and resembling hers when she sought the wedding-gifts—and at last criticizes her silence, she disclaims unfeelingness. Well she knows, she asserts, how he looked when he left, that fixed image that returned to her in dream. Yet, she says trying him, let Eurycleia prepare his old bed outside her room—at which he for the first time bridles, describing the great bed that on their marriage he himself had made from an olive tree, leaving as one leg a timber still rooted in earth and adorning the whole with gold, silver, and ivory (23.177–204). With the themes of the web and of the bow, this is the third fundamental theme of the story of return, describing reunion as the others describe waiting and test.

Convinced at last, she flies to him, and her most revealing speech follows. "Do not be angry with me, Odysseus, since in other ways you are wise beyond men. The gods gave us sorrow, who begrudged that remaining together we should take joy of our youth and reach age's threshold. And now do not take this ill and hold it against me that at first sight of you I did not greet you with love. The heart in my breast always shuddered lest someone might arrive and deceive me with his tales. Many plan evil gains. Even Argive Helen sprung from Zeus would not have joined in love and the bed with a man from another country, had she known that the warring sons of the Achaeans were to bring her home to her own land. A god surely stirred her to commit the unseemly act. Until then she did not set that folly in her heart, the calamitous folly whence sorrow first touched us also. But now, since you have uttered the clear tokens of our bed, which no other mortal saw but only you and I and one lone servant Actoris whom my father gave me on coming here and who kept the door of our strong chamber, you persuade my heart, obdurate though it is" (23.209–230).

A recent writer contrasts Athene's heeded warning to Achilles in *Iliad* 1 not to kill Agamemnon to Hermes' similar but unheeded warning to Aegisthus in *Odyssey* 1.[9] The interventions show breaking against men's passions the longer sense of consequences that the gods possess and embody. Admittedly the gods also understand a farther reality than any human mind can grasp; the equal ruin of Achilles' and Hector's hopes at Troy and the disasters that

9. Albin Lesky, "Göttliche und menschliche Motivation" 33.

overcame others there and on their return make that clear. But the divine view of reality is not wholly out of reach; the *Odyssey* is the obverse of the *Iliad* in showing what measure of attainability is possible. This kind of difference distinguishes Penelope from Helen in the present passage. She hesitates to criticize Helen, who did not yield to Paris until a god impelled her. Penelope's reply to Eurycleia's proof of the scar (23.81–82) shows her on guard even against the gods. She intensely realizes the danger from her own impulses, therefore speaks with sympathy for Helen, yet with tacit expectation or at least with stubborn hope that she herself might act otherwise. Like her husband, she emerges by tenacity and scepticism—which is to say that, like Achilles in *Iliad* 1 but more persistently and unlike Aegisthus in *Odyssey* 1, both husband and wife are guided by a vivid sense of consequences, she even more steadily than he. The modesty of her self-contrast to Helen is testimony to her sense of her own strong feelings and to what she thinks her brilliant fortune in her great husband. She will not assert that she is better than Helen, on the contrary apologizes for the obduracy that she has thought necessary. The contrast attests to the fact that the mysterious gods do finally grant a measure of intelligibility, though seemingly less on the big scale of states and armies than on the small scale of persons and households.

It is on the smaller scale at least that Penelope has succeeded with Athene's help in steering her dangerous course. The fact leads to ghostly Agamemnon's final praise of her in the Second Nekyia. As regards the unity of the poem, her obdurate fear of deception by others and even more of self-deception is crucial. In the one day comprised by Books 17 through 19 it meets two classes of events: those deriving from Telemachus' maturity and her husband's old command, if he should not return, to remarry when their son will be grown, but also the events concerned with signs, prophecies, and dreams, all strengthened by the beggar's credibility and converging on the next day, the first of the new month. Athene's hand in her, at the time, inexplicable impulse to dazzle the suitors and ask for wedding-gifts guides and accompanies her first response: namely, to break the lethargy of her waiting and to face tomorrow's outcome of either pain or joy. Nothing was yet said of the test of the bow, which apparently rises to her mind from vivid memories of Odysseus roused by the beggar's stories. His assurance that the voice at the end of the dream of the eagle and geese was truly Odysseus' amounts to a sixth sign. She no more expressed belief in it than in the previous five signs; on the contrary, resists both it and them, yet so far believes as to conceive of Odysseus' bow as something that would fit tomorrow. An upshot of disbelief that would equally serve if belief proved justified—what could better show the goddess's working or the magnitude of a scepticism that yet kept place for hope?

2. Characterization and Theme

Before following Odysseus' travels and the further events in Ithaca, it will be useful to pause with the related questions of the method of characterization in the poem and its guiding theme. Neither question is easy, and the resonance of the myth to inward-looking ages adds problems. Who shall catch the myriad overtones of the journey, the return, and what they jointly tell of human possibility? But a few points are clear. To Homer, unlike Dante, the journey and the return belong together. Dante's famous Ulysses of *Inferno* 26 is the endless quester. His unappeased Faustian search has no place for homecoming. Because for Homer the vast world and small Ithaca both claim part of Odysseus' mind, each describes him. Unlike the homestaying suitors, he partly belongs to the world. He is seen in its varied settings, responds to them singly and, in a more important sense, cumulatively, and becomes their pupil. But though he has lived with immortals and seen the dead, none of these holds him. He refuses Calypso's offer of agelessness and immortality for mortal Penelope in Ithaca. The questions of characterization and of theme belong together because, as a character, the hero becomes known by his situations. The adventures make him; he does not in a subjective sense make the adventures.

The overarching theme meanwhile declares that as a mortal he must somehow unite the immense, immensely varied world with his inborn identity. That he does so makes him the jointly enduring and emerging hero that he is.

To start with the mode of characterization, even Penelope, who is seen against a stabler background than is her traveled husband, several times assumes ideas that were not mentioned in her presence: that Telemachus wants her to remarry and, in the scene of gift-soliciting in Book 18, that she will announce her choice of a new husband from among the suitors. "You have what you have prayed the gods for, a son at last bearded," says the servant Eurynome (18.175–176), but it is only later, on telling of Odysseus' parting command, that the queen repeats these words (18.269) by saying that the sad time has come when she must marry and leave the house of her youth and happiness. The intention of the scene is further clouded because other themes intrude: her beauty, Athene's inspiration, her mingled resentment and concern toward Telemachus, and the comment "her mind intended other things" (18.283). She in fact achieves postponement, but that too involves something not yet said: namely, the beggar's assurance, previously given Eumaeus but to be given her only that evening in the firelit conversation (19.306–307), that Odysseus will return on the first day of the new month, tomorrow. To the poet's mind, the story should evidently take certain turns at certain times, and the characters should act accordingly. The story dictates their actions, not their actions the story.

Again, what at first glance seems a quite minor point on second thought shows the method. It concerns the time when Penelope may have had her crucial dream of the geese and eagle. She tells it to the beggar on the early night of the day that began in Book 17 with Telemachus', then the beggar's arrival from the swineherd's hut, the day when hopeful signs and prophecies first agitate her. The suitors have surrounded her for three years, and it might be thought that she could have had the dream on any night then. But her previous dream of her sister showed her quite vague about Odysseus. Telemachus was her pressing concern; at questions about Odysseus, the dream vanished by the door-bolt (4.804–839). Her way of speaking of him conveyed a fixed and famous image; even in her third dream later in the present night he appears as he was when he left for Troy (20.87–90). The mood of night and dream conveys inwardness. The nightingale's changeful song resembled her nightly question whether to stay or leave; the gates whence dreams issue, of deceptive ivory or credible horn, repeat the dilemma. The good signs were what prompted her laughing impulse, misunderstood by Eurynome and mysterious even to herself, to declare to the suitors her decision to remarry and to rebuke their withholding wedding-gifts. That evening the beggar's credibility and, more important, his evoked memories of her husband and confident assertion of his next day's coming issue in her decision for the test of the bow. As is clear when she rejects his interpretation of the dream of the geese and eagle, she still will not let herself believe; in spite of all her wishes, she says, the dire dream came from the ivory gates. Yet she partly believes. The present point is, when could she have had the dream that expresses this anguish between doubt and hope? Evidently not before today. Then in the moment when Athene turned her gaze from the footwashing? But the question is meaningless. The poet clearly bent his full resources, of night and dream especially, to the great scene. He no more thought to fix the dream in time than to fix in space the gifts that, though most suitors lived far off, at once appeared when she invited them. One again sees the story dictating words and emotions, not the reverse.

For one more among many possible examples, Athene-Mentes' initial advice to Telemachus, which has long disturbed critics,[1] shows the same dominance of the scene over what, from the point of view of the characters, might seem subjectively likely. The goddess begins with a recollection of Odysseus as, in her guise of Mentes, she claims to have seen him long ago standing at the door with helmet, shield, and two spears. If he should reappear thus, she says, the suitors would be fast-dead and bitter-wed (1.266). But, though divine, she speaks like Mentes and concludes that whether or not he will return lies on the knees of the gods. Her

1. D. L. Page, *The Homeric Odyssey* 52–64, carries forward old objections. The passage is freshly interpreted by the late Klaus Rüter, *Odysseeinterpretationen* edited by Kjeld Matthiessen, and also by Marion Müller, *Athene als göttliche Helferin in der Odyssee* 32–35, who rightly says that Athene's purpose toward Telemachus is not to inform him what he will accomplish but to set in motion her plan, announced at the initial divine assembly, for Odysseus' return. The goddess partly, though not fundamentally, deceives Telemachus for her own ends and for those of the poem.

advice follows (1.269–305): first, summon the council and with the gods as witness bid the suitors return to their houses. If Penelope wishes to remarry, let her also return to her father's house, who will hold the marriage and give suitable wedding-gifts. The points look to Book 2; neither eventuality will occur, and Penelope will keep the element of inner choice that characterizes her. All that Telemachus will gain is attestation before the gods, a point of importance to his development and in the poem. The goddess goes on: seek news from Nestor and Menelaus; if you learn that Odysseus is dead, build him a tomb and make large offerings, then give your mother in marriage. The former point looks to Book 3 and 4 and especially to Menelaus' report that Proteus saw Odysseus alive. The latter point touches Penelope's future dilemma. She will not surely believe her husband alive and by reason of Telemachus' maturity must face the remarriage that she thinks that he wishes and that Odysseus once commanded. The goddess then concludes: after giving your mother in marriage, take thought how you may kill the suitors, whether by guile or openly, an option that three times later faces Odysseus (11.120, 455, 14.330 = 19.299). It describes his resourcefulness, which his maturing son is to emulate. Consider the fame, Athene says, that Orestes got by killing his father's murderer Aegisthus, whom Zeus censured at the start; you too must be brave that posterity may speak well of you. It is objected that, if his mother will have remarried, he will have no need to kill the suitors, though in the second later council to plot his death, they hope to divide his property, leaving only the house to the successful suitor (16.371–392). He earlier told Mentes of their wish to kill him, and their presence remains ambiguous; they want Penelope but also wealth. In sum, the speech looks to the rest of the poem. It reverts by so-called ring-composition to Mentes' initial vision of Odysseus killing the suitors and to Zeus's approval of Orestes' vengeance. Though Athene is omniscient, her advice neither shows her full knowledge nor—what concerns the question of characterization—is limited by what, from a subjective point of view, a mortal character might resonably say. It looks rather to the myth than, in a narrow sense, to the moment. Telemachus is to act toward situations that the poem will unfold.

This way of seeing human postures as issuing from events rather than events as issuing from sharply defined personal consciousness appears in some similes. Before the dream of her sister, Penelope ponders like a huntsmen-encircled lion her son's possible escape or death on return from abroad (4.791–792). The beggar compares her to a just king under whom nature abounds and the people flourishes (19.109–114). On her final recognition of Odysseus, he is as welcome to her as is land to the few brine-covered survivors of a wreck who reach shore (23.233–238). Odysseus at Scheria weeps at Demodocus' song of the Trojan horse as a woman whom enemy drag into slavery weeps over her dead husband (8.523–530). When earlier between Ogygia and Scheria he has been swimming for two days and nights, the sight of land is as welcome to him as to children is the life of a father long wasted in illness whom the gods finally free (5.394–397). Greeting Telemachus on his safe return and while the still unrecognized Odysseus stands by, Eumaeus weeps over him as a father weeps over an only son returned from a ten-year absence (16.17–19). The common trait of these similes is that age, sex, and state of kinship, usually fundamental to identity, drop out before more universal emotions that in turn relate to the poem. Odysseus as a sorrowing woman is parted from home and marriage; as a son he sees land from the sea; Penelope as a wrecked and brine-covered sailor reaches land; as a just king, she rules a happy land and people; to Eumaeus Telemachus is like a ten-year absent son. Penelope as an encircled lion may be less odd, but in the *Iliad* warriors evoke lions, as does Odysseus thrice in the poem (4.335 = 17.126, 6.130, 22.402 = 23.48). The simile of the octopus has something in common with these (5.432–435). When Odysseus is borne to sea again from below the cliffs of Scheria, skin from his hands stays on the rocks as pebbles cling to the tentacles of an octopus that has been torn from its bed. The tearing is similar, but the pebbles leave whereas the skin stays, nor does the octopus' loss match his gain. In all these cases the poet again seems not to feel elements that to later minds help fix unique experience. What is important to him seems less the character's exact identity than his stance toward governing conditions of life that equally touch men and women, young and old. Such conditions are loss, recovery, parting, return, worry, power to benefit. A person thus touched declares the nature of things more fully than by his lone individuality, as if behind the accidents of age, sex, and circumstance stand common categories of experience in which an individual shares and by sharing becomes illustratively human. An experience does not become real because a person feels it, rather a person becomes real because he undergoes what exists. The emphasis is on the human condition, not on private consciousness of it.

The principle is at work in the portrayal of Odysseus. Many strands, some of which are clearly traditional, are interwoven to reveal the many-sided man, and it will be useful to review the more important of them, for two reasons, to observe the poet's method and to come nearer his weight of emphasis. Different settings evoke different sides of Odysseus, which in turn carry distinct themes and often correspond to his various epithets. A scholiast on the first line discusses the meaning of the epithet *polutropos,* "of many turns," which is absent from the *Iliad* and reappears in the *Odyssey* only in Circe's recognition of the gifted man who resists her drug and whose coming had been foretold her by Hermes (10.330). The scholiast's question is whether the term is pejorative, and he concludes that is is not; it fits, rather, the wise man who understands and can deal with many minds. But, he rightly says, such a man differs from undeflected people like Achilles and Ajax, and W. B. Stanford in his commentary well contrasts the concentrated wrath that speaks in the first line of the *Iliad* to the adaptability first suggested of Odysseus. The four-times repeated "many" of the first four lines of the poem states a connection: Odysseus has many turns, was driven to many wanderings, saw the cities of many men and learned their minds, and endured many sufferings. Part of the poet's theme is thus the vicissitudes that relate to and have fostered the hero's many-sidedness. Yet the adventures are not random like Sinbad's; they reach a goal, which in turn implies unity of character. Thus the present question concerns both variety and unity: the one in the themes surrounding Odysseus, the other in the poet's weight of emphasis.

He can be clever in the sense of deceitful; the trait has to do with words. It seems traditional to the character; a Trojan in the *Iliad,* like Athene at the Bay of Phorkys, calls him "insatiate of wiles" (13.293, *Il.*11.430). In Hesiod's *Works and Days* (788–789) a man born on the propitious sixth day of the month will like "to speak taunts, lies, deceptive words, and privy secrets." Helen tells of Odysseus' entering Troy as a disfigured spy (4.244–258), a role not unlike his in *Iliad* 10. The second line of the poem alludes to the device of the Trojan horse, his chief part in which Menelaus and Demodocus describe (4.265–289, 8.499–520). The theme fits his repeated position as outsider. He laughs to have tricked the Cyclops by calling himself No-one (9.413–414), and as beggar he both tests Eumaeus and on a cold night gets a warm cloak by a story to the effect that, on such a night at Troy, Odysseus sent a man back to camp from an ambush in order that the purported Cretan might inherit his cloak (14.468–506). His disguise as beggar is in the spirit of this deceptiveness, and the great statement of his guile is his first interchange with Athene at the Bay of Phorkys which ends in his transformation as beggar. She appears as a handsome young shepherd, and he tells his first deceptive story of himself as a Cretan, she meanwhile changing into a woman beautiful, tall, and skilled in fine works. "Sharp and cunning would he be who outdid you in all ruses, even if it were a god that met you. Scamp, devious-witted, insatiate of wiles, even in your own land you were not to give up trickery and cunning words, which are dear to you from the ground" (13.291–295). That is their bond, she goes on, because she is the cleverest of gods. She helps him hide the gifts that by her intention the Phaeacians gave him and describes the pains that he must endure without self-revelation on reaching his house. Cunning and secrecy are of the essence of the speech, and both will mark the beggar into which she changes him.

He replies that, though he felt her presence at Scheria as he did at Troy, she had been absent from the many sufferings that befell him "when we boarded the ships and a god scattered the Acheans" (13.317). He is thinking of the storm roused by her anger that carried him into Poseidon's distant world. But the instruction of his wanderings has healed the estrangement, and she speaks as if it had not occurred. To his doubt whether she might still be deceiving him she affectingly replies, "the mind in your breast is ever such. Therefore I cannot desert you in misfortune, because you are controlled and closewitted and mind-keeping" (13.330–332). The tone has changed; he has needed his cleverness to survive and shows it now by impulse not to rush home before testing his wife. It is this impulse that the goddess helps effect by changing his looks to a beggar's; her hand is in the dictates and result of his intelligence. The theme of his shrewdness thus becomes allied with other traits that are revealed and partly begotten by his travels and that show in his attainment of home. His deceiving Penelope by lies that resemble truth creates in her the half-credence that in turn elicits the test of the bow. In her gift-soliciting she shows similar deviousness, yet for the more important purpose of postponement. The theme may seem overdone in his final meeting with Laertes; yet, as before with Penelope, he brings the old man to the tears that are the necessary proof of feeling. As traditional to the character, the theme was inescapable to the poet; he has no impulse to reject it. But, as in the *Iliad* Achilles becomes much more than the traditional destroyer, becomes rather the one figure who clearly sees his own and others' human fate, so Odysseus' cleverness shrinks as a separate theme, to show among the several traits that win him knowledge and survival. Yet as theme it dominates some incidents; it is one strand from which the poet weaves the narrative.

His shrewdness verges, among other traits, to an eye for wealth, which again marks him in the *Iliad*. Greek legend subtly makes social judgments. In *Iliad* 9 (269–299) Achilles spurns Agamemnon's vast offer that Odysseus has carefully itemized. The young hero chiefly speaks from self-fidelity but also as the heir to a fertile kingdom. Wealth means little to him because, as he says (*Il*.9.400), he can have it in Phthia. He exemplifies Aristotle's view that people of high station make fittest tragic heroes, partly because, if they possess what life can give in material ways, their choices more purely reflect the human condition. Odysseus from rocky Ithaca makes his way by ability among the rich and in great enterprises. He has more reason than his associates at Troy to heed what the world can give. His respectful itemizing of the offer of *Iliad* 9 fits not only his clarity of mind but his beginnings, as does his concern during the reconciliation of *Iliad* 19 (172–179) that the offer in fact be paid Achilles. By origin he comes naturally by his appraisiveness.

In the *Odyssey* Athene helps him return with Phaeacian treasure which she then helps him hide. She likewise inspires Penelope to her gift-getting. The goddess is mindful of much else, but wealth fits the royal pair's station, and she gives it due heed. She and Odysseus are of one mind. When at Scheria he is promised still greater gifts if he will postpone departure for a day to finish his entrancing story, he exaggerates by saying that he would gladly stay a year for such a purpose: "I should prefer that and it would be much more advantageous to reach my fatherland with fuller hand. I should be more revered and more welcome to those who beheld me returned Ithacawards" (11.358–361). Yet on the next afternoon while the changeless Phaeacian life of song, wine, and feasting continues, he keeps watching the sun, yearning for its setting as a man who all day has ploughed new ground yearns for supper and whose knees waver as he goes (13.29–35). Desire for wealth and yearning for home both describe Odysseus. The themes are not compared when each arises; only the progress of the poem states which is the more descriptive. Odysseus has lost the loot that he brought from Troy, but it is more than replaced by the Phaeacians' freely given gifts. The substitution reflects his own change from the recent conqueror fresh from Troy to the afflicted yet instructed man who has seen even the dead. The change corresponds to Athene's restored favor. Eumaeus, to be sure, with pride in his old master enumerates to the beggar Odysseus' former wealth: on the mainland, twelve herds of cattle and as many flocks each of sheep, swine, and goats, and further flocks of the last two on the island (14.98–108). But Telemachus at Sparta is amazed at the brilliance of the palace, which he compares to Zeus's dwellings (4.71–75). Though the rich Menelaus makes modest disclaimers, the youth had known nothing of the sort in Ithaca, and he refuses his host's proffered gift of horses because the island would not support them (4.600–608). Yet Odysseus is not least among the Trojan heroes, and wealth is part of what he went to obtain. The gift-giving society of the poems posits wealth of its leaders. It is part of their description and, as such, with Athene's help is accorded both Penelope's beauty and Odysseus' intelligence, which source imparts a certain immateriality.

His Iliadic gift of eloquence also continues. In *Iliad* 2 (265–335) having been roused by Athene to stem the flight to the ships after Agamemnon's misleading dream from Zeus and deceptive speech to the army and having got rough merriment by striking Thersites, he becomes both critical and sympathetic. The army, he says, forgets its oath to Agamemnon, yet understandably; people chafe at a month's absence from home, but they are in the tenth year away. He recalls the portent at Aulis of the snake eating eight chicks and finally the mother bird and Calchas' ensuing prophecy that they would take Troy in the tenth year. He concludes with the words with which Penelope describes her husband's parting command, "all is now coming to pass" (18.271, *Il*.2.330), and the army answers with a great shout that echoes on the ships. The old Trojan Antenor recalls from an early embassy concerning Helen his memory of Odysseus' eloquence (*Il*.3.204–224). On rising to speak he would gaze silently down, as he does in the scene of Penelope's final recognition (23.91, *Il*.3.217), but when his great voice came from his chest and words like snow-flakes in winter, no man could rival him.

His indignity in addressing Nausicaa more than matches his plight after Thersites' mutiny, and the half-smile of the *Odyssey* is nowhere lighter. The brine-covered hero shields his nakedness with a branch; after pondering whether to clasp the fair maiden's knees or from a distance address her with smooth words, he wisely decides to do the latter; then his indignity vanishes in his words (6.149–185). Is she a goddess?—then Artemis. Is she a mortal?—then happy her parents and kindred and happiest her future bride-groom. He never saw a thing so beautiful, unless it was the young palm by Apollo's altar at Delos that he and his men saw on the way to Troy. She is the first human being whom he has met after twenty days at sea from Ogygia; let her give him the wrapper of the clothes that she and her friends have brought to wash, and may the gods grant her in return all that her heart wishes. "Husband and house and happy oneness may they give. For nothing is nobler and better than when two keep house in oneness of mind, man and woman. Much sorrow to their foes and joy to their friends, but they themselves best know." He has shown that he feels her beauty and youth, shown that he was once a man of position, shown especially that he knows how happy people live. His feeling praise of marriage equally fits her youthful thoughts, his desire for home, and the theme of the poem. The slight first amusement at his plight and his skill in extricating himself has yielded to sense of his humanity. His eloquence will indeed effect what he wants but toward a right goal. If the gods sanction some mortal joys and if intelligence can grasp the gods' intentions, it proves of human use, though much of its effort goes simply to keeping a man alive.

In the process of verse-making his epithets, like others, vary by position in the line, grammatical case, and speed of pronunciation (whether the name Odysseus has one or two initial s's). Five epithets concern these traits of guile, wealth-getting, and eloquence: *daiphron* "wise-hearted," *poikilometis* "devious-minded," *polumechanos* "much-devising," *polumetis* "of many thoughts," and the epithet of the first line, *polutropos* "of many turns." They relate to actions as well as words, to his whole power of successful survival. Most important, they suggest his indestructibility, his mounting capacity to have learned the position of place and home not merely toward great public and political events such as took place at Troy but toward the vast unhistorical world of nature. The five epithets vary in tone, *poikilometis* most suggesting guile, *polumechanos* ingenuity, *polumetis* a wider capacity for idea, *polutropos* a many-sided humanity, and *daiphron* wisdom. Each trait is uppermost at one or another moment, but the poet feels no inconsistency when they merge. By the theme of the poem, of the hero's return not merely to wife and house but to a finally flowering Ithaca, the last two epithets come to dominate.

Odysseus' curiosity, though not specified by one of these epithets, reflects the speed of mind that they variously describe. His ardor at once hurts and saves him. Eager as he is for home, he is interested in what he sees. It is as if he would not have learned had his fate not so decreed, yet that as watched over by Athene at Troy he, in spite of her anger after the sack or, more truly, by reason of it, was chosen for the test of further instruction. He meets the test by endurance but also by curiosity, to emerge having seen the divine, enormous world but in that very experience having understood that it finally has no place for him. Only home has that. The travels temper but do not quench his confident vitality. Near the start, curiosity and hope of gain first take him to the Cyclops' cave, then make him stay when his twelve companions want to seize cheeses and leave (9.224–229). His later disasters follow from his boastful revelation of his name (9.528–536, 1.68–75). Dangerous as Circe declares the Sirens to be, he contrives to hear their song and in spite of her warning would have yielded to it (12.39–54, 192–194). The silence of his seven years with Calypso did not wholly change him. Though he approached the Phaeacians with notable reserve, his eagerness as beggar to differentiate himself in Penelope's eyes from venal people who got gifts by false tales of her husband made him reject soft treatment but then, in his eagerness, to add that he would let his feet be washed only by some old woman who had suffered as had he—which nearly undid him by Eurycleia's recognition. Ardent as Penelope likewise is, she emerges the more sceptical. Yet Odysseus' epithets express a mental nature that gains even from dangers and indignities. Pindar compares himself to a cork (Py.2.79–80), and Odysseus shares that unsinkability.

His power of survival leads over to another class of epithets: *po-*

lutlas "much-enduring," *talasiphron* "enduring-hearted," *megaletor* "great-hearted," and *megathumos* "great-spirited." Wandering and suffering are joined in the first lines with many-sidedness, sight of men's cities, and knowledge of minds. Endurance is the precondition of knowledge. At Troy he rebuked Agamemnon's weak thoughts of flight: he is of the breed, he says, that winds the skein of bitter wars until each shall die (*Il*.14.83–87). He contrasts to Menelaus when each is left alone against many Trojans: Menelaus reluctantly draws back; Odysseus ponders the danger, yet the disgrace and knows that he must stay (*Il*.17.91–108, 11.404–408). He is not conceived as a man of blind courage but as thinking, yet persisting. He lacks the titanic emotion that, Hera says (*Il*.20.125–127), will make Achilles invincible for a day and that shows in the ruinous fire of his advance, the fire that wastes the rivers and portends the destruction of the city.

The engulfing sea is Odysseus' peril in the *Odyssey*, and fire becomes benign. Its former tone chiefly returns in Zeus's fiery bolt, with attendant smell of sulphur, that destroys the last ship (12.417); at home after the carnage Odysseus cleans the house with sulphur (22.481–482). But fire is more commonly a mark of habitation and human life. The fragrance of burning cedar spreads from Calypso's hearth; Circe's servants heat water to bathe him; at Ithaca he sits by Penelope in the firelight, and at the final recognition she takes her place by the hearth. This tone of attainment and safety marks the famous simile when, in Scheria after twenty days at sea, he creeps under a pile of fallen olive leaves, "as when a man on a distant farm, one who has few neighbors, hides a brand in the black ashes, saving the seed of fire, that he may not seek it from elsewhere" (5.488–490). Not that in the *Iliad* fire cannot be benign—Andromache was heating a bath for Hector when she heard the wail for his death (*Il*.22.442–446)—but that home is lost. Its attainment asks a persistence different from that in war. In the Underworld his mother Anticleia's first question to him is, "my child, how have you come beneath the nether gloom still alive? These things are hard for the living to gaze on" (11.155–156). Heracles' greeting is similar, "Zeus-born son of Laertes, much-devising Odysseus, poor wretch, you too lead a bitter life, such as I led beneath the sun's rays" (11.617–619). At the storm that wrecks his raft between Ogygia and Scheria, he calls those who died at Troy thrice and four times blessed; they got burial and fame (5.306–

312). That is in the mood of his story to Eumaeus as a Cretan beggar (14.196–359). Troy was definite; it did not, in the story at least, teach such bitter truths as did wandering; on reaching home from Troy, the Cretan after a month confidently and restlessly put off for Egypt. As contrasted to the fire of the *Iliad,* the water of the *Odyssey* imports time and disappointment and chiefly asks endurance.

The stamina expressed in this class of epithets fosters the mental scope expressed in the previous epithets, but one trait of Odysseus seems mixed of both classes, his suspicion of the future. He has learned to doubt that any new event will turn out well. At the Bay of Phorkys his reply to Athene's raillery is guarded; he is still not sure that he is in Ithaca. The protective mist with which she obscures the familiar places fits his ingrained doubt (13.352). The blinded Cyclops had prayed, and Poseidon had heeded and Zeus ratified that if he were to reach home, it should be late and ill (9.528–535), and the long delay followed. Even when waked at Scheria by the amiable cries of Nausicaa and her girls, he first speculates whether he has reached a land of violent, wild, and unjust people (6.120). Earlier just before he clung to the reef from which he is torn like an octopus, he reflects that, if he swims in, waves may dash him against the cliffs but, if he swims out in hope of a better landing, a tempest may catch him or some great sea-creature, many kinds of which Amphitrite rears, may devour him (5.417–422). Antithesis does credit to one who has sailed for seventeen and swum for three days, and the poet's mood, as later in the speech to Nausicaa, seems smiling. So also on his landing when he has prayed the river to abate its flow, has been kindly received, and has kissed the land, worn and brine-crusted though he is, he can still dourly reflect that, if he should sleep near the shore, the cold morning wind could kill him in his weak state but, if he should go inland, he might fall prey to beasts (5.465–473). If in the *Iliad* he thought why he should fight, yet fought nevertheless, this mixed trait of dubitation yet action now marks him more strongly, and with reason. Though the *Odyssey* is much the more optimistic of the poems, its outcome is not won by optimism. On the contrary, the wear of years lies behind both his and the still warier Penelope's success. The trait is at once mental and moral, a stubborn clinging that teaches the cost of hope.

Two further traits accompany his endurance: loyalty and considerateness. The former is stressed in the prologue: "and many pains at sea he suffered in his heart, striving to win his life and his companions' return. Even so he did not save them; they died by their own follies, silly men who ate the cattle of Helius son of Hyperion, and he took from them the day of their return." There is continual lament for lost companions. On waking at Thrinacia to the smell of roasting cattle, he cries to the gods that they have lulled him in a cruel sleep (12.371–373). He grants his companions' folly, yet feels for them in spite of their rebellions. Gentleness of feeling marks him at main moments. Misfortune and perhaps years teach kindness, but the trait marks characters of the *Iliad* and may have seemed to the poet native to him. His gesture of taking Penelope's hand when, on leaving, he told her what she should do in his absence and if he should not return, is gentle (18.258). Her love evidently draws from more than his eminence. In the scene of recognition, her plea that he forgive her obdurate scepticism shows entire faith that he will understand. His mother in the Underworld, to his question how she died, replies that she neither wasted in long illness nor fell to Artemis' mild arrows, "but yearning for you, your thoughts, radiant Odysseus, your gentleness of mind took away my honey-sweet spirit" (11.202–203). Somewhat in the tone of Odysseus' parting from Penelope, Hector deflects Andromache's extreme and immediate anxiety by recalling his duty; he too can envisage his death but in his prayer for Astyanax evokes a brighter hope (*Il*.6.476–493). In the next-to-last speech of the *Iliad* Helen says that Hector rebuked others' criticism of her and himself spoke only gently; she uses of his gentleness the same word that Anticleia uses of Odysseus (*Il*.24.772). Patroclus spoke with like kindness to Briseis (*Il*.19.287–300). In the fight over his body Menelaus cries for loyalty to one who in life was pleasant to all men (*Il*.17.671–672).

Three speeches of the *Odysssey* notably show this feeling. After promising to help him go, Calypso asks in a final plea whether he fully understands the dangers ahead; if so, he might prefer to stay immortally with her; she is not less beautiful than Penelope (5.203–213). In reply he asks her not to be angry; well he knows that Penelope is not her equal. If he must suffer more by waves and war, so be it. The gulf between man and goddess exists and he does not obscure it, but his quietness acknowledges the sorrow of parting. He speaks similarly to Nausicaa. As W. J. Woodhouse once said,[2] the handsome stranger of fairy stories commonly marries the princess, as does Bellerophon in the story of him in the *Iliad* (6.192), and both Nausicaa and her father conceive such thoughts toward Odysseus. But, again, though he knows himself to be who he is and knows his purpose and age, his feeling matches his debt to her. She stands by a pillar when he is about to enter the hall where he will tell his long tale, and bids him remember her when he has reached home because he owes her the price of life. He replies, "Nausicaa, daughter of great-hearted Alcinous, so may Zeus, Hera's loud-crashing husband, bring it to pass that I reach home and see the day of my return. For that I should ever pray to you there as to a goddess. For you gave me life, girl" (8.464–468). Finally, when in the scene of recognition Penelope is not yet wholly sure and Telemachus bitterly criticizes her hesitation, he gently bids him let her find her own means of test, then speaks to him of the danger from the dead suitors' kinsmen. He is kind to both her and him. This awareness of others evokes equally his labors and his intelligence. It relates to his knowledge of minds but, as Penelope's and Anticleia's memories make clear, springs from a more private source. It is the inward counterpart of his long search for home. The poem recounts not only experience of the wide world and capacity to cope with it but quiet of mind as goal. The *Odyssey* is the great poem of onward years. The present passages carry over to Teiresias' prophecy of a bright old age among a happy people. They suggest what will be Odysseus' tone of life then.

Other epithets express either his heroic role and station, "bold," "worthy," "blameless," "Zeus-born," "glorious," "godlike," and "sacker of cities," or his origin, "son of Laertes" and "Ithacan." The latter two epithets are more basic to the story, but the former show in the suitor-slaying, which occupies the same relative position as the slaying of Hector in the *Iliad*. It is similarly the climax but very different. Odysseus starts with something like Achilles' unforgiving wrath. As Hector seeks agreement to return the loser's body only to meet the cold answer that wolves and sheep make no compacts (*Il.*22.260–272), so Odysseus spurns Eurymachus' offer to repay his loss. If you and the others paid me all that you have and yet more, he says as did Achilles on spurning Agamemnon's offer (22.62, *Il.*9.380), I should still kill you because of your out-

---

2. *The Composition of Homer's Odyssey* 63.

rage; you must fight. Athene supports him as she did Achilles. Deaths carry details from the previous dining but also from battles of the *Iliad*. Yet the differences are greater. Athene in *Iliad* 22 was not in the least testing Achilles—she enhances or, better, expresses his irresistible might—but she tests Odysseus for a last time. His anger, unlike Achilles', does not last. He spares the herald Medon and the bard Phemius and forbids Eurycleia to whoop in triumph: "be glad in heart, old woman, and check yourself, do not whoop. It is not holy to exult over dead men" (22.411–412). He sees himself as the exactor of just punishment. The twelve faithless servant girls who are hanged in the court by Telemachus, not by him, are not true counterparts of the twelve Trojans whom Achilles ritually kills at Patroclus' pyre, an act that the poet censures (*Il*.23.175–176). The slaves' and, perhaps, Telemachus' disfiguring of the goatherd Melanthius echoes Antinous' threat to the beggar when he proposed trying the bow (21.299–301).

What has been judged a simple moralism that distinguishes the *Odyssey*, as concerned with right and wrong people, from the *Iliad*, as concerned with fated heroes, may seem confirmed here. Yet though heroic and carrying his epithet "sacker of cities," Odysseus has appeared in other lights and with his other epithets. What in the suitor-slaying appears as justice is rather the proof and manifestation of a god-given order that by long tuition he has come to understand. His double character as both wise man and hero, both reduced and effective man, persists in the climax. Even the fated heroes of the *Iliad* remember home or appear against the lucid sanctities of city and family. The sorrow is that, given human desires and the brevity of life, these securities are perishable. Odysseus' outrage through the latter half of the poem is that this minimum, brief as it is, is disordered and unvalued. He is the hero defending the last human possibility. His epithets "Ithacan" and "son of Laertes" assert that. After all that has gone before, he is not simply vindicating property or common civic order. In having seen the Underworld and renounced Calypso's proffered agelessness and immortality, he alone has fully regained what was lost in the *Iliad*. His anger in the suitor-slaying is not least a mental anger. He understands as tested man but must still act as powerful man. His two sides meet in the scene.

We thus return to the mode of characterization. Story and scene have been seen to outweigh sense of actions as issuing from inwardly conceived feeling. That in turn asserts that the story makes the characters, not the characters the story. In Odysseus' mixed role as hero, wanderer, and returner he at different times shows one or another of his attributes. The fact does not make him less convincingly human. Greek myth, as seen at least by chief poets, fills history with illustrative figures. Though they were thought to have lived and in fact carry relics of past eras, history as such is not their home, rather history become paradigm. From the auditors' point of view and to the poet, the effect is to translate into a half-timeless past emotions and stances that seem generically and presently human but which, thus translated, take on objectivity. The characters become as descriptive of the world as are seas and mountains. The step is not taken that might make of them mere figures of the imagination; rather, they once existed or, in the case of gods, still exist. They show the possibilities of human life; by hearing of them, one knows what is. But as auditors gain touch with guiding reality by tales of great events, so do the characters by living the events. Their fame is that they enact or endure what is necessary to human beings. They become, so to speak, characters in a humane and peopled Euclid, living exemplars of natural conditions: youth/age, male/female, gain/loss, instruction/change, expectation/outcome. The great poet sees farthest into these mortal axioms. As taught by the Muses, he is the inspired geometer of the human state.

The characterization follows from the theme of the poem. The two elements are inseparable. In the height of battle at Troy Hera descends as fast as darts the mind of a man "who having traveled widely over earth thinks in his shrewd mind 'would that I were there or there' and purposes many things" (*Il.*15.80–82). The assumption of the first lines of the *Odyssey* is similar: experience of the wide earth and of men's cities and minds gives knowledge. But given the size of the world and the strength of people's feelings, others' and a man's own, travel is dangerous and wisdom hard to acquire. The tale of Troy has many people, the chief heroes especially, failing to bring home the fruit of their experience. The dire story of Bellerophon is in the spirit of the *Iliad:* after leaving Greece for Lycia, he killed the Chimaera, conquered the Solymi, and did other feats, but in later years became hated of the gods and "roved alone on the Alean plain, eating his heart, shunning the track of men" (*Il.*6.201–202). The example may be extreme, but whether by actual dangers or by the pitfalls of the emotions necessary to meeting them, few achieve sane and serene late years, a dark vision of human possibility. It is at best the brief illumination and resultant self-demand that heroes, Achilles supremely, are shown achieving at Troy, people who rise to heights but do not survive to report what they came to understand. Therefore, as is conveyed in the vision of the Second Nekyia of the Muses singing at Achilles' pyre and as Pindar believed (*Is.*8.65–66), only the Muses report such people's understanding. It is Homer's theme in the *Iliad*. The idea is related to the Aeschylean doctrine of learning by suffering (*Ag.*176–178) if, whether or not the sufferer has time to learn, the poet and audience do so. Though more distantly, it is even related to the Aristotelian doctrine that poetry is more philosophical than history (*Poet.*9,1451b), as explaining the natural configurations of events and showing human probabilities. But if a traveler may reach home with his experience intact, something better is said of life. It can be, if not permanently or wholly, at least partly understood, and the traveler can himself report what he has found. The knowledge is bought at the price of his acceptance of mortal limits. Travel and return are in this sense the subject of the *Odyssey*, a limitedly optimistic contrast to the dark *Iliad*.

So conceived, the poem is less moralistic than has been asserted. According to the gifted Karl Reinhardt, the moral difference between Odysseus' right-minded side in Ithaca and the suitors' flagitious side corresponds to nothing in the *Iliad*.[3] If Paris implicated Troy, Helen too was guilty; gods support both sides, and a sovereign fatality overhangs. To Reinhardt the *Odyssey* suggested rather the moralistic *Thebais*. It reflects a more settled age and society than does the *Iliad* and a poet more concerned with the harmonies and proportions, not the savage disproportions, of the world. Much this view was widely held by excellent German Hellenists,[4] to some of whom the Telemacheia seemed particularly given to the niceties of wealth and manners.[5] But if the central question is not the relation of justice to injustice but of home to distance, the two poems will seem less far apart. Whether for

---

3. *Tradition und Geist* 14–15.

4. In addition to the writers mentioned in Ch. 1, n. 3, and as an eminent example, Felix Jacoby, "Die geistige Physiognomie der Odyssee."

5. Friedrich Focke, *Die Odyssee*, and Wolfgang Schadewaldt, in an essay appended to his *Die Odyssee Übersetzt*.

wealth or reputation or by a code that demands leadership in adventure, a hero cannot tamely stay home. In the so-called shame-society[6] and at a time before the protections of formal law, a man's standing with dependents and rivals turns on his will to demonstrate his power. Nothing will protect him if he fails to do so. But if he leaves home, he moves into a world the width and complexity of which only the gods fully know, yet which as a man of position he expects to master. The task will prove impossible on those assumptions. Great heroes will owe their fame to their self-fidelity in face of the fact. True to themselves, they will have moved out toward command and glory and will die when it becomes evident that safe return was not among the first conditions. On this view, the *Iliad* as much as the *Odyssey* concerns the relationship of home to the world. Both poems turn on the hard paradox that to stay home will, by a man's loss of wealth and reputation, undermine home and obscure its relation to the gods' wide world, yet to venture out will reveal enormity and danger and make return unlikely.

Geography frames the difference between the poems. In Hesiod's *Theogony* (337–370) Oceanus begets the known rivers, including Trojan rivers of the *Iliad*, also the three thousand slender-ankled Oceaninae, nurturing spirits of the waters of home. The distances thus conveyed are wide; in his anger at Agamemnon Achilles speaks of passing shadowy mountains and echoing seas on the way to Troy (*Il.*1.157), and on the return Nestor anxiously ponders the risk of crossing the open sea from above Chios to Cape Geraistus in Euboea (3.173–175). In reaching Phoenicia, Cyprus, Egypt, and Libya, Menelaus saw the limits of the civilized world. Birds, Nestor says, would not cross those seas in a year (3.321–322). By contrast to Oceanus, Pontus in the *Theogony* (233–279) is the god of unknown farther seas. He begets Nereus father of fifty Nereids, Thaumas father of the Harpies and of cyclonic Aello and Ocupete, and Phorkys father of the Graiae and Gorgons, terrible residents of the unknown. The *Iliad* takes place within the known world—within, for Homer, the geography of history—Odysseus' travels take place outside that world in Pontus' untracked domain.

6. M. I. Finley, *The World of Odysseus* 62–64, 103, 129–130. A. W. H. Adkins, *Merit and Responsibility* 30–57, 154–156. E. R. Dodds, *The Greeks and the Irrational* 48–49. The terms "shame culture" and "guilt culture" are carefully discussed by Hugh Lloyd–Jones, *The Justice of Zeus* 23–27.

The reason why he gets there, the storm that blows his twelve ships from Cap Malea to the country of the Lotuseaters, is only indirectly explained but taken for granted. It is the famous storm described in the lost *Nostoi* and later prominent in the *Agamemnon* and *Trojan Women* which, as Phemius sings and Nestor and Menelaus amplify, arose from the gods' anger at the Achaeans' impiety during the sack. The divine will that orderly peace follow war is also assumed. Agamemnon vainly and foolishly, Nestor says (3.130–166), hoped to placate Athene, but Zeus decreed the storm and it was effected by Poseidon. Nestor enumerates those who, like himself, by fast departure got home before it: Diomedes, Neoptolemus, Philoctetes, and Idomeneus, though according to later legend the first two and the last even of these did not long enjoy home. The cost of the war reverberated. But Agamemnon, Menelaus, and Odysseus became the storm's immediate victims. The fact relates to the sea-god's continuing anger against Odysseus. Poseidon has close ties with Pontus; he does not commonly consort with his fellow Olympians. In the *Theogony* (930, 819, 732) he has as consort the Nereid Amphitrite, has further union with Cymopoleia, daughter of the hundred-handed Briareos, a sea-figure, and after the defeat of the Titans imprisoned them in Tartarus at the roots of earth and sea. Poseidon is absent at the start of the *Odyssey*, among the farthest Ethiopians who dividedly inhabit the lands of the sun's rising and setting. By Phorkys' daughter Thoosa, he begot the monstrous Cyclops Polyphemus (1.22–24, 71–73). His enmity to Odysseus, begun in the initial storm which the god joined with Zeus and Athene to cause, mounted with Odysseus' blinding of Polyphemus. It is anger for mortal intrusion into the god's untouched world, and in turning to stone the Phaeacian ship that brought the voyager home, he wishes to prevent further such invasion.

Agamemnon's and Menelaus' implication in the storm is more transparent than that of Odysseus. They caused the carnage which, though in some respects just, loosed devastation and impiety and on any reasonable view of the gods entailed repayment. Aeschylus' sense of the intermixture of right and wrong at Troy is not absent from the epics: Achilles speaks of fighting Trojans who are only defending their wives (*Il.*9.327), and in the *Odyssey* Nestor's and Menelaus' memories are full of pain. Eumaeus wishes that Helen had never been born, and Penelope rues evil Troy (14.68–69,

19.260). Odysseus in the *Iliad* was closest to the commanders. It is characteristic of him that, in Nestor's report to Telemachus, though with the old hero on Tenedos on the drunken and quarrelsome night after the sack and thus, as events worked out, in a position to sail home as safely as Nestor himself, he showed his loyalty by rejoining Agamemnon (3.159–164). This is another instance of the story dictating. Only the instruction of his journey and its result in Athene's restored favor give the explanation. A deeper need launched him: that the most intelligent of the Achaeans who had successfully seen what human history and active affairs could teach was, by his very ability up to that point, marked out for fuller knowledge. That is not to say that some guilt from Troy did not pursue him; his looting of the Cicones and Cyclops and violence to the latter show him at the start the same successful warrior as in the *Iliad*. If to the gods' mind his former powers sufficed, he would have returned triumphant. Athene's absence from him during his earlier travels is in the spirit of Zeus's, her, and Poseidon's anger after the sack. But in the events of the *Odyssey* near the end of his ten years' wandering that first cause has sunk away, to survive only in Athene's wonder at her father's long affliction of him (1.59–62) and in the accounts of the first storm. Zeus puts the blame on Poseidon, on the sea itself, to which the hero first brought his violent habits. Much more important is what he has undergone and seen in a period as long as that which he spent at Troy but in a less fixed and more revelatory world, the world of nature rather than of history.

His return as beggar fits his painfully acquired knowledge of his mortal place in the world. The disguise is partly description. As Helen's and Circe's drugs match and accompany their transporting beauty, the disguise expresses his mind. In both poems the characters' minds appear in the actions to which their motives led. After Achilles' quarrel with Agamemnon in *Iliad* 1 and his vow to withdraw from battle, his inward mood appears only in *Iliad* 9 in his intensely felt refusal of the king's offer to him to return. His achieved self-understanding similarly accompanies his final mercy to Priam. But the *Odyssey* gives one informative variant of this practice: the half-true, half-false stories that Odysseus tells in Ithaca in his disguise as Cretan beggar, especially his longest such story to Eumaeus (14.199–359). He was, he says, a rich Cretan's son by a concubine and, though ill treated by his legitimate brothers after his father's death, excelled in war and leadership and married well. "Yet, I think, to look at me you see only a straw. Immense affliction grips me. Truly Ares and Athene gave me vitality and man-breaking. When I would choose champions for an ambush hatching evil for enemies, my confident heart never looked toward death but, leaping out far first, I would take foemen with a spear or as one fled. Such was I in battle, but work was not congenial to me, nor house-tending which rears glad young. Rather oared ships were ever my delight, and battles and polished spears and arrows, grim things that chill others. But my pleasures were what a god put in my heart; one man has different joys from another." Together with Idomeneus he led the Cretans at Troy, but when a god scattered the returning Achaeans, "for my wretched self counseling Zeus devised evils. A month only I stayed taking pleasure in my children and wedded wife and possessions. Then my heart bade me sail for Egypt after equipping ships, with godlike companions." Like Menelaus and Helen, he at first got riches, then met misadventures complexly resembling those of Odysseus. On betrayal by a false Phoenician, he was similarly wrecked by Zeus's avenging bolt. Cast up in Thesprotia and kindly saved by the Nausicaa-like king's son, he learned, he says, that Odysseus had just been there, about to return with riches but absent at Dodona seeking Zeus's counsel whether to return openly or secretly. Sent on by the Thesprotian king, he was again tricked by sailors, but escaped and thus reached the swineherd's hut. The straw of a man now before Eumaeus was once a confident warrior. Troy had not changed him as did his wandering.

This contrast between bold youth and worn age describes the hero's mind rather than his strength. He girds up his rags before the fight with Irus to reveal great thighs, shoulders, chest, and arms (18.67–69), and at the crisis after the suitors have vainly labored at the bow, he as lightly strings it as a singer replaces a string on a new peg of a lyre. He is the same Odysseus who in the second line of the poem is said to have sacked Troy. Yet as old beggar he contrasts to the suitors, who are repeatedly called young. His famous speech to the mild suitor Amphinomus sets the tone: "Earth rears nothing frailer than a man, of all creatures as many as on earth breathe and fare. He says that he will never later suffer evil, so long as the gods furnish merit and his knees spring. But when the blessed gods bring disasters too, he bears even these against his will with a stubborn heart. Such is the mind of mortal men as the father of gods and men brings on their day. I too on a time was like to be prosperous among men, and heeding my strength and power did many reckless acts, confident of my father and brothers. Therefore let no man ever be wholly lawless but quietly bear the gods' gifts, whatever they give" (18.130–142). Again, as the beggar and Eumaeus two days before sat talking after supper and the latter's three helpers thought of sleep, Eumaeus calls nights at this season endless and talk pleasant. "Let us two in the hut drinking and eating please each other with our bitter pains, recalling them. For afterwards a man takes joy even in sorrows, one who has suffered very much and wandered much" (15.398–401). He in turn tells of his kidnapping as a child and of being sold to Laertes. The story partly matches the beggar's; both appear old men taught by misfortune. The tone of retrospection that marks much of the *Odyssey* is strong in these passages. It implies years, as years imply suffering and suffering knowledge.

It follows that the theme of the *Odyssey* is instruction. Instruction takes time and is wearing, therefore includes the theme of battered age. The sobering character of the experience no doubt has moral implications; the survivor has had reason to learn his stance toward the timeless gods. So much may be granted the view of the *Odyssey* as a moral poem. But the *Iliad* is in this sense not less moral. Everyone learns, Achilles and Hector chiefly, that what the gods give, not what men expect, takes place, and they accommodate their actions to this reality. When Achilles prays Dodonian Zeus for Patroclus' glory and safe return, Zeus grants only half the prayer (*Il.*16.233–250), but at the end, in the fable of the jars of Zeus, the hero expounds just this truth to Priam: the god never gives wholly from the jar of good gifts but dividedly (*Il.*24.525–533). In Hector's splendid final soliloquy when he looks for support but finds none, he sees that his death has long been Zeus's and Apollo's intention (*Il.*22.297–305). Odysseus as survivor has painfully learned a like truth, sense of which sharply distinguishes him from the suitors. But the fact makes the poem no more moral than the other, except as a more optimistic poem in which the mighty storm of suffering at Troy is at last subsiding and the reality behind both storm and calm grows more visible. If comedy and tragedy show the world as viable and unviable to human hopes, the *Odyssey* is the comedy to the *Iliad's* tragedy. A like but dif-

ferently seen reality, of human hopes striking against the gods'
fixed order, animates both. They concern stages of understanding,
the one by young men, the other in later years. That outcomes follow from conscious choice, though not totally since death is a fact
not subject to choice, gives experience a moral character. Men
learn to act in ways that they did not initially expect because these
are in the condition of things. But the upshot of such experience is
mental, an act of seeing. In this sense the *Odyssey* is chiefly a mental, not a moral, poem. It is the history of the one survivor of Troy,
and of the woman who effected his full survival, who traced to a
farther stage the sudden truths shown in the fighting. Odysseus becomes, as it were, a fulfilled Hector in learning the conditions
under which home and family may be kept. If he lacks the flame of
Achilles' young heroism, he attains the humanity of home and
place that Achilles once imagined compatible with heroism
(*Il.*9.360–367, 393–400). The price at which expectations are
bought is at the root of both poems, and awareness of the price is
knowledge of what the gods grant.

Odysseus is thus both the mighty man who fought at Troy and
an old beggarly man. Because the poem chiefly sets forth events,
the two sides never quite merge in his reflective comment. His contrast to the young untraveled suitors makes a main comment: essentially that of his story to Eumaeus, of his own reckless and
confident youth as contrasted to his present straw-like state. To an
insult by the rich suitor Eurymachus he replies by proposing a contest of work in the fields and by stating and partly prophesying
how he would show himself in battle, then concludes: "But you are
insulting and have a hard mind. You no doubt seem great and
powerful because you consort with few and paltry people. If Odysseus should come and reach his fatherland, the door-posts, though
wide, would be narrow for you fleeing abroad by the fore-door"
(18.366–386). Travel in the poems thus appears in two stages,
alike painful. The Trojan expedition, which proved long and dangerous beyond expectation, enlisted the hardy, and Odysseus'
wanderings, wider than those of Menelaus and in regions replete
with the wonder and enormity that surround normal human habitation, framed the fixity of home in still more daunting horizons. It
is of these widths that the suitors have no inkling. Like Odysseus'
instruction, their blindness is mental; they have not lived, traveled,
endured or seen, but snatch at local wealth without sense of its
value in the huge world.

Age in the *Odyssey* thus takes on a quality of metaphor. Odysseus is not physically old, but his mind is old, and his disguise so portrays him. Women and working people, or some of them, seem not to need the instruction necessary to rich and well-born men. For all his retrospectiveness Eumaeus may be slightly younger than Odysseus. Enslaved as a child, he was kindly reared by Laertes and Anticleia with their younger child Ctimene, at whose marriage he was established in his present place and occupation (15.361–370). The cowherd Philoitius, who remembers his former master and is loyal to his son, may be of about the same age (20.199–205). The nurse Eurycleia, who came to the house in Laertes' prime and tended Odysseus as a child (1.429–433, 19.482–490), is in fact old, as is the dog Argus. Penelope and Helen are special cases. Their beauty still enchants, but Helen praises the husband whom she left for ten years (4.263–264) and looks back with wondering interest on the events of her fabled past. In all Penelope's dangers and still harder uncertainty of mind, she never loses either purpose or kindness. Her laughter at Telemachus' sneeze and in her wondrous impulse to appear before the suitors is nearly a girl's. Like her husband, she is her former self but old in mind. A catalogue of the old will include Nestor, Laertes, the seer Haliserthes, and Aegyptius of the first Ithacan assembly who remembers assemblies in Odysseus' time and had a son who accompanied him. It is not surprising and seems correct that pseudo-Longinus, doubtless reflecting some ancient opinion, portrays the *Odyssey* as the poem of Homer's later years (*On the Sublime* 9.11–14). As less a state of years than of mind, age performs in the *Odyssey* something like the metaphorical function that, in the analysis of C. H. Whitman,[7] fire plays in the *Iliad*. As there a god descending like a star enflames battle and Hephaestus accompanies Achilles' supreme onset, so in guiding Telemachus and later Odysseus Athene takes the guise of the sage Mentor. The flame that invests Diomedes' head in his great moment of battle (*Il*.5.1–8) and still more intensely rises above Achilles when he is about to resume war (*Il*.18.203–214) is the emanation of their glowing youth, as age, actual or by suggestion, expresses awareness beyond the confining present. Both fire and age convey higher realities, whether of a god-given brilliance, which of the many hopes entertained at Troy was the one chiefly fulfilled, or of the existence of a finally visible order. Both themes

7. *Homer and the Heroic Tradition* 128–153.

convey, relatively to the two poems, what the gods offer men, hence touch the substance of the poems.

The tone of age and retrospection in the *Odyssey* inheres in the story, but that the poet from many other possibilities chose just this story cannot be without meaning. In addition to his praise of the singers Phemius and Demodocus, he twice compares Odysseus to a singer: in the interlude of the hero's tale to the Phaeacians when the king praises his powers and the joy of hearing him (11.363–376), and in Eumaeus' like praise to Penelope of the beggar's words: "As when one gazes toward a bard who taught by the gods sings to mortals his lovely words, and they ceaselessly yearn to hear him as he sings, so with me in my house that man charmed me" (17.518–521). Does this suggest the poet's identification with Odysseus? The suggestion fits the notion of the poet as himself now older. If so, the themes of the two poems, of the young and the old hero, might give some inkling of the poet's onward mind. Such at least must have been pseudo-Longinus' view. The parallels of Sophocles and Shakespeare, and somewhat more intangibly of Pindar, present themselves. The suitors, though called young, are not young in the sense of Telemachus, Nestor's son Peisistratus, and Nausicaa; they are hardening toward ambitious maturity. The characters of the poem, other than the magical characters, thus divide into three classes: the old in years or experience, those just leaving youth, and those at neither the one stage nor the other.

Set about the old and the young is the marvel of the world. The description of Calypso' island concludes, "Even an immortal coming there would marvel as he saw and feel joy of heart" (5.73–74). Hermes' wonder at Ogygia resembles Telemachus' young delight in his travels and Nausicaa's at the shipwrecked mariner. The beauty of the world evokes youthful joy as counterpart to old experience. The suitors have lost the one and not reached the other. Such an alliance between tested age and fresh youth, with the beauty of the world as intermediary, variously marks the *Philoctetes* and *Oedipus at Colonus* and *The Tempest*. In the Sophoclean plays, the island-bound and injured hero finds bonds with the young son of Achilles that neither feels with the worldly Odysseus, and at the end salutes the island's rough beauty. Oedipus attains at the last a flowering garden, and the love of daughters has sustained him. The young lovers of *The Tempest* are seen through the old Prospero's eyes—they are not at the center as in the early *As You Like It*—and Miranda's "O brave new world, that has such people in't" is a near equivalent to Hermes' marvel at Ogygia. Pindar in late poems sees in the joy of young victors a renewing brightness among the world's disorders (*Is.* 7.40–42, *Py.* 8.88–94). If the *Odyssey* is the older Homer's poem, it would express this alliance between age and youth in the surrounding marvel of the natural world.

Troy and travel thus describe two stages of experience. The speed of the demanded response chiefly distinguishes the poems. The *Iliad* is not tragic in the sense that nothing is affirmed to the greatest heroes. Their greatness in rising to see their lives almost with the gods' eyes even achieves something denied to the timeless gods, an understanding bought by accomplishment and death. That is the price of the heroism that in the poems becomes their endless fame. Fame in turn replaces the beauty of the world that once lured them outward. Achilles at the end loses much of his former joy. In spite of the happy end of the *Odyssey,* the movement is similar. The famous travels show where much of the poet's heart lay—necessarily so, poetry being response to the world. The Iliadic narrative of deeds and loyalties and their refraction in the descriptions and similes thus correspond to the travels. But poetry is not only response to the world but understanding of it, and Homer shares with Achilles and Odysseus the remove from actuality to meaning. The Muses give memory, and the glad end of the *Odyssey* celebrates a wisdom on the other side of former action. The tone of the poem as comedy is in this emergence. Yet the greater beauty of the travels speaks of something lost—if not life itself, which in the Underworld dead Achilles yearns for, yet something once wide and brilliant. In the example of the poems, highest tragedy and comedy do not wholly differ. Each leaves comprehension as summary of living, with mixed gain and loss that differ only in proportion.

The structural parallels between the poems were well summarized by Alfred Heubeck.[8] In both, a sharp break in the expected order of things is righted in a bow-like movement toward final calm, and in a relatively few days of which fewer still are decisive. The two climaxes of Books 22 correspond; divine decisions start and close; the Second Nekyia of *Odyssey* 24 serves the function of review performed by the funeral games of *Iliad* 23. The repeated divine assemblies of *Odyssey* 1 and 5 apply to the poem's

---

8. *Der Odyssee-Dichter und die Ilias.*

double action and disparate geography a device used on a smaller scale in *Iliad* 15 and 24, where in each case two divine messengers are dispatched to effect a decision of Zeus. In *Iliad* 15 (168–245) Iris descends to restrain Poseidon, and Apollo to rouse Hector; in *Iliad* 24 (133–158, 187–199) Thetis goes to prepare Achilles to return Hector's body, and Iris to inspire Priam to seek it. In Homer's linear manner, each of the two first messages is at once carried out, but so quickly that the scenes may return to Zeus before the second messengers leave. The device is a near-approach to simultaneity. But in the *Odyssey*, though it is planned at the first divine council that Hermes shall rouse Odysseus on Ogygia and Athene Telemachus in Ithaca (1.81–95, as at *Il*.24.104–119). Telemachus' resultant doings are traced through six days—in Ithaca, on shipboard, in Pylos, at Pherae, and two days at Sparta—before Hermes leaves for Ogygia on the seventh day. Epic linearity and the fact that the suitors by then plan to intercept and kill Telemachus on his return dictate the second divine council of Book 5. A familiar device has been stretched to fit the double plot and wider scale of the *Odyssey*. The lists of Myrmidons in *Iliad* 16 (171–197) and of the ghostly heroines of *Odyssey* 11 (225–330) are a further instance. The Odyssean list is again more elaborate, but both lists start with mortal women's unions with gods from which heroes are born, then go on to purely mortal heroes. These and other parallels were noted before the recent study of oral themes and methods. Their prominence in the *Odyssey* was thought to mark a sedulous but creative pupil of the great author of the *Iliad*, and a further sign of him was found in what was judged the different social and religious outlooks of the two poems.

Zeus's opening speech in *Odyssey* 1 was taken to show the change.[9] Mortals, he says, unjustly blame the gods for evils that they bring upon themselves by their own follies. They die *huper moron*, "beyond their mortal lot" (1.34)—which is not to say that mortals may be spared death, only that they perversely invite it. This purely human causation seemed different from the union of act and fate that marks deaths in the *Iliad*. The first lines of the poem announce the nexus: Achilles' wrath and the resulting deaths of many mighty heroes fulfill Zeus's plan.[10] The wrath and deaths

9. Werner Jaeger, "Solons Eunomie" 73–74.
10. Albin Lesky, "Göttliche und menschliche Motivation" 23–24.

and the plan constitute a kind of mirror-image, the same action seen from two sides, and the poem keeps showing both sides. Agamemnon's rejection of Chryses and quarrel with Achilles constitute a fault that he later admits, though in self-exoneration he blames his act on divinely sent Madness, *Ate* (*Il*.19.86–136). Achilles likewise curses his anger (*Il*.18.107–111), which causes his fated early death. Examples may be multiplied; both Patroclus and Hector neglect advice that might have saved them, yet they die by Zeus's will. But Odysseus too suffers alike for his confident cleverness in blinding the Cyclops and by his fate, which Athene sees prefigured in his name, "wrath-felt" (1.62). The goddess imputes this anger to Zeus, and it is said at the start that the gods spun his homecoming only after years. His companions and the suitors want gain; neither are heroic. The peculiar union of fatality with human choice that marks death in battle hardly applies to lesser people over long events; nor, it seems, would it have occurred to Homer so to interpret their lives. Like Aegisthus who spurned the divine warning not to woo Clytemnestra and kill returning Agamemnon and like Odysseus' companions who neglect his warning not to kill the Sun's cattle, the suitors are blind to the appeals, prophecies, and omen of the Ithacan assembly of Book 2. All have had time to show what they want, and to declare that their fates were of their own choosing, *huper moron,* seems the only reasonable possibility. Abrupt fatality, seen as partly in character, partly god-given, fits war as longer choice fits peace.

Land and sea in the two poems set the conditions. Achilles' fated brevity of life reflects in only a minor way his fault of wrath, which also reflects Agamemnon's kingly stiffness. As the Nereid's half-divine son, Achilles is no firm inhabitant of the land to which his mortal father nevertheless commits him. His irridescent hopes are incommensurate with the tangible purposes of his associates. After his repulse at the first council, his lone stance by the shore and seaward cry to Thetis state his isolation. Briseis and Patroclus hold for him temporary bonds of love and friendship, and his mercy to Priam acknowledges his further human bond from his father Peleus. But these ties do not long keep him; the brief brilliance that the poem celebrates is far other than he first imagined. No more than his mother does he natively belong on land. Odysseus, by contrast, is certain that he belongs in Ithaca; his earth-rooted bed and the fruit trees of his youth declare him to Penelope and

Laertes. But as Ithaca is an island, so his final understanding of it is got from the sea. Though mortal, he has had to acquire, compulsorily and by gods' tuition, knowledge of the place of home in the vast world. It is this knowledge that distinguishes him from the suitors and will make Ithaca flower. If half-divinity is uneasily placed on earth, mortal wisdom must reach a like, though opposite, awareness: of horizons enlarging limits rather than, for Achilles, of limits hedging horizons. The poems are complementary not only in contrasting early death to late return and war to peace but in the reversed histories of the Nereid's son on land and the home-returner at sea. What may be judged the aristocratic tone of the *Iliad,* its concern with victory and glory, is less aristocratic than heroic: the brief glint of half-divinity on earth. What, conversely, may be thought the quotidian concern of the *Odyssey* with house and possessions is rather the recovery of a mortal place in the farflung world. Each poem has dimensions of the other, and the opposite outcomes describe the attainable best, which is neither an enduring state of godlike brilliance nor a narrowness untouched by gods.

Homer gathers in the brief days of the *Iliad* suggestion of the ten years.[11] The fact makes evident his long absorption with death and loss. In the persons of Achilles and only to a less degree of Hector, these are the outcomes for the best and most gifted. Even those who survive do so at similar cost; in the *Odyssey* Nestor mourns his eldest and best son Antilochus, and Menelaus his brother and companions. As attested by the *Iliad,* loss was Homer's long vision. If the *Odyssey* is his and from his later years, it shows what may be even rarer, not than the *Iliad,* but than a view of life as tragedy: a view, rather, of regained affirmation and of limited but serene attainment. This is in any case the contrast of the poems. The *Odyssey* follows Troy not only in subject but in mood, and the tone of retrospection fits that of age. Teiresias' prophecy to Odysseus in the Underworld, that after finally placating Poseidon he will reach a gentle death from the sea in bright old age among a prospering people, extends beyond the limit of the poem as the fall of Troy extends beyond the *Iliad,* but the homecoming is assured. The poem states the conditions of a homecoming that can exist on the other side of loss.

11. Wolfgang Schadewaldt, *Von Homers Welt und Werk* 155–163. C. H. Whitman, *Homer and the Heroic Tradition* 270.

3. Origins of the Tales of Travel

Interpretation of the famous travels can be as vagrant as they. To heed the hinted origins and latent tone of the stories simultaneously with their onward movement in the poem takes a kind of seamanship. The bright sea-shine of Books 5 through 12 hides the subcurrents.

Odysseus moves from the known and historical, though legendary, world of Troy into an unknown sphere beyond history. That sphere is to be imagined leading its untouched life while human societies struggle. It was noted that in Pontus and his progeny Hesiod lists a class of largely dangerous primal creatures, Gaia's parthenogenic issue, that are distinct from her issue by Ouranus. A still more primal class is listed in the *Theogony* (211–232) in the descendents of Chaos by Erebus and Night: Doom, Fates, Death, Sleep, the tribe of Dreams, down to Age, Strife, and her dire breed. In these lines of descent Bruno Snell saw a triple division of the world into, first, inresident powers such as sleep and death; second, drastic natural forces such as earthquake and hurricane; and, third, potentially orderly powers that Zeus and his lucid offspring came to embody.[1] It is into the second and even the first of these

1. "Die Welt der Götter bei Hesiod."

spheres that Odysseus penetrates and, though the beings that he meets largely differ from those listed by Hesiod, in meeting them he gains experience of something other than human interchange within a known and demarked world. If he ends as the most informed of men, he takes into account not only human affairs but their wider frame. Ithaca becomes for him a point at the center of two concentric circles, the human and the trans-human or the historical and the natural. If, further, his intelligence at Troy marked him for the test of completer knowledge—partly by reason of his intelligence itself but also because, able though he was, he shared guilt for the violence, therefore incurred Athene's initial anger—then his attainment of Ithaca shows what from the divine point of view a man should understand if he is justly to value home or keep it peacefully in late years. The suitors lacked inkling of these horizons, and even Hector, suited to home though his heart was, underestimated the dangers surrounding it. Odysseus' travels make up a necessary half of what a man should come to grasp who in youth conceived himself as belonging in a certain place among certain people.

The first adventure, the unhappy attack on the Cicones, Trojan allies on the Thracian coast mentioned in the Catalogue (*Il*.2.846–847), resembles raids about the Troad during the fighting like those that Achilles recalls to Aeneas in *Iliad* 20 and Andromache to Hector in *Iliad* 6. Though it begins Odysseus' tale at Scheria and sets his tone of misfortune, it preceded the storm that blew the twelve ships from Cape Malea westward. The onward adventures fall into four slightly overlapping classes. First, there are those involving his companions' errors: the outcome of the raid on the Cicones and, progressively, the fleet's near-return to Ithaca from Aeolus' island only to be blown back again when his men opened the bag in which Aeolus had bound all winds but Zephyrus; loss of eleven ships when these were heedlessly moored inside the bay of the Laestrygonians; loss of the last ship when, against Teiresias' and Circe's warnings, his hungry companions on Thrinacia killed and ate Cattle of the Sun. Desire by three men to stay with the Lotuseaters; general dejection when after loss of the eleven ships the remaining ship reached Circe's island; after Eurylochus saw half the crew disappear into her house, his and the others' refusal to accompany Odysseus thither; weak Elpenor's death: are further incidents. Second, some adventures chiefly concern natural wonders and perils: the wandering island whence Aeolus sends the winds, Scylla and Charybdis, the clashing and smoking rocks that they shun by Circe's advice, the fjordlike bay of the Laestrygonians where the paths of day and night are close, the island where the Sun keeps his seven herds, each of fifty immortal cattle, and like flocks of sheep. The preternatural character of the farther realm speaks in these marvels. Third, the Cyclopes and the Phaeacians show societies below and above the known societies of Greece. The Cyclopes neither plant nor plow; the earth and Zeus's rain give them wheat, barley, and grapes; they have neither assemblies nor laws but inhabit caves in the mountains; each rules children and wives, and they are heedless of one another (9.107–115). By contrast, the Phaeacians possess ships, swift as wing or thought, that are endowed with intelligence needing neither steersman nor tiller (8.555–563). An unfading garden surrounds the king's palace; they live with grace and ease; gods sometimes dine with them (7.201–203); they do not easily endure strangers but carry sleeping to his destination whomever they accept. The fourth class of adventures is of inward character; they concern states of mind. The gentle Lotuseaters offer food that brings forgetfulness of home. Circe's magic can change men to animals but also can rejuvenate them, and stay with her brings Hades as next journey. The Sirens sing of all that befell at Troy and of all things that come into existence on the much-nourishing earth. The Underworld gives a more personal knowledge concerning self, family, and former friends, also concerning the origins of great past figures and the acts of excessive figures. Calypso, though suggestive of Circe, is not like her; in the beauty of her flowering island and her promise of agelessness and immortality she offers the iteration of nature. These interior adventures—loss of will, sexuality, universal knowledge, personal knowledge, and the continuity of nature—though inward in tone, follow as factually in the limpid sequence.

He was blown westward and, near the end making toward Scheria whence he will reach home, sails eastward as Calypso had bidden him with the Pleiades, Bootes, the Bear, and Orion to his left (5.271–277). Yet some incidents are in the east. He returns from the Underworld to Circe's isle Aeaea "and to where are early-born Dawn's dwelling and dancing places and the Sun's risings" (12.3–4). In the country of the Laestrygonians the spring Artacia where his men meet the king's daughter (10.108) seems inspired by the like-named spring near Cyzicus which appears in the Argonautic story, and Meuli argued borrowing from those eastward travels.[2] Circe is a sister of king Aeetes and in warning Odysseus of the clashing rocks she mentions the Argo to him (12.61–72). The Underworld is on the other side of the stream of Oceanus from Circe's island, in the mist-covered land of the Cimmerians on which the rising or setting sun never looks (11.4–19). It has been argued that the name Cimmerians replaced that of a western Greek people,[3] but the known Cimmerians adjoin the north-eastern Scythians. The land of the dead is traditionally in the west beyond the setting sun, where Heracles sought the apples of the Hesperides, and Moulinier has Odysseus carried to and from the westward dead by the circling stream of Oceanus.[4] Aeolus' floating and unfixed island may be seen, as by Moulinier, as the point where Odysseus passes beyond ordinary direction, but in sending him homeward Aeolus left Zephyrus outside the bag (10.26). The island was then in the west, which is clearly the main region of the travels. Contradictions, even contamination with the story of the Argo, may not have concerned the poet. After the blinding of the Cyclops and his Zeus-ratified prayer to his father Poseidon for vengeance, Odysseus' full afflictions begin. The story concerns their variety and illustrativeness. They are travels in nature, societies, and the self.

Yet suggestions of geography are important because they bear on the date of the poem. Later generations took the travels as westward. Herodotus (4.177) puts the Lotuseaters on the Libyan coast near Lake Tritonis. Thucydides notes the local claim that Corcyra was Scheria (1.25.4), also Sicilian claims to the Cyclopes and Laes-

2. *Odyssee und Argonautika.*

3. G. L. Huxley ("Odysseus and the Thesprotian Oracle of the Dead" 245–248) sees the name Cimmerians as having displaced Cheimerions, inhabitants of the town Cheimerion on the Thesprotian river Acheron beside which Periander invoked the shade of his wife Melissa (*Herod.* 5.92). Pausanias (1.17.5) thinks the scene and rivers of *Odyssey* 11 inspired by this dark valley. Dodona, which the beggar says that Odysseus visited in order to inquire of his return (14.327; 19.296), is not far beyond. Tradition about these mysterious places might have included the folk and town of the Cheimerions on which the sun never looks. The Cimmerian migration from South Russia into Asia Minor in the early seventh century (*Herod.* 1.15) would have prompted the substitution, and their native north would have been thought equally mist-covered.

4. "Quelques hypotheses relatives a la géographie d'Homère dans l'Odyssée."

trygonians (6.2.1). Theocritus, born in Syracuse, calls the Cyclops "our countryman" (11.7) and in his amorous Polyphemus pursues a theme that the poet Philoxenus invented there in mockery of Dionysius I. To Apollonius (3.312–313, 4.661) and Virgil (*Aen.*7.20) Circei near Cumae was Circe's haunt, and non-Hesiodic lines near the end of the *Theogony* (1011–1016) list Agrius and Latinus as her sons by Odysseus. Polybius (34.2–5) identifies Scylla with the swordfish that were got in the Straits of Messina. Strabo gives part of his first book to arguing that the travels took place within, not outside the western Mediterranean.

Recent yachtsmen and the airman Mauricio Obregón have tried to trace Odysseus' poetic route exactly, with different results. Gilbert Pillot and A. Rousseau-Liessens take him outside the Mediterranean, respectively to the northern Irish and Scottish coasts and up the Adriatic Sea.[5] Both not surprisingly find places suggestive of the travels: a mountainous island with caves, lone islands, a deeply recessed bay, and a current-washed cliff opposite a whirlpool. Pillot adds evidence for early contacts between Mediterranean and northern peoples and for the mild climate of the post-Mycenaean age. The former British naval officer, Ernle Bradford,[6] comes nearer the route imagined in later antiquity. He takes Odysseus to the Lotuseaters on the island Jerba in the western Syrtis, the Cyclopes near Eryx at the western tip of Sicily, the Laestrygonians at Bonifacio in southern Corsica, Circe at Cape Circeo, the Underworld beyond Gibraltar, Scylla and Charybdis on the Italian and Sicilian sides of the Straits of Messina, the Sun's cattle at Taormina, Calypso on Malta, and the Phaeacians on Corfu. He writes in Strabo's spirit.

Obregón[7] starts by taking prudent Odysseus not north to the Cicones on the Thracian coast where the Catalogue has them, but south with the same favorable wind of which Nestor, Menelaus, and Diomedes took advantage. But whereas they risked the open crossing from above Chios to Euboea, he discreetly hugged the shore and avariciously attacked Ismarus, which Obregón connects with Smyrna-Izmir. The delay, like that of Menelaus at Sounium, then exposed him to the *meltimi*, Boreas, of which Obregón identi-

5. G. Pillot, *The Secret Code of the Odyssey*. A. Rousseau-Liessens, *Géographie de l'Odyssée*.

6. E. D. S. Bradford, *Ulysses Found*.

7. Mauricio Obregón, *Ulysses Airborne*.

fies two currents, a southward that took Menelaus to Crete and a south-westward that blew Odysseus beyond Cape Malea to the Lotuseaters in the eastern, southernmost Syrtis on the promontory Arae Philenorum. After following the Libyan coast westward, Odysseus is then borne by the south-easter, the sirocco, to the Cyclopes on Majorca, near which Cabrera across a narrow strait is the Isle of Goats, and thence to Aeolus on the high-cliffed, seemingly bronze-walled Minorca. Sent homeward by Aeolus, he mistakes islands off western Sicily for Ithaca, whence he is blown back. Like Bradford, Obregón puts the Laestrygonians at Bonifacio but differs by placing Circe on the island Ischia off Cape Circeo. For him as for Bradford, the Underworld lies outside Gibraltar, specifically at caverns near Tangiers. On leaving Circe, Odysseus evades the Clashing Rocks at Lipari, meets Scylla and Charybdis at the straits of Messina, finds the Sun's cattle at Catania, and after retracing the Straits drifts southward again to Calypso on Malta. Obregón's chief novelty is to place the Phaeacians and Homer himself on Cyprus, because Mycenaean tradition and relics of Linear-B survived there and because at 700 B.C. only the constellation of the Bear was visible from Cyprus always above the horizon. Further, Poseidon wrecks Odysseus' raft, for Obregón a boat, from Mt. Solyma in eastern Lycia.

These travelers vary the wake of Bérard's *Dans le sillage d'Ulysse*. But the question seems not whether Mycenaean and later reports of outer lands descended by the poetic tradition, as they doubtless did, but in what spirit they descended. Nothing suggests that Homer conceived the world with modern exactitude. As Obregón says, the days of Odysseus' journeys tend to familiar poetic numbers. It may be added that the naiads' cave in Ithaca reflects an actual cave but in another position and that Ithaca is not, as Odysseus says, the westernmost among the neighboring islands. The *Odyssey* traces the instruction of one who saw the cities of many men and learned their minds. The travels are real to the poet in a mental, not a geographical sense. The rock into which the Phaeacian ship was changed makes Odysseus the last voyager on those mind-forming seas. The fall of Troy similarly brought to an end the revelatory generation of the heroes, and the voyages framed the siege within a greater scheme. The *Odyssey* is a summary of the Trojan age. Without denying the possible correctness of some of these modern reports, or conceivably their hybrid, interwoven correctness, one may hardly judge between them because their spirit and purpose are not the poet's.

The traditional date of settlement of both Corcyra and Syracuse was 734, and Blakeway's tabulation of Proto-Corinthian pottery at Italian and Sicilian sites supports such a date.[8] Although the main era of Greek colonization was yet to come, curiosity about the west could not have been absent from Homer's audience, and the start of the adventure with the Cyclops shows that mood. Odysseus and his men reach by night an uninhabited but goat-filled island from which on the next day they see smoke and bleating flocks across the water. In the usual proleptic manner of the narrative the inhabitants have already been described. "The Cyclopes have no ruddle-cheeked ships, nor are men among them shipwrights who might build well-benched ships that could meet each need in reaching the cities of mankind, even as men travel much over the sea in ships toward one another—who would also have built them a well-established island. For it is not at all contemptible but would yield all crops in season. In it are meadows by the banks of the gray sea watered and soft. Grapes would be boundless. There is smooth ploughland; they would reap a heavy harvest year after year because the soil beneath is rich. It has a sheltered harbor where there is no need for a cable nor to cast bed-stones nor attach hausers, but to beach and stay until sailors' impulse bids and winds blow" (9.125–139). The invitation of new lands seems in these lines.

To be sure, they have another purpose. Paolo Vivante excellently describes the reciprocity in the *Odyssey* between landscape and inhabitants.[9] Thus the alluring first description of Calypso's distant island—her cave whence spreads the fragrance of burning cedar, herself within singing with a clear voice and weaving with a golden shuttle, groves of alder, poplar, and fragrant cypress where owls, hawks, and sea-crows nest, wild vine above the cave heavy with clusters, bright streams spreading from four springs, meadows with violets and parsley—serves to set the changeless nymph in her ever-blooming world (5.55–75). Similarly the description of Alcinous' palace and gardens—of cultivated as con-

8. "Greek Commerce with the West, 800–600 B.C.," *Annual of the British School at Athens*, 33, 170–208. See also T. J. Dunbabin, "The Early History of Corinth," 65.

9. *The Homeric Imagination* 72–78.

trasted to Calypso's wild abundance—exhibits the Phaeacian ease
(7.81–132). The remote forest surrounding Circe's house conveys
her mystery and secrecy (10.196–197). The landscapes of Odysseus' travels, though full of danger and surprise, are not inoppor-
tune to intelligence but themselves intimate what he will find. Thus
in the account of the Cyclopes their ignorance of ship-building and
civilized arts even while they adjoin good land chiefly serves to introduce the formidable but primitive giant.

Even so, the emphasis on happy lands awaiting settlers seems
evident and, when taken with the generally fabulous nature of the
story, points to an era when colonization was in fact beginning but
when the new regions still wore an air of mystery. The example of
The Tempest again applies. Early accounts of the New World gave
it in 1611 an aura of marvel that it lost in the course of even fifty
years. Trade soon developed; families at home had connections in
the colonies; some would have returned; there would have been
messages and news. But at an earlier stage imagination could place
a former king of Milan and his daughter with Ariel and Caliban
near "the still-vex'd Bermoothes" and have a tempest blow to the
island ships returning from Tunis to Naples. The New World supplied a place of beauty and instruction which included strange
creatures; not unreal geography accommodated imagination's
travel. The *Odyssey* catches a like moment, of an era when enough
was known of the western Mediterranean to stir wonder but not
enough to shed practicality. Odysseus reaches mentally illustrative
places, and the fact puts the poem at the dawn rather than in the
full day of Greek colonization, in the eighth rather than the seventh century. If so, it would seem, as on grounds of language,
roughly contemporary with the *Iliad*. From the tales of Egypt and
using Herodotus' date of about 650 for when the Ionian and
Carian so-called bronze men first reached there (2.154.4), Rhys
Carpenter like others put the poem much later, and he ingeniously
found a terminal date in Menelaus' account of the island of Pharos
as a day's sail off shore (4.354–357), though the founders of Nau-
cratis at about 610 knew it close to land.[10] But the Mycenaeans
knew Egypt. Tradition of Egyptian Thebes, the decline of which
roughly parallels that of Mycenae, echoes in Achilles' reference to
its vast wealth (*Il.*9.381–384) and, in the *Odyssey*, in the splendid

10. *Folk Tale, Fiction, and Saga in the Homeric Epics* 92–100.

gifts that the king and queen gave Menelaus and Helen (4.125–132).[11] Dunbabin has shown much earlier Greek contacts with Egypt in the archaic age than Herodotus suggests.[12] In sum, the marvels of travel in the *Odyssey* and their character as less geographical than mental best fix its date. The world was opening intellectually as well as spatially.

Attempt to fix the origins of the several stories, hence their latent emphasis, is much harder. The term folktale is commonly used of them, doubtless rightly in a general sense, but the term is itself ambiguous. Malinowski took chief folktales for faded ritual.[13] While granting occasional such origin, G. S. Kirk rejects it as universal.[14] Lévi-Strauss sees early intelligence giving order to the world by means of myth.[15] D. L. Page sees historical memory occasionally working.[16] Several forces seem intertwined. Gabriel Germain's very full treatment of parallels among other peoples to the stories of the *Odyssey* gives, if not clarification of the peculiarly Greek mind, vivid sense of what it shared and worked on.[17] Under these circumstances a few first principles seem worth attempting. First, thought is by nature an act of categorization. We cannot grasp the infinite particularity of things but put them into classes: man/woman, spring/autumn, oak/pine, though no member of these or of any other class of things exactly resembles another thing. Second, it makes a difference from what source categorization chiefly derives. The contrast of Hebraism to Hellenism reflects the fact that the ancient Jews had the vision of a single God which was further strengthened by holy books and priestly castes, whereas the Greeks lacked these. Writers of the Old Testament therefore tended to see the working of God in an otherwise unanalyzed world. His will was their clarification whereas the Greeks tried to analyze the world. Ancient Jewish thought tended to move from

11. T. B. L. Webster, *From Mycenae to Homer* 65. H. L. Lorimer, *Homer and the Monuments* 86–87, 96–99. Webster notes the pictured record of such a bath on a tablet from Pylos.

12. *The Greeks and Their Eastern Neighbors.*

13. *Argonauts of the Western Pacific* and *Myth in Primitive Psychology.*

14. *Myth: Its Meaning and Function in Ancient and Other Cultures.*

15. In addition to, among other writings, *La pensée sauvage* and *Le cru et le cuit* (both also in English translations), a useful short statement is "The Structural Study of Myth."

16. *Folktales in Homer's Odyssey* Ch. 1 and Appendix.

17. *Genèse de l'Odyssée.*

home outward; ancient Greek thought moved from the world homeward. Third, the Greek need to see man's place in the world, by thus inducing categorization of the varieties and conditions of life, of human fates, and of their setting in nature, tended to illustrative stories. Though entertaining, these stories were at bottom diagnostic; they related what characteristically happens to people in a world that operates characteristically. That is not to say that the heroes were only or chiefly acted upon; in their deeds they showed reaches of human possibility but also, in contrast to the timeless gods, human limits. Auerbach's *Mimesis* may overstate the Greek concern with visible presents and with foregrounds; pasts are invoked by reminiscence and events reflect motives. Yet foregrounds recur because they invoke the conditions that frame any act. It follows that folktale, of whatever origin, served for the early Greeks as means for conveying the nature of things and the probable outcome of actions. In its generic forms, the evolved Greek classic drew in part from folktale. Both sought intelligibility through classification.

The terms "legend," "myth," and "folktale" connote areas of this analysis, though in practice the areas merge. Legend looks to history: not to history positivistically conceived, but to history nevertheless as describing great events that were believed to have occurred. The fact that, from among the many wars and expeditions of the Mycenaean Age, Greek legend chiefly fixed on two, the overseas struggle at Troy and the domestic struggle at Thebes, shows its illustrative purpose. Actions and agents gathered to a great event; details were elaborated; while conceived as historical, the event displayed human situations, motives, and fates. From the representation of a siege on the silver rhyton from the shaft-graves and from fragmentary suggestions of such a scene at Knossos and Pylos, T. B. L. Webster inferred that siege was an existent topic of poetry to which any further siege, including that of Troy VII A, would be adapted.[18] But in the process, legend drew to itself elements of myth and folktale. Myth, in a narrow sense, connotes divine happenings: Zeus weighs in his golden scales the fates of Achilles and Hector and sheds bloody dew about Sarpedon (*Il.*22.209–213, 16.459). Folktale, among much else, expresses recurrent human postures: Achilles must choose between a long in-

18. *From Mycenae to Homer* 58–61.

glorious and a short glorious life (*Il.*9.410–416). The *Iliad* is a legend that includes elements of myth and folktale. Conversely, the *Odyssey* is a folktale that attaches to legend because Odysseus was a known warrior at Troy and which includes myth because he visits the haunts, if not of the greatest gods, yet of gods that operate in nature. Though thus distinct, the themes of the two poems overlap, and Odysseus' character as an Achaean king and fighter at Troy, though progressively extended and nearly submerged at the end of his travels, unites the strands. Folk themes guide the Ithacan narrative also—Penelope's web, the trial of the bow, and the token of the bed—which, though opposite in outcome, are comparable in nature to Achilles' choice in the *Iliad*. The fact that legend, myth, and folktale, however logically distinct, in practice merge connects the two poems. Illustrativeness is their common purpose, whether of the exigencies of heroism or the dimensions and hazards of the world.

That the story of travel, which on the surface seems to come from folktale, has its origins in cult has been argued on linguistic grounds by D. G. Frame. He derives *noos*, "mind," and the verb *neomai*, "return home," from the same verbal root *nes-*, from which he also draws, by vocalization of the initial consonant, *asmenoi*.[19] That word appears three times in the formula, *asmenoi ek thanatoio*, which to Homer means "grateful (gratefully released) from death" but which, Frame infers, once meant "returned from death." The poet and current speech would thus have lost exact sense of a mind formed by travel to and from death, but aura of an old belief would have survived in the story of the man who was famous for his mind, who visited the dead, and who on return brought order and prosperity. Since the name Nestor derives from the same root, the mysterious account in the *Iliad* (5.397) of Heracles wounding Hades "in Pylos among the dead" suggests that both Nestor and his city may have shared these associations. Pylos as "gate" would then have admitted to the dead. The city of the Laestrygonians, Telepylos, at the end of the long bay where the eleven ships were destroyed, might show the same origin. Whence would such associations derive? Absence of Mycenaean temples and the lists in Linear-B of revenues from cults and cult-lands suggest that a Mycenaean king had two functions, as war-king and as

19. *The Myth of Return* 9–19.

priest-king. If his deeds as the former passed into legend, his deeds as the latter, deeds having to do with powers below the earth and on which earthly prosperity depended, may also have been told. Such a figure as Melampus, who healed the roving frenzy of the Argive women, then became king of Argos, shows this union of priestship and kingship (15.225–240, Herod.9.34). But after the fall of Mycenae, when such ruling figures ceased to exist, the report of warlike deeds remained more comprehensible than that of priestly deeds. Transplanted Greeks in Asia Minor saw in the legend of Mycenaean war the prototype and sanction of their own merits and the praise of forebears. But to the degree that half-religious kings had vanished, their doings would have survived as mere tale, not as belief. The mixture of retention with gradual change that marks any system of oral poetry would have kept old words and themes but in a half-disembodied sense. Stories would be told of a king who visited the dead, tried vainly to save many, yet by endurance or intelligence or both returned home bringing order and prosperity. The tale would carry the sanction of antiquity but not of acceptance in the former sense. Beyond antiquity, its sanction would lie in its relevance to the world and to experience. Travel, even to the dead, would be illustrative, no longer sacral travel.

Calypso etymologically means the "veiled one," and *phaiax* later meant "gray," hence may once have given the Phaeacians a dimness that they lack in the poem, except in the mist that is magically cast about Odysseus when he enters the palace and in the fact that they swiftly carry him home asleep and as swiftly vanish. Firmer inference from Greek and especially Sanskrit myth has to do with sacred cattle.[20] The chief reason why Odysseus, unlike his men, gets home is that he alone resists killing the Sun's cattle. The fact is given prominence in the prologue, and Teiresias' and Circe's warnings are emphatic (11.105–115, 12.127–141). Gregory Nagy, who shares Frame's linguistic search into the poetic language, shows common use but different development in Greek and Sanskrit of some meters and formulae.[21] In Vedic myth Indra's second great deed, after the winning of waters, is the winning of cattle,[22] and whether the cattle signify the sun's rays after night or

20. *Ibid.* 41–44.
21. *Comparative Studies in Greek and Indic Meter.*
22. Frame, *The Myth of Return*, 44–46.

water-giving clouds in an otherwise stark sky, their liberation is benignant; life depends on their safety. In Western myth Heracles thus
frees the cattle that had been hid in caves by the three-bodied
Geryon and by Cacus, and Hermes tries to hide Apollo's cattle in a
cave. Frame sees in Vedic myth the further motif of knowledge, in
the triumph of priests and their reward by cattle. Odysseus' sparing of Helius' cattle notably reflects the knowledge that he has
gained in the course of his unearthly travel. Helius "who sees all
and hears all" expresses illumination, and Heracles and Apollo as
Zeus's sons have like roles. They and Odysseus in his due reverence
for Helius ensure life-giving light and abundance. The nymphs,
Helius' daughters, who guard the sacred herds and flocks are
named Phaethousa and Lampetie, Beaming and Radiant (12.132).
If, in the derivation of "mind" from "return home" and the connection of the latter with "returned from death," Odysseus carried
to Homer the aura of a former sacral journey, the Sun's cattle were
part of it, and the hero's return included the safety of the bright
herds.

Limits to this line of derivation are unclear. The destructive Cyclops' dark cave, the dangerous Laestrygonians' confining bay,
veiled Calypso who seeks to retain, gray Phaeacians who occasionally carry back and who specifically mention carrying Rhadamanthys, an inhabitant, Proteus told Menelaus, of "the Elysian
plain and farthest reaches of earth" (7.323, 4.564): all in various
ways suggest a journey to and from death. The suggestion is stron-
gest of the Laestrygonians. Their city Telepylus is situated "where
shepherd in-driving greets shepherd, and he out-driving answers. A
sleepless man might there have earned two wages, the one cattle-
herding, the other shepherding bright flocks. For the paths of day
and night are close" (10.82–86). In the *Theogony* (748–757) Day
and Night thus meet where Atlas stands at the springs and limits of
earth, Tartarus, sea, and sky. "Drawing near, Night and Day address each other as they cross the great bronze threshold. The one
will descend within, the other fares abroad. The house never holds
both, but ever outside the house the one wanders the earth, and the
other waits within until the hour of her journey shall come: the one
bearing to earthly creatures far-seeing light, the other holding in
her arms Sleep, Death's brother, baleful Night veiled with misty
cloud." M. L. West cites parallels from the *Rig Veda,* and Frame
sees such origins, rather than any intimation of nordic summer, in

the account of the Laestrygonian bay. Like language descends to Parmenides, whom daughters of Helius bear in a chariot from the halls of darkness into light. "Gates of the paths of Night and Day stand there, which lintel and stony threshold keep apart, and high in air they are closed by mighty doors, of which much-punishing Justice holds the alternate keys" (1.6–14, Diels). Having been admitted, Parmenides is addressed by the goddess, "Hail, for no ill fate has guided you to travel this road—and remote it is from mankind's path—but right and justice. You must wholly learn both circled Truth's unmoving spirit and mortals' opinions wherein is no true surety." Hesiod's gates of Day and Night standing at the juncture of earth, underworld, sea, and sky stand for the philosopher at the juncture of truth and error.

In the *Odyssey* the Laestrygonian bay and city evoke these associations, but lightly and passingly. That a man could earn two wages there reduces the role of night, yet the place is dangerous; the gigantic inhabitants shatter eleven ships with rocks and spear the men like fish. In act and stature they nearly repeat the Cyclops but prove more destructive. Much as he later does on Thrinacia, Odysseus does not follow the others but prudently halts his ship outside the bay. On reaching Circe's island after the disaster, they have lost common bearings: "Friends, we know not whither is the nether dark nor whither dawn, neither where the mortal-lighting sun fares beneath earth nor where it ascends" (10.190–192). They seem to have passed beyond night's and day's meeting-place among the Laestrygonians, yet the statement is vague. Hesiod's and Parmenides' house where night and day greet each other but within which they never meet has become double daylight, and lost direction at Circe's island does not preclude Odysseus' rising at dawn to explore. The lines may mean that they no longer grasp in which direction home lies relatively to dusk and dawn. Yet the ties with clearer passages in Greek and Sanskrit are evident. As with Helius' cattle and with the etymological suggestions of travel to and from death, the poet seems aware of tones in the story that he neither wholly omits nor wholly reproduces. The fact tells something alike of his tradition and of his mind. He did not abandon preternatural overtones, rather felt in them the scope of a story that yet concerned a purely mortal man. Hesiod's mind was on powers and processes, Homer's was on persons, yet on persons who inhabit a world of powers and processes.

A further line of argument concerns rather the nature of the traveler than of the travel. Writing of the overtones of words that descended to archaic Greece, M. Detienne sees in *aletheia,* "truth," the antonym not to *pseudos,* "falsehood," but to *lethe,* "forgetfulness."[23] The poet as possessor of words and inspired by Mnemosyne and the Muses could give men permanence or let them sink into oblivion. But he in turn was the lesser partner of kings who by sacral knowledge asserted and helped maintain a prospering order. King Minos was said to have slept in the Idaean Cave, Zeus's birthplace, where the nature of things was revealed to him in dream; like beliefs were held of the cave of Trophonius, the Nourisher, at Lebadia. To Detienne the sea-god Nereus is the arch-example of such conveyors of truth, perhaps by remote connection with the tests by water over which Mesopotamian kings presided. In contrast to the dangerous descendants of Pontus listed by Hesiod, Nereus and his fifty daughters are benignant. The term *nemertes,* infallible, that describes him often applies, as M. L. West notes, to oracles; "he does not forget ordinances, but knows just and gentle wiles" (*Theog.*235–236). In Menelaus' account to Telemachus, Proteus, Nereus' near-equivalent, is hard to lay hold of, but when the hero clung to him, at noon drowsing among his seals, in the many forms that he took on, the old man of the sea told Menelaus what he must do to reach home, what he would find there, and what awaited him after death (4.471–570). In directing him to seek her father, Proteus' daughter Eidothea uses the same words that Circe uses in directing Odysseus to seek Teiresias in the Underworld: "who will relate to you your journey and the measures of your route and your home-returning, how you will pass over the fishy sea" (4.389–390, 10.539–540). Teiresias, "whose wits are firm, to whom alone, though dead, Persephone gave knowledge" (10.493–495), is in the *Odyssey* such another figure as Proteus. Neither in fact tells his questioner the details of the journey home, yet tells the essential condition, for Menelaus return to Egypt to make sacrifice, for Odysseus abstention from Helius' sacred cattle. Each then similarly goes on to what will be found at home and what the end of life will be. As returned king, the former traveler will have learned from a wise figure who was hard to reach but who, once reached, gives sure knowledge. Menelaus is pictured

23. *Les maîtres de vérité dans la Grèce archaïque.*

at home in abundance; it is more precisely said of Odysseus that the people will prosper under him. Such a view of the king as a recipient of other-worldly knowledge is to Detienne a survival of old belief. Like the journey, the journeyer of the *Odyssey* would thus wear to the poet the aura of notions no longer clearly understood, yet present to the language and the story and in an intangible way describing the hero. Odysseus in this sense would be a reverse example of Oedipus at Thebes, a blessing, not an infecting king.

These parts of the travel would thus express faded belief, perhaps faded ritual, which in fading would have passed into folktale. They had become descriptive of the world but in no narrow sense; rather, the world wore in them a tone of widest possibility which in turn opened to a mortal man. As the fighting of the *Iliad* becomes the concern of gods and by so doing takes on something of their diagnostic timelessness, so the journeys of the *Odyssey* carry the mortal traveler to representative stations. His travels are not random; they clarify. The fact fits the views of Lévi-Strauss, if not his strictly structural theory of myth, yet his contention that early thought is within its own methods as analytical as later thought. The relation of Odysseus' stay with Circe to his journey to the Underworld is a case in point. Myths concerning the union of gods with mortal women are very numerous, evidently as explanation of greatness; the offspring brings brilliance into the world. Union of mortal men with goddesses is much rarer and dangerous. Calypso, when commanded by Hermes to let Odysseus go, laments the gods' hostility to such loves: Artemis killed Orion after he had slept with the Dawn, Zeus killed Iasion whom Demeter loved (5.118–128). In the *Hymn to Aphrodite* Anchises on learning that it was Aphrodite with whom he had slept fears withering away; she tells him that Tithonous, whom the Dawn loved, thus withered and warns him to be silent lest Zeus strike him with a bolt (*H.H.*5.185–190). Gilgamesh refuses union with the goddess Ishtar because his companion Enkidu, the former friend of animals, was fled by them after he had known love; he soon died, and Gilgamesh vainly sought to reach him in the Underworld. In Theocritus' mysterious *Idyl I* (109) Daphnis' refusal of Aphrodite may show like fears; he pointedly mentions Adonis, who was loved by the goddess and died young.

The divine decision that Odysseus shall reach home is stated at the start of the *Odyssey;* even so he makes both Calypso and Circe swear not to bring him harm (5.177–179, 10.342–344). His stay with Circe brings him near forgetfulness; his men have to remind him that he has been with her a year (10.469). Her shattering reply that in order to reach home he must visit the dwelling of Hades and dread Persephone to inquire the way from dead Teiresias repeats the sequence of love of a goddess and death. As in the *Iliad* Patroclus is the part-self of Achilles and his death presages his friend's, and as a like vicariousness takes Gilgamesh toward the dead to seek Enkidu, so Elpenor's death in Circe's house accompanies Odysseus' journey to the Underworld. Elpenor lacks Odysseus' temporarily lost purpose; he is a figure of entire heedlessness; yet the oar that Odysseus is to plant on his grave marks their common travel. The island where they had lost sense of direction is the fit place of love. More than the land of the Lotuseaters, it conveys abeyance and cessation, and its sequence by death can hardly be accidental. This sequence too might imply lost ritual, but a mortal's attainment of a goddess seems chiefly a folk theme expressing the impossibility of supernal happiness. "Do not seek to wed golden Aphrodite," writes Alcman (1.17), and Peleus' attainment of Thetis marks to Pindar a more-than-mortal, transient brilliance (*Py.*3.92–96, *Ne.*4.62–68, 5.22–25). The emphasis differs on the two sides: sorrow on that of the goddess, danger on that of the man. Both sides are expressed in the *Odyssey,* and for Odysseus the sequel is the Underworld. In this case too the poet seems faithful to a mythical train of causation, but passingly rather than expressly. His art is toward the nature of the experience, in which emphasis he approaches the diagnostic mood stressed by Lévi-Strauss.

Problems of origin of the stories thus more concern the tradition than the poet. Or at least they more concern what he worked with than what he made. They are nevertheless important as suggesting the dimensions that, he could assume, surround a hero. Such a man was the concern of gods; he coped with a partly practical world in which death, sleep, hunger, the labor of travel and much else were real, but also with a spirit-filled world where encounters were momentous. It is this union of the human with the larger-than-human that gives the *Odyssey* its tone. If Achilles' sense of home and Hector's setting among the decencies of city and family, also many similes, show the poet of the *Iliad* deeply sensible of common reality, the same assumption marks the *Odyssey,* not only in the Ithacan parts but in the travels. "Afflicted though I am, let me take supper," Odysseus tells Alcinous. "Nothing is more shameless than the bitter belly that bids a man perforce think of it, worn though he is and with sorrow in his heart" (7.215–218). But this sense of the immediate and ordinary is set in a hugely outflung world, in both poems and in the *Odyssey* especially in the account of the travels. It is this scope that seems given by the tradition. To call the travels folktales thus amounts to saying not only that Homer has lost sense of the former sacral import of some of the stories but that he positively seeks something else. The term folktale then signifies his diagnostic purpose. Odysseus is conceived as a man who needs the teaching of the travels in order to return instructed. The tales of travel relate what a man can learn of the world. They are not the mere jetsam of beliefs that would have been lost if themes and phrases had not descended by the tradition; they shine in their own right as descriptive of experience. Nor, as the term folktale might imply, are they simply attractive popular stories. As the battles of the *Iliad* show for the poet the nexus of intentions with outcomes, so the travels show for him a wider, silenter dimension surrounding social enterprise. Achilles at the end of the *Iliad* has been forced toward loneliness; as seen at the start of the *Odyssey,* Odysseus has long reached that state. Homer is concerned with what a lone man must come to understand, and heroism to him is what brings a man to the acknowledgment. The so-called folktales in function thus resemble the battle tales; both descend by the tradition and both illuminate mortal necessity.

Faded history as well as faded myth could pass into folktale. In the account of the Lotuseaters D. L. Page sees knowledge deriving from Mycenaean times that Egyptians ate lotus, yet knowledge now so dim as to have become fused with the widespread theme that to accept food from the dead or from spirits binds the eater to stay with them.[24] Walter Burkert adduces a carving and inscription of the pharaoh Amenophis II shooting an arrow through bronze shields.[25] Germain cites from the *Mahabharata* the story of the suc-

---

24. *Folktales in Homer's Odyssey* Ch. 1.
25. "Von Amenophis II. Zur Bogenprobe des Odysseus."

cessful suitor bending a stiff bow and with five arrows striking an elevated target through a hole, also the marriage-feat of the future Buddha, who in the manner of the Pharaoh pierces bronze drums.[26] Germain cites the belief that winds may be controlled by tying knots in a string, then by untying when a breeze is needed.[27] Aeolus thus binds winds, though by knotting a bag; the story would be pure folk theme. But report of places might, like faded historical report, combine with story. Herodotus describes ritual gifts that reached Delos from the far north (4.33–35). Such contacts might help explain why at the Laestrygonian bay night and day do not alternate as with Hesiod and Parmenides, but day is long enough for a sleepless man to earn two wages. Though Frame sees only echo of a sacral journey to the end of earth and to the dead, it might be overlaid with the report of nordic summer. Similarly, though Polyphemus evidently repeats the universal story of the terrible giant outwitted by the clever small man, his one eye might, as Bérard thought, suggest a volcano winking in the night.[28] Non-Homeric myth has gigantic smiths working at volcanic forges. Man-fishing Scylla will express another kind of danger. Odysseus clinging to the reef at Scheria evokes the simile of the octopus; reefs suggest sea-creatures. But if such geographical explanations seem easy, perhaps too easy, their use in the poem hardly implies specific places. The Cyclopes' caves across a strait from an island might be imagined of many coastal mountains; so also the returning Phaeacian ship halted by Poseidon to become a rock in a bay. Calypso's flowering meadow and Circe's secret grove no more identify a place than does Persephone's wooded shore dense with poplars and willows. The diagnostic Greek mind, though fixed in the actualities of labor or hunger or danger, verged toward analysis, and Homer's mind notably. G. L. Huxley's reconstruction of non-Homeric epics shows them much more given to local detail; he enhances the impression of Homer's uniqueness.[29] Herodotus' view (2.53) that Hesiod and Homer fixed the Greek pantheon implies sense of the exemplary, and to turn from problems of origin to the poem itself is to enter that kind of clarifying travel.

26. *Genèse de l'Odyssée* 14–20.
27. *Ibid.* 179–189.
28. *Les navigations d'Ulysse* III 154–158.
29. *Greek Epic Poetry, from Eumelus to Panyassis.*

4. Ogygia and Scheria

Odysseus' evolution in the course of travel is evident. He starts as the effective fighter fresh from Troy, leading back the twelve ships that in the Catalogue of the *Iliad* he is listed as having brought; he ends alone on the beach of the Bay of Phorkys. He has lost his share of the Trojan booty, the increment that, together with heightened reputation, would take a Mycenaean king to overseas war and which in the Cretan tale to Eumaeus is so described. But the Phaeacian gifts that with Athene's help he hides in the naiads' cave more than compensate. They were increased by reason of the eloquence that, in the interlude of his speech, for the first time fully wins the queen Arete's admiration and which the less firm-minded king Alcinous calls truthful and sensible, like a knowing bard's (11.363–369). Athene at the Bay of Phorkys says that she prompted the gifts; her lucid spirit was evidently in the speech as just earlier in his performance at the games. He has moved from a warrior to a man of wisdom of whom the goddess approves. Not that he lacked intelligence, eloquence or Athene's guidance at Troy —it was he whom she chose to stem the flight to the ships after Agamemnon's abortive speech (*Il.*2.166–181)—but that she has long neglected him, evidently in some mixture of anger at the sack and consequent sense that he had more to learn. His beggarly role in Ithaca is anticipated at Scheria; there too he begins as a lone figure on a beach to end with acceptance by a sceptical woman. But this movement from fighter reliant on violence to lone man possessor of wisdom appears rather in the myth than in the hero's express words. Not, again, that he lacks eloquence at the banquet or tact and gratitude to Nausicaa or, in Athene's eyes, discretion in his plan to test the household at home or feeling intuition in his test of Penelope. Rather, these and other words and deeds show him in action; except indirectly in his Cretan stories, he does not personally assert what he had learned. Even the famous lines to Amphinomus, "Such is the mind of men on earth as the father of men and gods brings on their day," appear as advice, not as self-expression. Thus the journeys themselves carry the import of his instruction, and the freely given gifts that accompany his return express its result, something not won from fighting but from diminution.

To Plato poetry, as fixed in sense-impression, falls far below dialectic as means of seeing and describing reality. A difficulty of the view is its implication that the seen is unreal, whereas the real is unseen. The recurrences of the oral style help meet that difficulty because objects and actions, being repeatedly put in similar ways, express stable and recognizable identities, yet by standing in a series also express novelty. The style accommodates both the stable and the emergent. In common experience today resembles yesterday, hence allows some mental security; yet does not wholly resemble yesterday but almost by surprise forces movement into the unknown. Poetry characteristically deals with this surprising novelty, which necessarily comes clothed in sense impression. If already known, it would have acquired familiar language, would fit smoothly into yesterday's scheme. The emergent is a kind of riddle for which the mind is unprepared—not, to repeat, wholly unprepared, since if the new lacked any bond with the old it would simply stupefy; there would be no way of accommodating it. Yet, being new, it breaks on experience as something stumbled on, something seen and felt but still unnamed. It compels rearrangement; what was previously fixed and comprehensible must move over to accept it, by old language taking on new overtones, by changed emphasis and train of priority, and by new words. All these changes clearly took place in the course of the oral tradition, and Homer certainly made them—his command assures that—but in what ways is unknown. The present point is that the tradition gave him marvelous means of expressing such change. Its recurrences gave the world a comprehensibility that outcomes of the stories kept enlarging. In the stories as in experience novelty intrudes as event wearing the colors of sense and feeling. By his command he keeps unfolding further episodes which, while by language reminiscent of former episodes and thus implying stable comprehensibility, in fact destroy the past order. How far the poet surprised himself as he surprised his imagined characters escapes understanding, but creativity involves just such a brush with the unforeseen. But as regards the two poems, it is clear that the tradition supplied a huge instrument for conveying both order and surprise. A received scheme of identifiable reality by which alone nature and the past carry shape speaks in the recurrent language, yet by standing in a successive order the language continually expresses new contexts and takes on new tones. The process is not endless; a more inclusive meaning must emerge as goal, though even there, the works being poems, attainment lies rather in act and feeling than in idea. Achilles with Priam and Odysseus in Ithaca convey this change from first assumptions. Their route to that end lies through alterations, their own and others', of what had appeared fixed and had been suggested as such by the language. The combination of recurrent language with unfolding event leaves the world stable but in a sense not initially understood.

This progression, which marks the mounting battles of the *Iliad*, almost schematically guides Odysseus' travels, yet not obviously because by ring-composition the two last steps come first. It is central to the poem that the journey to the Underworld stands midmost among the thirteen adventures: before it, Cicones, Lotus-eaters, Cyclops, Aeolus, Laestrygonians, and Circe; after it Sirens, Scylla, Cattle of the Sun, Charybdis, Calypso, and Phaeacians. Spatially the Underworld is farthest; mentally it is most diminishing; as regards return it first gives guidance. From then on the hero divides from his companions. The first storm that blew them west involved them all in the fate of recent victors (9.67–81). The second storm off Thrinacia destroys the cattle-eaters but spares Odysseus who in the Underworld learned from Teiresias, as again from Circe, not to kill and eat and who so warned the others (12.405–419). With the third storm between Ogygia and Scheria Poseidon's anger subsides, to change to mercy with Odysseus' final act of placation after his return (5.291–296). But the sea-god's anger carries the poem back to the start, to the decision of the other gods in his absence that Odysseus shall return. Why was Zeus angry at him, Athene there asks with word-play on the name Odysseus, "the man who endured anger" (1.59–62).[1] Because, Zeus replies, he blinded Polyphemus, Poseidon's son by the sea-nymph Thoosa. The blind Cyclops' prayer to his father for vengeance and Zeus's ratification of it conclude Odysseus' narrative of that adventure (9.526–555). The sequence is clear: Poseidon's and Athene's wrath for the violence at the sack of Troy, expounded by Nestor (3.141–152, 286–290), mentioned by Hermes to Calypso (5.105–109), and assumed by Odysseus in the conversation at the Bay of Phorkys (13.314–319), took them far from home; Athene's anger, shown in her long absence, is now gone but Poseidon's has mounted. A man kept at sea for ten years is necessarily the sea-god's foe, but Odysseus is specifically such because he damages the god's previously serene, unvisited sphere. The damage, shown also in Calypso's sorrow and the Phaeacian ship turned to stone, is the obverse of the hero's gain. Mortal ingenuity harms and destroys even while it profits; nature resents, a penalty must be paid, and a placation must be reached. E. R. Dodds thus describes the tragic hero as a creative man who disturbs a pre-existent order.[2] The journey to the Underworld both shows Odysseus his mortality and commends future restraint toward divine things and future placation of Poseidon. The result for him approaches an option: having seen the gods' changeless world, he may remain with it and is so invited by Calypso or by refusing may choose at once his identity and mortality. The quiet of his seven years with her conveys his half-entrance into timelessness; his recovery at Scheria of his old heroic power is slow, a kind of rebirth. But though his speech there traces him from Troy, as speaker he is no longer simply the Trojan hero but something more. The familiar repetitive language expresses a still recognizable world but a world dauntingly enlarged to include more than battles and kingly decisions, dangerous as these were. Timeless nature and death seen no longer as sudden personal fate but as general condition have been added, and it is with this knowledge that the beggar at home still must act.

1. G. E. Dimock, Jr., "The Name of Odysseus."
2. *The Greeks and the Irrational* 43–50.

The beauty of the poem is nowhere more affecting than in the first sight of the farther world of Calypso's isle (5.55–75). As with the first mighty battle of *Iliad* 5 old reality enters a new dimension, so in this far scene does the postwar world of home with which the poem opened. Menelaus' account of his wanderings makes a transition much as the muster and initial deaths of *Iliad* 4 lead to the god-heightened crash of the next Book. But the transitions are opposite, there to closer, direr spaces, here to distance and isolation. It is a paradox of the *Odyssey* that the hero, for all the circumstances in which he is seen, may be less intimately knowable than the main figures of the *Iliad*. The fact relates to the spaces of the poem and to its nature as comedy; Penelope alone at home, though mysterious in dreams and devices, is more singly felt than is her many-circumstanced husband. Comedy has a mental tone; it shows the world as desirable and finally attainable, but in the process puts the emphasis on the world. The hero is one who sees and assents to its variety. Calypso's island, we learn at the start of the poem, has grown tedious to Odysseus, who would gladly die if he could see the smoke upleaping in his native land (1.55–59). But its beauty states the other side of his adventures, their privilege and the wonder that they reveal. That this side of the travels speaks thus purely in the first scene heightens the desirability of the world that showed beneath Penelope's clouded beauty and in Telemachus' young travels. It is a world in which the gods might justly expect mortals to take pleasure if they could learn how. Thus Hermes, who brings the decision that Odysseus shall leave, wonders at the island; "even a deathless god on coming there would marvel as he saw and feel joy in his heart" (5.73–74). The description of its wild serenity had been cited; so also the gods' displeasure at goddesses' love of mortals, Calypso's chafing regret, yet her offer to Odysseus to help him leave, his suspicion, the oath that he exacts of her, and the final gentleness of his statement that, more beautiful though she is than Penelope and dangerous though his course may be, as mortal he still must go. "Much have I already suffered and much toiled in waves and war. Let this too follow" (5.223–224). This is the other side of the adventures; to know the size and wonder of the world does violence to the self, even when after sight of the Underworld the self is known to stand in a pale succession. The compulsory widening that knowledge asks has its outward counterpart in storm, wreck at sea, swimming, near-

death on cliffs, and naked, almost de-selfed arrival. Something inveterate, whether native or acquired, persists: skill, suspicion,
physical endurance, the habit of alertness. But these are strained;
they are seen as hardship, while being in fact both the means and
the outcome of knowledge. In the process the mind, as commonly
in Homeric language, is hardly more instrumental than legs or
arms; faculties are jointly strained in the survival that becomes instruction. Yet the beauty that marked the first description of Calypso's island sets the tone of the effort and keeps inducing it. The
simile of the spark saved for relighting which describes Odysseus
on Scheria safe at last under fallen olive-leaves carries the response.
The dimmed but potential fire relates to the fiery heroism of the
Iliad, but the present danger has been the dimming element of
water.

Calypso's offer of agelessness and immortality may have been
delusive; the gods disapprove such offers to mortals (5.136, 208–
210). Lesky nicely notes her failure to tell Odysseus that she had
been instructed to help him onward.[3] That may be Homeric omis-
sion (the hero later shows knowledge of Hermes' visit, 12.389–
390), but the simplicity of her feminine reliance on her love and
beauty, his sense of these, yet sense also of his difference from her
profoundly put his condition at the near-end of travel. He has seen
and almost merged with the green freedom that she inhabits—a
desire that recurs in Euripides' free Bacchants and in Hippolytus'
and Daphnis' wish to keep their youth—but being the kind of man
that he is in other parts of his mind, he can acknowledge the privilege but does not seriously heed it. The implied optimism of the
Homeric style, that the world is beautiful and worth knowing but
also reconcilable with action, identity, and self-demand—the optimism that is denied in the *Iliad,* confirmed in the *Odyssey*—speaks
in the parting. The half-cultivated, half-wild olive sprung from a
single root under which he finally sleeps at Scheria prefigures the
new stage (5.476–477). Homer surely had no language consciously to explain such natural intimations. As the sceptre in *Iliad*
1 (234–237) that will never again put forth leaves or twigs once it
has left its place of cutting on the mountains expresses in Achilles'
hand the fatal consequence of his reply to Agamemnon, so the
double-natured olive foreshadows Odysseus' half-return at Scheria

3. "Göttliche und menschliche Motivation" 36.

to civilization and self. The sceptre and tree quite simply show the poet's immersion. The young figure of Nausicaa, also Athene as little girl on this her resumption of guidance, further fit the hero's emergence.

If Ogygia was timeless, Scheria has the brightness and some of the sorrow of youth. Nausicaa charmingly conceals from her parents the dream of approaching marriage that Athene sent her (at Sparta the goddess has Telemachus dream of his mother's marriage, 15.16–23, fit thoughts of youth). She asserts virtuous concern that her married and unmarried brothers have clean clothes for dances, and asks her father for the mule-cart (6.57–65). But he understands; fathers come off well in him. The sparkling scene follows: clothes-washing, ball-playing, the ball fallen into the deep eddy, girls' cries waking the suspicious hero, his first thought that he has again reached wild people but precaution to shield his nakedness with a branch, his approach to the gentle company like a wind-blown, rain-wetted, hungry lion, speculation whether he had best clasp the fair maiden's knees or from a distance address her with smooth words and correct decision to do the latter, then in these graceless circumstances his supremely graceful speech. Homer smiles. Even in the highest kind of comedy exemplified by this poem, to keep the desirable world means to stay alive, and staying alive can mean indignity. The poet sees Odysseus in many ways—necessarily so, considering his experience—and one way is amusement at his indomitability. Is this a further sign of Homer's age? The young tend to take themselves more seriously than the old or than some of the old. Time at least shows everyone solemnly repeating predictable acts. To Bergson sense of the mechanical is the root of humor. Yet life remains beautiful and desirable. The contrast between assent to it and the pertinacity that the assent takes on can evoke a smile, not of condemnation but of fellow-feeling and human recognition. Odysseus appears in other, more serious lights; the beggar at home can be noble. But as occasionally there, so notably here he is seen with smiling affection as from the outside. The worn lion among girls who prettily cried out when their ball fell into the eddy is absurdly cast, and his rallying to call Nausicaa a goddess or, if mortal, a luckiest suitor's bride, to hint of his better days and Trojan past in likening her to the palm at Delos, and to end with sterling praise of marriage still evokes a smile but now of approval (6.149–185). He is indomitable but a great man. As Penelope at home matches him in shrewdness, so Nausicaa had her covert plans. She too is seen amusedly but with admiration. The poet's sense of the beauty of the world includes assent to mortal devices. The approval, if not a proof, is at least a sign of age, vision of an order that would be less winning if it were less human.

As in the night-scene with Penelope Odysseus will reject being washed by young servants, so he refuses the girls' offer (6.218–222). Together with his attractive speech, that politic act is not lost on Nausicaa, and his transformation by Athene as by a gold-smith putting gold on silver (6.229–235) tells something of the girl as well as of him. At least his full impressiveness emerges only slowly to the Phaeacians but is already clear to her. Telemachus will thus later acknowledge his great father and Penelope her husband. Observation in Homer subtly includes the observer. She tells the girls that he looks god-like; "would that such a man might be called my husband dwelling here, would that he would choose to stay" (6.244–245). Alcinous later repeats the hope, which then vanishes in the assumption, though Odysseus had not said so, that he has wife and children at home (7.313–314, 8.243). The theme is as fugitive as Nausicaa's dream, with light overtone of sorrow like Calypso's and the Phaeacians' in their ship turned to stone. He is afflicted, yet afflicts; instruction leaves a trail of loss, which most obviously includes the suitors but others also. The point is important as further showing that the killing of the suitors is not an act of property-saving moralism, such as would differentiate the *Odyssey* from the *Iliad*, but part of the inherent cost of order. The order keeps setting limits. But in bright Scheria Nausicaa's disappointment, though prophetic of the ship turned to stone, is quickly overlaid.

In saving the afflicted stranger who soon appears great, she resembles Keleus's daughters of the *Hymn to Demeter* (99–183) who meet the sorrowing goddess as an old woman and guide her to their parents' house at Eleusis where her divinity is revealed. They share Nausicaa's young generosity. Oral themes treated the ages of women's lives. In the *Iliad* Thetis tells her memory of Achilles as a child, Briseis her lost hope of return to Phthia as Achilles' wife, Andromache her fears for Astyanax without a father (*Il.*18.56–60, 19.287–300, 22.477–514). Nausicaa is the mirror of late girlhood. She spiritedly awaits the startling stranger when her companions flee, hides her secret hopes from her parents, yet ingenuously confides to her friends her feelings about the transformed handsome man. She shows a charmingly practical mind as they return to town, describes it with youthful factuality, will have him accompany them while they are still in the country but no farther since she fears gossip, imagines people reading her hopes of the godlike stranger and resenting the affront to local suitors, yet admits that she herself would think ill of a girl who thus brought home a stranger, ends with thought of her mother near whom her father will be found drinking wine and who, if well disposed, will chiefly benefit him (6.255–315). All happens as she said; she is seen safe at home where the old servant Ampimedousa lights a fire for her (as safe as the girl that Hesiod describes indoors in winter, *Erg.* 519–525), then is seen again only as Odysseus is about to enter the banquet. Standing, as did Penelope, by a pillar, that mark of home, she bids him not to forget her in his own country, and he replies that he would pray to her there all his days as to a goddess; "For you gave me life, girl" (8.464–468). Throughout the travels characters disappear as the hero and the poet move on, and this final sight of Nausicaa is exceptional. Important as she is for the plot and for the mood of renewal at Scheria, there is something more. The suggestion of her disappointed hope less describes her as a person, since health and vitality clearly lead her on, than it describes her youth. She will someday lose what Odysseus has already lost; meanwhile keeps in actuality for her, in future memory for him, that complete yet incomplete moment. In literature only Miranda and Natasha equal her, but they progress while she stays a girl. From the point of view of the poem, her youth conveys what as older figures Odysseus and Penelope have moved from, yet remember. The gods, says Penelope in her speech of recognition, "begrudged us that abiding with each other we take joy of youth and reach age's threshold" (23.210–212). Given the permitted terms, only the static image survives; youth stays as memory. As regards the poet, Nausicaa's moment of life, like the moments of the lives of Thetis, Briseis, and Andromache, imports the static into the changing narrative, but unlike theirs her moment has only the touch of sorrow. In both poems Homer verges to such fixed and, as such, timeless states of being. The young figure of Nausicaa as contrasted to women of the *Iliad* is at the heart of the difference between the poems.

Wilhelm Mattes well describes Odysseus' evolution at Scheria as
from self-awakening to self-revelation.[4] Nausicaa had told him of
the town—entered by a gate, divided by an isthmus with beached
ships on either side, beyond the isthmus a stone-fringed assembly-
place with a shrine of Poseidon and much ship-gear (6.262–269).
Athene as a little girl directs him to the palace still farther on. The
narrative has two main stages, both bearing on his return: at the
palace his initial evasion of the queen's question, "who are you,"
and, in the interlude of his self-revealing speech, postponement of
his return to the night of the third day. The return had been set for
the second night (7.317–318), but his night-long speech gets him
higher regard and more riches. The evolution starts against obsta-
cles: the local suspicion of strangers of which Athene warns him
and against which she gives him the protective mist, and the brilliance of life in the palace, something alien to the surprised and
surprising stranger. But, as the little girl sagely advises, "a bold
man does better in all enterprises, even though he come from some
place far," and so it proves (7.51–52). As with Calypso, description comes first but not now of cave, bird-filled trees, and watered
meadows, rather of an opulence beyond that of Menelaus' palace
that dazzled Telemachus: bronze walls, cyanite frieze, gold doors,
silver door-frames, gold guardian dogs outside made by Hephaestus, ranged seats within where the leading Phaeacians sit eating and drinking, gold youths with light-giving torches; fifty
serving women, some busy at grinding, others as quick as poplar
leaves at weaving, wherein Phaeacian women excel as the men in
ships; an unfading garden beyond, where successive fruits forever
ripen. The gold dogs and youths resemble Hephaestus' gold girls of
Iliad 18 (417–421), and as Achilles' shield shows the outspread
world that he will briefly keep, Odysseus in the marvelous palace
will relive his travels. The description contrasts to that of Calypso's
wild island: art as against nature, memory as against continuity.
But since Odysseus will not stay, time pauses suspended at Scheria
also, not with tone of oblivion as with Calypso, rather in review of
a past from which he will return, changed but still himself, to Ithaca. The magic of the ship that will take him home extends to his
sleep on board; the ship travels by night and he wakes to find it
gone. Once he is home, the travels recede like a dream, in some

4. *Odysseus bei den Phaaken* 162.

sense counterparts of Penelope's dreams and a further mark of likeness between the two. This tone of, for the future, half-unreality surrounds the Phaeacians but in the moment of the speech brings back the past engrossingly.

If Odysseus did not know himself invisible, the surprise in the palace when the mist drops heightens the mood on both sides. The Phaeacians think him perhaps a god such as those who in the past graced their feasts, but he remains to himself simply a hungry home-seeker. Nausicaa had told her girls to give him food and drink and to wash him in the river, but little more was said of food when he refused their help; they left him a cloak and chiton and oil in a gold flask. Hunger is in his mind on this night of his fourth day since his raft sank. She had also bidden him pass by her father seated at his wine and as a suppliant address her mother. From Nausicaa the advice partly conveyed a girl's feeling for her mother, but Athene as precocious child expounded Arete's ancestry and importance. Like her husband, she descends from a destructive king of Giants by whose daughter Poseidon begot the late Phaeacian king, Alcinous' father and Arete's grandfather. Husband and children defer to her; the people greet her like a goddess as she walks in the town; she adjudicates even men's quarrels; a home-seeker's hope lies chiefly in her (7.54–77). In Sparta Helen, unlike her husband, quickly recognized Telemachus as his father's son and dispelled sorrow by knowledge of an Egyptian drug; she is more intelligent than Menelaus. Odysseus in Ithaca will owe his success to Penelope. Arete is another such presiding woman, but why is obscure: whether the idea of home evokes women as means and goal, or in the pre-city age when men's position depended on loot and raiding (or so the poetic tradition held) women in fact managed half-rural households, or pre-Greek vestiges survive of a religion dominated by goddesses. Further, by the nature of the story Odysseus wants something beyond war; as peace-bringer he understands women and their world. He contrasts to Sophocles' honor-dominated Ajax who bids Tecmessa be silent (*Aj*.585–595), more resembles the dying Oedipus who leaves to his daughters as last possession the word love (*O.C.*1617). The women of the *Odyssey* reflect his wish for conciliation, complicated though it is by his other wishes for knowledge and survival. Arete's high position foreshadows Penelope's or what Penelope's will be with husband beside her in an orderly Ithaca, and her final approval marks his success.

Alcinous unbends sooner. There is silence while after his appeal Odysseus sits in the ashes, until an old Phaeacian, as did Aegyptius in the Ithacan assembly, breaks the pause by bidding Alcinous seat him and command wine for libation to Zeus the protector of suppliants (7.159–166). In doing so the king proposes entertainment and convoy for the next day unless the stranger be a god—which Odysseus somberly denies, asserting his misery, asking to be let eat, and calling nothing so shameless as the belly. If this is slight rebuke to Alcinous, his general conduct is approved by all except Arete, who recognizes his clothes. In the conversation by fire-light suspicious Penelope has a like question. When the others have gone, Arete asks who he is and who gave him the clothes (7.237–239); did he not say that he got here from sea? He avoids the first question by answering the second two, and the reply equally illuminates the three people. For himself, his mind is on his sufferings. Though he does not say so, he may be suspicious of descendents of his persecutor Poseidon, but on the next day it takes taunts to make him show his old strength. Demodocus' song about an early quarrel between Achilles and himself, termed best of the Achaeans (8.78)—the quarrel in which Agamemnon saw good omen—then begins to revive his past. Nagy imaginatively sees in the song Homer's conscious pairing of the two poems and heroes.[5] It in fact first rouses Odysseus to himself; he solicits the second song about the wooden horse, the sack of Troy, and his going with Menelaus to Deiphobus' house to retrieve Helen (8.492–495). Sense of who he was and still is grows in him during the second day to culminate at the banquet in his self-revelation and tale of sufferings, but he is now not yet himself. There may be inconsistency in his earlier mention of Troy to Nausicaa and his handsome transformation; he remains a shipwrecked suppliant at the hearth, though in the clothes that Nausicaa gave him and that Arete with her servants made. But if he evades the question who he is, he tells how he reached and after seven years left Calypso's island, finally to attain Scheria and receive food and clothes from Nausicaa. Trustingly and as a genial

---

5. In a still unpublished paper, "Demodocus, Odyssey-Iliad," delivered at the meeting of the American Philological Association in 1975.

host Alcinous criticizes her for herself not bringing him in, but Odysseus combines compliment and knowledge of the world by falsely saying that she invited him but he refused, fearing her father's disapproval; "the breed of us men on earth is irritable" (7.307). He implies that he did not then understand Alcinous' courtesy, with the result that the king repeats his daughter's hope of him as her husband but, if he wishes to go, firmly sets return for the morrow, even if to beyond Euboea, their farthest point of sail when they took Rhadamanthys. But again like Penelope in the night-scene, Arete simply notes that it is bed-time; her trust in him is slower.

In the *Odyssey* taken as a whole, Odysseus lives three stages: famous man, lone man, and man at home. The stages concern not only periods of life but a process of self-recognition. To heed in youth the call of effort fits and describes a man of spirit; response could then be imagined compatible with first identity. Hector protects home and Achilles expects to return. Contrast of them to Agamemnon is made at the start of the *Iliad* when the king says that he prefers the war-won Chryseis to his wife Clytemnestra. A man does not choose who he is or where he comes from; as with Oedipus, greater forces make some lucky, others unlucky, but the fact does not spare them the necessity of lone choice. It is this necessity that Achilles and Hector in different ways both meet; the outcome was unforeseen but the choice was inescapable. Though both are unlucky, Oedipus is superior to Agamemnon in seeking what seemed a forever opening future, whereas Agamemnon judges fixed and certain his power as king; he thinks himself by position spared privacy. The affirmation of the *Iliad* is in the heroes' answers to the isolating moment, its darkness is in that moment's sure arrival. The third stage of home regained and first identity resumed implies some loss of position as a fighter and personage among important men, the position that Agamemnon thought firm. But his delusion that he was spared the equalizing fate of isolation marked him at Troy and in his death. Diminution of public personality, though a fact of age, is more than that; it is encounter with a reality beyond the self and fixed in nature. In this encounter Odysseus is at one with Achilles. Nagy well notes that the two are linked in Demodocus' song as the best of the Achaeans. That the one dies young, the other moves to a later stage of life, seems not in Homer's mind to divide them. Both behold the self in its lone stance toward something greater. The wide sea by which Achilles walks at Troy partly conveys his half-divine nature and Nereid mother, partly his fame, but partly also the greater and, as such, unsocial necessity with which he lives. Odysseus meets this reality less fast; the travels, so to speak, analyze it; but he equally perceives. His regained sense of self in the second day at Scheria, then his account of his sufferings give the necessary prelude to homecoming. That in turn is not restored self-assertion, rather an adaptation of self to a fixed order not unlike Achilles' adaptation in his final meeting with Priam. In Homer attainment is mental in tone, giving sight of what is and quiet by acknowledgment of it.

The Phaeacians once lived near the Cyclopes who molested them but found peace by moving to Scheria under the king's father Nausithous (6.4–8); even so remain related to the Cyclopes and Giants. Ease has not quite erased their inherited dangerousness. Athene warned of their hostility to strangers, and on the bright second day of feasting, dance, song, and games Odysseus is first taunted, then tested. The day foreshadows Ithaca: in the theme of testing, in opprobrium by young men of an old man and his show of strength, in Odysseus' self-praise as an archer and his reference to the bow of Eurytus (8.224–225), and in Demodocus' light song of Ares' adultery with Aphrodite as contrasted to Odysseus weeping like a woman torn by captors from a husband dead in war. This last contrast is general; the epithet of gods as those who live at ease nearly fits the Phaeacians. When Odysseus has thrown a discus well beyond local marks and goes on to challenge competitors in other feats, except running because the sea has undone his legs, Alcinous admits them inferior in rough sports. "We are not blameless boxers nor wrestlers but run fast and are matchless with ships; ever dear to us are feast and lyre and dances, changed clothes, warm baths, and beds" (8.246–249). This lightness of life suggests but surpasses the suitors' ease at home; Odysseus has been reared in a harder school. But the king's dignity of mind imparts more than mere ease; the Phaeacians have something like Paris's charm in the *Iliad* but, except in Laodamas and Euryalus, not his lightmindedness. The king notices Odysseus' secret tears at the bard's first song of Troy, that of himself and Achilles quarreling, and courteously proposes games, in which the sea-worn hero at first declines to take part. Charmingly ship-named contestants (ships being all that Homer knew of them) spring up; the king's son Laodamas tries Odysseus; he replies that afflictions, not games are in his heart. Young Euryalus (the two talk together like Telemachus and Peisistratus at Sparta) calls him just a trader ignorant of games; and as to Eurymachus at home, he answers with a fine insult. The gods, he says, give varied merits: looks to some, fair speech to others, "even as your looks are distinguished and not even a god would fashion otherwise, but in mind you are vaporous" (8.176–178). He seizes and throws the heaviest discus; the ship-famed company stoops; Athene fixes the mark that even a blind man would recognize as far in front; and the hero boastfully and with mention of games at Troy proposes other contests, except in running. There may be conscious contrast to the funeral games of *Iliad* 23 (782–793), where he wins the foot-race and of which two other themes seem echoed here: Nestor's son Antilochus called him an older man and Ajax Oileus called him favored by Athene. The success is a further step in his self-revival; with his words, it also impresses the king. Alcinous would have Odysseus see their unrivaled dancing in order some day to tell another hero when dining with wife and children at home. On sight of the dancing and after Demodocus' song of Ares and Aphrodite, he readily grants this superiority. Pleased, the king proposes gifts by himself and the twelve other kings to be ready by the evening; Euryalus gives in amends a sword with silver handle and ivory sheath. Odysseus gracefully accepts and puts on the sword, mark of revived heroism.

The king bids his wife have water heated for Odysseus' bath and fetch their gifts of a gold goblet and clothes and a box in which to pack them. She simply does so; her assent still awaits. Odysseus' self-revival draws from Troy and the travels; memories of both induce his speech. First, he ties the box with a knot that Circe taught him (8.448). In the manner of Achilles' withered sceptre and the double-natured Scherian olive tree, that knot comes near expressing the whole gain of his wanderings. Demodocus' song of Ares and Aphrodite so far bears on Ithaca as having to do with a wife, but also and peculiarly shows the Phaeacian lightness. Merriment is brightest when the adulterous pair is held in bed by subtle chains that the outraged husband Hephaestus laid as a trap. The goddesses shrink from coming to see; Zeus too stays away, but Apollo and Hermes feel quenchless laughter. Apollo asks Hermes if he would thus sleep in chains with golden Aphrodite, and the scampish god replies: "Be it so, lord far-darter Apollo. Let thrice as many boundless chains surround. Let you gods and all the goddesses look. Still would I sleep with golden Aphrodite" (8.339–342). The outraged husband's vindication does not cancel the laughter.

But Odysseus wants from Demodocus another kind of song. He praises the blind singer as taught and beloved by the Muses and sends him meat from his own portion. The bard's blindness, like the smith-god's lameness, has social origins; both pursue arts that their impaired faculties still allow. But blindness chiefly conveys sight beyond the present; it is visionary. This is Demodocus' tie and that of the blind Chian poet of the *Hymn to Apollo* (172) with the tradition of Homer's blindness: vision of a greater world than seeing eyes behold, the world of gods and heroes. It is to that world that Odysseus recalls the bard: "Demodocus, I praise you beyond all mortals. In due order you sing the Achaeans' doom, the many things that they did and suffered and toiled, as had you yourself been somewhere present or heard from another" (8.487–491). In fact Demodocus has not sung the full tale of Troy; it is simply assumed, as later by Alcinous of Odysseus' speech. It is in the hero's mind and he imputes it of the bard; it is not a tale of victory but of pain. The further song for which Odysseus asks, of the wooden horse and the capture, leads to his weeping like a captured woman torn from her dead husband (8.521–530). The song and simile convey the reverse of the song of Ares and Aphrodite. Both songs concern marriage, not only in Odysseus' tears but in the tale of his going with Menelaus to Deiphobus' house to retrieve Helen. His weeping like a lorn woman states his present position between Troy and home, his position toward the full poem. The box tied with Circe's knot and the farewell to Nausicaa add his recent to his former past. He is himself again as regards these pasts, but the Phaeacian lightness marks his distance from the third stage of return.

To postpone discussion of the speech, he has told of reaching the Underworld, speaking with Elpenor, Teiresias, and his mother Anticleia, and seeing the famous heroines who lay with gods and bore demigods, when he suddenly declares that it is time for sleep and stops. Arete first breaks the raptness: "Phaeacians, how appears this man here to you in looks, stature, and balanced wits within? Also, he is my guest, though each shares the honor. Therefore do

not press to send him on nor stint your gifts to one thus needy. By
the gods' will many possessions lie in your halls" (11.336–341).
The just previous accounts of his mother and the heroines echo in
Arete; his world of desired peace has place for women, who prove
his salvation. The contrast with the *Iliad*, in Hector's gentle dismissal of Andromache (*Il.*6.486–493), is evident; the initially
sceptical Arete foreshadows Penelope. Old Echeneos, who the
night before first urged raising the suppliant from the ashes, agrees,
and Alcinous proposes a day's delay and further gifts—to which
Odysseus exaggeratedly consents by saying that he would wait a
year for the wealth that would win him regard at home. The reply
illustrates Homer's way of fixing on one point at a time which can
soon yield to another equally real point. On the next day Odysseus
sits at the banquet yearning for sunset. The reply no doubt also
shows his conciliatory side, which however Alcinous takes to harbor no lying: "Odysseus, as we gaze we do not fancy you a cheat
and deceiver, such as the black earth rears many mortals far and
wide, offering lies of things that none can see. With you is shape of
words and in you good wits. You told your tale from knowledge
like a bard, the grim pains of all the Argives and yourself"
(11.363–369). He essentially repeats Odysseus' praise of Demodocus; the swineherd will say much the same of the beggar.

A question of poetic truth arises. Odysseus can deceive: in the
firelit scene with Penelope "he feigned many lies telling them like
truth" (19.203); so also in the other Cretan stories. He told Alcinous that he refused Nausicaa's invitation to the palace. To be
sure, the Cretan stories have elements of truth, but that is not the
issue. They show him making his way as a beggar and, though he is
making his way here, the fact that praise of him as a bard matches
his own praise of Demodocus puts the question of poetry, not of
deception. Homer in effect treats Hesiod's problem that the Muses
can inspire either falsehood or truth. The line of the *Theogony* (27)
about their power to deceive is nearly the same as that of Odysseus
in the firelit scene. But in the Phaeacian speech he has not only told
his tale like a bard with form in his words and good intelligence; he
told "the grim pains of all the Argives and yourself" (11.369). Like
Demodocus, he is assumed to have told the Trojan story of which
his travels are an integral part. The tale nearly asserts Hesiod's
claim to truth. Arete's and Alcinous' praise of his powers and his

truthfulness may be accepted. It comes near to being Homer's praise of his own theme, the heroes and their world.

He finishes his story; further gifts of a tripod and cauldron are given by Alcinous and each of the twelve kings, which the people will help pay for. Alcinous sees to their packing; the Phaeacian life of feast and song continues on the third day as before while Odysseus looks to the bright sun yearning for its setting. At last he rises, places the wine-cup in Arete's hand, and wishes her her joy until age and death in house, children, folk, and the king Alcinous (13.56–62). They embark in silence; sweetest sleep, nearly like death, comes upon him. The ship speeds as fast as a hawk bearing the man of godlike mind who formerly endured pains of war and wave but now slept unmoving, forgetful of his sufferings (13.79–92). The lines are one summary; Poseidon makes another. If Odysseus was to return, the sea-god wished him wretched, but the Phaeacians have given a wealth that he would not have brought from Troy (13.131–138). Alcinous knew an old prophecy that one day a ship of theirs would not come back but be shattered at sea and a mountain would be set about the town. The god now gains Zeus's consent to change the returning ship to stone while the Phaeacians watch from shore. Alcinous cries aloud the remembered prophecy and commands sacrifice and prayer to Poseidon that the mountain not enclose the city (13.163–187). They shall never again give transport from the unknown to the known world, but it is not stated that the mountain descends.

What is being said? The passage suggests the opening of *Iliad* 12 (3–33) where it is foreseen that Poseidon and Apollo, champions of the two sides, will one day destroy the Achaean wall at Troy. The rivers beside which shields and helmets and the breed of demigods fell in the dust will drive against it. The earth-shaker will sweep downstream the timbers and foundations that the Achaeans toiled to set in place and will again strew the great beach with sand. Like Alcinous, the Cyclops and Circe knew prophecies of one whose arrival would bring change (9.507–510, 10.330–332). Two ideas converge, the trail of harm that follows the voyager and the end of an era. Like the destruction of the Achaean wall, the Phaeacian ship turned to stone closes an age. The theme is echoed at the end of the poem in the compared figures of Achilles and, jointly, of Penelope and Odysseus, themes of poetry. Alcinous' and

Arete's praise of the true tale of travel and the lines on Odysseus' return asleep complete for Homer the next-to-last stage of the Trojan era. In *Iliad* 12 (445–449) Hector hurls a rock that two men such as live now could not easily pry from the ground into a cart. The heroic age to Homer stands above the weaker present as to Hesiod it divides the bronze from the iron age. Odysseus most fully saw and could report its actuality and consequence.

5. Odysseus' Tale

The tale of travel, long delayed and at last told not of but by Odysseus, marks his emergence in his hosts' and his own eyes and promises his change from traveler to returner. But also and chiefly it enlarges the tone of memory that suffuses the poem. Memory imports remove and intellection; "We enjoy seeing exactest likenesses of things that in themselves we dislike seeing," says Aristotle of *mimesis* (*Poet.*4,1448b10). The swineherd tells the beggar nearly that: "Afterwards a man takes joy even in sorrows, one who has suffered very much and wandered much" (15.398–401). The poem is partly backward-looking. "All the others, as many as escaped steep death, were then at home clear of war and sea. Him only, yearning for return and wife, the nymph queenly Calypso, divine of goddesses, held in hollow caves desiring as her husband" (1.11–15). Phemius in Ithaca sings the doom of Danaans; Nestor enumerates the famous dead; Menelaus and Helen tell of Troy; Odysseus in the Underworld sees his former comrades; the Second Nekyia summarizes the war in its protagonists. Summary was one of the poet's purposes; the great disturbance is dying. As sung by him, the *Iliad* is an act of memory. "Now tell me Muses who inhabit Olympus; for you are goddesses and attend and know all things, we hear only the fame and do not know" (*Il.*2.484–486). But to the warriors events are continually and direly present; the poet, not they, sees the gods that drive the action. Ajax's prayer for sunlight to die in (*Il.*17.645–647) comes near fitting them all. Except the old figures, only Achilles and in the last books moves from involvement to reflection. His remove at the funeral games sets him apart from the others, and his generosity as contrasted to their continuing will to win carries something like regret for his own former passion.

Isolation, shipwreck, arrival among strangers, maltreatment at home, the suitor-slaying and much else show Odysseus too coping with the uncertain present, but the adventures that he tells at Scheria are past; he testifies in his person to the stored experience. Athene tests him in the suitor-slaying, watching as a swallow from a beam. To that extent even such experience as his does not make a mortal secure of the present; he will need to leave Ithaca again in order finally to placate Poseidon. Yet relatively to the *Iliad*, visibility is widening and life opens to effort because the past has left its lessons. Nestor and Menelaus at home live with the past; much more will Odysseus to the degree that he has seen more. But in this awareness the hero moves almost to the position of the poet of the *Iliad* which Achilles approaches at the end. Having lived with the history of the heroes, the poet wants it not simply as song but in some degree as translatable to experience. The knowledge of the world that Odysseus brings with him becomes a key to living with it.

At issue is the nature of heroic poetry, or its nature to Homer. In his astonishing *Homo Necans* Walter Burkert detailedly expounds a ritual alternation of payment and renewal. The payment involves sacrificial bloodshed, carries sense of guilt, is sometimes made at night and by secret groups, conveys an alienation that must continually be re-endured and reacknowledged as price of renewal and affirmation. He cites[1] a myth from Orchomenus, how Leukippe, daughter of Minyas and priestess of Athena Ergane, resisted Dionysus and being maddened by him tore apart her child. The crime caused a priest of Dionysus every second year at the ceremony Agrionia to chase women of that family with a sword and, Plutarch says, in his own time inspired a priest to kill a woman (*Aet.*

1. P. 197.

Gr. 299). Burkert imagines the priest in religious zeal confusing ceremony with reality; the many rituals that he cites carry a heavy emotional burden. The burden survives, he argues, as legacy from a hunting era some ten times longer than the agricultural era, itself of ten millennia; the price of life is bloodshed, at once guilt and renewal. To be added is the tension between the sexual tie of family and the aggressive tie of the hunting and fighting group. The question then arises, what is the relation of poetry to this continually relived emotion. Gilbert Murray judged popular beliefs consciously omitted from the epic poems, but the impulse may be unconscious and subtler.[2] Mind is the final solace; by liberating even temporarily from present obsession, it gives sight of longer realities not unrelated to any present but cooler because more spacious and less personal. In the epics direct speech, estimated at half the *Iliad*, three-fifths of the *Odyssey*,[3] recreates a present, as does the action of tragedy. But a frame surrounds even this immediacy, whether in the remove of poetic language, knowledge of gods and the past, narrative, simile, or the tragic choruses. Greek philosophy perpetuates this search for mental distance, gift of sight and perspective, which was already in Greek poetry. The retrospection of the *Odyssey* dominantly expresses this lucid impulse first among Greek works. Odysseus' labors keep the vision from being purely mental; yet that he both looks back on most of them and that they have given him knowledge imports scope both to experience and to the mind formed by it. The tragedy of the *Iliad* shows this sight already the poet's; heroes reach it only through loss and briefly. In the *Odyssey* the poet's sight more nearly becomes the hero's, vision survives passion, mind finds escape from emotion, by partial transfer from experience as endured to experience as remembered.

Odysseus begins by praising the calm of the banquet; he refers to Demodocus' just finished song, but implication carries to his own tale which the king later compares to a singer's. "I call no consummation gladder than when joy reigns among all a people and serried diners in a hall give ear to a bard, and beside them tables abound with bread and meat, and a wine-bearer drawing wine from the mixing bowl carries and pours to the cups. To my mind this seems a fairest thing. But your heart was moved to ask of my

2. *Rise of the Greek Epic* 136–140.

3. In a doctoral dissertation by Stephen B. Kelly, summarized in *H.S.C.P.* 79 (1975) 363–364.

bitter sorrows that lamenting I may groan yet more. What then shall I tell first, what after? The heavenly gods have given me many pains" (9.5–15). Pain and pleasure are juxtaposed, each distinct yet to be connected in the act of telling. The connection extends to his name, which he proceeds to tell. He is Odysseus son of Laertes, known to all men for his guiles; his fame reaches the sky; he lives in Ithaca beneath Mount Neriton, low-lying and farthest toward the nether dark among the islands Doulichium, Same, and wooded Zacynthus, a rough island but good nurse of young, fairer to him as his land than any other (9.19–28). The heroes can be aware of their later fame; it resembles a light reflected back upon them. Speaking of herself and Paris, Helen in the *Iliad* (6.357–358) says that Zeus gave them an evil fate that they might be subjects of song to posterity; Achilles tells Agamemnon that the Achaeans will long remember their quarrel (*Il.*19.63–64). Odysseus here knows this reflexive fame which marks him as his father's son from Ithaca; he knows himself to be the legendary home-seeker. The information will direct the Phaeacian ship and to that extent is functional but, more than that, makes the coming story exemplary. He will tell what the most famous of home-returners has seen of the world. The much-discussed error about the site of Ithaca partakes of this assumption that the hero has of himself because the poet has it of him. Ithaca is not in fact farthest west nor do the other three islands, as he says, lie apart toward the dawn and sun.[4] As here described, it lies farthest toward Odysseus' journeys; the poet does not conceive Ithaca geographically but thematically. Legend gave certain facts about it—Mount Neriton, the Bay of Phorkys, a cave, ridges—but these were known for their place in the story. The opposite was not true; the story did not exist to fix Ithaca exactly. Somewhat similar confusion marks the medium of the speech. Demodocus sang to the lyre; Odysseus speaks; yet his tale is likened to a singer's, evidently because Homer sang and the speech becomes his poem. The hero's self-awareness as famous in legend, the partly incorrect but feeling description of Ithaca, and the speech that is tantamount to song share a poetic reality. The tale of travel is illustrative of the world and of the mind that has survived wide sight of it. The man, his home, and his account occupy an explanatory plane.

4. Lord Rennell of Rodd, "The Ithaca of the Odyssey," gives a contrary view justifying the geographical position.

Until the last episodes violence and languor alternate in the journey: Cicones yield to Lotuseaters, Cyclops to Aeolus, Laestrygonians to Circe, and chiastically after the central Underworld, Sirens to Scylla. With the Underworld the theme of his own as contrasted to his comrades' return supervenes, but the alternation mutedly holds as between Cattle of the Sun and Charybdis, Calypso and the Phaeacians, in at least their covert dangerousness. Such abstract words as violence and languor would not have occurred to Homer, who thought in stories. The generation of Socrates first systematically pursued abstractions, with the difficulty not only that abstractions are hard to fix but that not yet existent terms for them were partly coined from neuter adjectives and participles. Homer's stories are not allegorical, allegory implying abstractions consciously presented in human colors: for example, the sophist Prodicus' description of Heracles' choice of the life of effort over that of ease, the one as an austere woman, the other a voluptuous woman meeting him at a cross-road and each urging her rewards (Xenophon, *Mem.* 2.1.21–34). Needless to say, greatest future allegories, Dante's supremely, so identify life as lived with life as idea that the two are inextricable. But Homer's language lacked the abstractions that could thus take on a sensate tone; it expressed the sensed, done, and seen, his terminology. The alternations that mark Odysseus' voyage show a narrative scheme not unlike the battles and deaths of the *Iliad;* successive events somewhat echo the earlier, yet differ both as immediately felt and as cumulative. Thus Odysseus moves from a confident warrior to a lone afflicted man, but the adventures themselves comprise the movement as each step brings its partly repeated but incremental and presently novel plight. As in the language thought comes clothed in sense, so in the adventures meaning slowly uncovers itself from circumstance. Alternations of activity and passivity shows a man's power as against the world's power. The two forces keep some relation, but the balance slowly changes, and the man who emerges reflects more of the world, less of his initial self. The adventure with Aeolus foretells the shift of balance, which becomes dominant with the Underworld.

The raid on the Cicones at Ismarus on the Thracian coast, made when Odysseus and his companions have just left Troy, gets them cattle, wine, and women but ends in disaster when they sit eating and drinking and the Cicones rally. The lines describing their defeat echo the cattle-raid shown on the shield of Achilles (9.54–55; *Il*.18.533–534); both tell the dangers of aggression. Further comment is given in the beggar's Cretan tale to Eumaeus in which a like raid in Egypt brings a like defeat. In both, Odysseus distinguishes himself from his followers: at Ismarus he urges leaving fast, a scouting party did the damage in Egypt (9.43–44, 14.262–265). But in the tale to Eumaeus the very enterprise describes the Cretan's confident youth or, if not his actual youth since he was ten years at Troy, his still unsatisfied vigor; he was content to spend only a month at home taking pleasure in children, wife, and possessions. The Odysseus of the *Iliad* is a generation older than the ardent Antilochus, Nestor's son and Achilles' friend (*Il*.23.790); his discretion implies some years, but the Cretan tale shows him in retrospect and to his own mind still appetitive. The great storm that Athene and Poseidon angrily raised after the sack then follows. Odysseus left Nestor and Menelaus on Tenedos to rejoin Agamemnon at Troy; together with the delay at Ismarus, that act implicated him in the storm. Menelaus was delayed by the death and burial of his steersman Phrontis at Sounium (3.278–285); like much else in his life, his implication has a passive tone. That of Odysseus shows choice; his active intelligence, though great, still insufficiently reckons with gods. Buffeted for two days and nights and on the third day carried beyond Cape Malea for nine further days, they reach the country of the Lotuseaters where, as soon with the Cyclops, he keeps his decisiveness. His companions will later need to tell him that he has spent a year with Circe; here he quickly retrieves the scouts who had found the gentle natives and after eating the honey-sweet fruit of the lotus sent no message back but would have stayed forever forgetful of home (9.94–97). The refrain of death that mounts throughout the travels began at Ismarus where they lamented six men from each ship. Mounting languor accompanies these deaths, but not yet in him. The adventure broaches the persistent alternation between deathly violence and deathlike quiet, but briefly and simply. He has the unwilling three tied to the thwarts of a ship, and they proceed.

Burkert sees in the adventure with the Cyclops re-enactment of the primitive guilt of alienating bloodshed.[5] Variants that he cites make the escaper first share the cannibal feast that in the *Odyssey*

5. *Homo Necans* 148–149.

the Cyclops alone eats. But Odysseus sacrifices the ram under whose belly he escapes. To Burkert he is the grandson of Autolycus, the wolf-man (19.394), and repeats the werewolf's exile from humanity that in Plato's story of Lykaon visits the eater of human flesh (*Rep.*8,565d), except that the shed blood is here the ram's and the Cyclops' blinding. In Greek belief night precedes rather than follows day, and the fugitives from the cave re-enact a debt to night. Burkert goes on to adduce rituals in Boeotia and Samothrace with which Odysseus was connected: the former associate him with Hephaestus and the Cyclopes, Hephaestus' servants; the latter with ram-sacrifice for saving from drowning. If, like the name Odysseus or Olytteus, these connections are pre-Greek in origin, sense of the debt of life to bloodshed survives in him; the fire-hardened olive pole with which he blinds the Cyclops is the primal weapon. His return to Ithaca and victory on Apollo's day will then express day got from night, civilization got, with ritual atonement, from killing. But, as with the previously noted suggestions of the cattle-saving king's journey to and from death, such overtones seem inherent in the story rather than imposed by the poet. Or they were only so far consciously imposed by him that he conceived alienation a necessary prelude to return and, further, that alienation should include encounter with elemental beings and the dead. As dreams take character not so much because they recreate words or persons lately in mind as because these appear in strange settings not consciously conceived by day, so the personages that Odysseus meets seem less significant than the tone of his adventures with them. It is in this sense that parallels to ritual convince. The stories do not merely evoke fabulous persons, they put them in a certain light and have them do certain things, which light and which actions hint of buried beliefs. The poet gives his personal emphasis but in so doing recreates implanted colors of feeling.

Some god, Odysseus says, brought them on a misty night to the gentle and fertile island abounding in wild goats across the water from which they looked toward the Cyclopes' smoke and bleating flocks (9.142–143). His fate is soon to turn, and a god is already working. Beyond his previous activism and acquisitiveness the episode shows two traits: his pioneering eye for good land and, more important, his curiosity. He on the second morning leaves the eleven ships on the outer island and with the twelfth seeks the inhabited land. He leaves most of the crew at the ship and with twelve men reaches a laurel-shaded cave entered from a walled sheep-fold high on the hill nearest shore. The occupant is away, but there are lambs and kids outside, milk-pails and cheeses inside; his companions urge seizing these and leaving, but he refuses (9.224–230). He is curious to see the occupant and hopes for a gift; he had imagined possible use for the strong wine that they had seized at Ismarus and had brought as his gift (9.196–215). All his first optimism speaks in these acts; he resembles the still eager Cretan of his later story. He admits as much here, saying that he would better have heeded his companions, but that is in retrospect. His joint acquisitiveness and curiosity seem undifferentiated; together they look to a world that is itself inviting and that holds gain for him. At this stage he somewhat resembles the young Achilles of before the war whom Nestor described as eager for Troy and glory (*Il.*11.777–782). The folktale of the giant is familiar in many forms.[6] The Cyclops' one eye and pastoral wealth may distinguish him, but not his jocose ferocity. He returns with a great load of wood, milks his flock, sets a huge doorstone in place, lights a fire, then sees the men and takes them for what in effect they are, seafaring ravagers. But to Odysseus' mind the ravaging of Troy was glorious, as he tells the Cyclops soliciting a gift and invoking Zeus the god of hospitality. But the Cyclops cares nothing for Zeus (9.273–278); in Burkert's perspective the god of civilization is on the other side of primitive killing as day is on the other side of night. The theme of littleness besting bigness by means of wits puts in simplest form the human posture; for all its elaboration, the present episode may be the least memorable, because the most obvious, of the adventures until the reversal at the end. Though he keeps outwitting the giant, Odysseus does not end, except briefly, in joy and triumph; his troubles begin, and his later success finds him a different man. The outwitter is outwitted; the world proves more testing than he fancied, and his cleverness, though necessary and provoked, is elementary. The tone carries Homeric obbligato to the contrast between night-blood-primitive and day-renewal-Olympians. After the suitor-slaying Odysseus' unwillingness to whoop over the dead shows the difference.

6. O. Hackman, *Die Polyphemsage in der Volksüberlieferung.* Germain, *Genèse de l'Odyssée* 55–129.

He keeps using his wits, first by lying, as to Alcinous about Nausicaa's failure to bring him with her, about his ship which he says
was wrecked. Then when the Cyclops has dashed to the ground,
torn up, and eaten two men, to the primitive accompaniment of
unmixed milk, and has fallen asleep, Odysseus feels his chest but
resists stabbing him because they would not be able to move the
doorstone. Still imprisoned on the second day, he finds an olive
pole as long as a mast, thinks of cutting off a length and hardening
it in the fire, then hides it under the multitudinous dung and receives the Cyclops pleasantly on his return at evening. But this
time, perhaps by a god's prompting (9.339)—another of the turns
that can shatter but that also force power of survival, therefore
show a latent divine intent—the giant does not divide the flock but
brings the males in. As on that morning, he kills and eats two men,
but while inveighing at him Odysseus offers the wine as a guest-gift
in professed hope of convoy homeward—this though he has called
the Cyclopes ignorant of ships. Tell me your name, Polyphemus
says, that I may give you my gift, and Odysseus replies Outis, No-
one (9.366). The simple trick fits a child's story. Giant, blood, sar-
donic humor (the gift will be to eat Odysseus last), and childish
deception give the poet's view of Odysseus at this stage. In Dante's
Inferno crimes of violence precede more mental crimes; the *Odyssey* is not at all an *Inferno*—it is nearer the *Purgatorio*—but there
is a like movement from harsh to subtle experience. Unused to
such strong wine, the giant drinks, sleeps, vomits; the pole is
heated nearly to flame and twirled in his eye like a ship-auger; the
roots of the eye sizzle like tempering iron. He cries aloud; neighboring Cyclopes ask why he disturbs the ambrosial night; is someone killing him by guile or might? He replies, No-one is killing
him; they leave saying that Zeus-sent ills are inescapable and bidding him pray to his father Poseidon. The hero's heart laughs
"how my name and faultless trick deceived" (9.413–414). In the
other negative form Outis punningly becomes Metis, which means
both no one and sharp mind.

Then comes the turn. Burkert sees in the next morning's device
whereby they leave, the six surviving men bound by Odysseus beneath rams, himself last clinging to the biggest ram's belly, a poetic
extension of sacrifants decked as victims and identification of killer
with killed. When on return to the island Odysseus sacrifices the
saving ram, Zeus rejects the offer (9.553–555). The bloody events

of the cave—in tone bloody rites—carry alienation. But in the poem the explanation is more simply human. Groping at the flock, the now pathetic Cyclops asks the ram (9.447–455) why he leaves last who always led to the soft grass and rivers and was first to the cave at evening; does he miss his master's eye that the cursed Outis blinded? In Theophrastus' *Characters* (4.10) the countryman is awkward in town but loquacious to his dog at home; the simple Cyclops is talking to his friend. But Odysseus cannot resist like an artist signing the canvas. He cries taunts from the boat which the giant nearly capsizes with a rock. From farther out and against his followers' second protest he cries again that, if anyone asks who blinded him, he shall say Odysseus the city-sacker, Laertes' son from Ithaca (9.502–505). Like Alcinous and Circe, Polyphemus recognizes the fulfillment of an old prophecy, but had expected a big man. In a formula of prayer like that of Chryses that initiates the quarrel of the *Iliad* (1.37), he prays to Poseidon that Odysseus not reach home but, if that be fated, "may he come late and ill after losing all his comrades, on an alien ship, and find sorrows in the house" (9.534–535), the prayer that Zeus ratifies. As in the *Iliad*, the outcome follows from both fate and character. Though Odysseus tells the story, his companions' protests give comment; Eurylochus later blames him for the men's death in the cave (10.437). He is the Odysseus of the start, not of the end, and Zeus's refusal of the sacrifice looks both to his change and to Poseidon. The damage that he leaves in the sea-god's untouched realm explains its future closing to intruders; that comes near being its retreat into myth. In Faulkner's *The Bear,* the killing of the great creature in the primeval forest ends the ageless past. Civilization brings some evils, including slavery; the youth who was guided to the bear by an old half-black, half-Indian is so shaken that he frees his slaves; sight of the primeval changes him. The Ithaca that Odysseus reaches is full of small men; the war, terrible as it was, has not touched them. If the war and, with it, the realm of his travels will have retreated into legend, memory of both imparts sense of watchful gods that were once more visible but still operate. Though Odysseus will have damaged Poseidon's now closed world, he becomes its beneficiary, the peace-bringer to Ithaca. Zeus's refusal of the sacrifice of the ram, in looking to both him and Poseidon, at once penalizes and by means of memory, the hero's and the poet's, comes to instruct.

Arrived at Aeolus' floating bronze-walled island and boun-
teously entertained for a month by the wind-king, his wife, six
sons, and their wives the six daughters, he tells to eager listeners as
now to the Phaeacians the tale of Troy and the Achaeans' return.
Aeolus sends them on with an ox-skin bag tied with a silver cord
wherein he confines all the winds except homeward-blowing
Zephyrus. On the tenth day they come near enough Ithaca to see
fires when Odysseus after continuous steering falls asleep. The men
compare their labors to his but contrast their empty hands to his
loot and gifts. They open the bag to spy gold and silver, and the
escaping winds blow them back whence they came. He contemplates jumping overboard but covers his head and endures (10.38–
55). The festive family is still dining; he blames his bad companions and wretched sleep and asks for remedy. There is silence until
Aeolus answers: "Quit the island fast, most cursed of mortals. It is
not righteous for me to speed and convey a man detested of the
blessed gods. Go, you come here hated of the immortals" (10.72–
75). The circular notion that success attests to merit and merit to
divine approval must be universal. Faith in virtue because it fits the
scheme of things would otherwise lack support. If gods ordain the
scheme, they reward virtue; misfortune shows lack of virtue.
Odysseus has so far assumed this clear code; his hosts' lively interest in Troy, Aeolus' fit if unusual gift, and the smooth homeward
course, all of which will be repeated at Scheria, show his confident
expectation. But the opposite intervenes and Aeolus draws the natural inference, in part rightly since Zeus has rejected the ram-sacrifice.

"Dear Zeus, I wonder at you," says Theognis (373) as in comment on the Book of Job. Hesiod momentarily contemplates but
rejects the vision of a world without justice: "Now let neither me
nor my son be just among mankind, since it is an evil thing for a
man to be just if the unjuster man gains the greater right. But I still
do not expect counseling Zeus to bring that to pass" (*Erg.*270–
273). Glaukon asks Socrates to show that the just man, though
maltreated and scorned, fares better than the unjust man, though
prosperous and esteemed (*Rep.*360e–361d). It is assumed in these
and other cases that someone is already just, therefore that society
is out of joint. That is not the assumption of the *Odyssey,* in which
misfortune is instructive, existing as part of an order that is initially
too big to be grasped but must be grown into. The austerity of edu-

cation prescribed in the *Republic* may carry that assumption, but it is clearer in tragedy, clearest in the figure of the old Oedipus. In expounding to Priam the jars of Zeus and Niobe's history (*Il.*24.527–534, 602–617), Achilles states different truths from those that he himself once grasped. It is a paradox that the great heroes do not become such by physical powers but by an understanding that supervenes on the acts to which their powers led. Courage is the first step, awareness the farther step. Aeolus' rejection of Odysseus is thus both correct and incorrect; he is indeed condemned by Zeus, as the storm after Troy made clear, but condemned in order that as the wisest survivor of Troy he might grasp its implication. Aeolus' assumption that bad luck attests to bad character and both to rejection by the gods would make life simple; the old question why the wicked flourish would not arise since misfortune would identify them. Achilles' tale of the jars of Zeus tells a different story. Zeus never gives wholly from the good jar, sometimes wholly from the bad jar, at best from both. The hero sees in this law his human bond with Priam: it marks the human condition. Athene at the start of the *Odyssey* rebukes Zeus for neglecting the worthy Odysseus. Her interest in him reflects his intelligence, as she expressly says at the Bay of Phorkys. Yet his first confidence shows even him taking Zeus's gaze lightly. The question concerns sheer dimension. Intelligent as a man may be, he cannot grasp the width of things; prudence and piety will always fall short, and confidence will prompt false steps. This delusion of security in a huge world is what chiefly marks the suitors in provincial Ithaca; they die not essentially from injustice but from insouciance. In his very intelligence and vigor Odysseus best exhibits Zeus's daunting law. The change of fortune that begins with Aeolus carries him to sight of the dead. As hero he keeps his vigor but as wise man returns a beggar. In invoking the jars of Zeus Achilles feels two bonds with Priam: old age which the king shares with Achilles' father Peleus and death which will soon be his and which Hector shares with Patroclus. By sight of the Underworld and as a beggar Odysseus recognizes the same.

The giant Laestrygonians more massively repeat the Cyclops' violence. As Meuli saw borrowing from the eastward voyage of the Argonauts, he saw further parallel in the reduction of the fleet to one ship. The twelve ships that began the homeward journey were those listed in the *Iliad;* they were in fact never functional to the story of return, unless possibly with the Cicones. In the introduction the foolish companions that he cannot save are those who ate Helius' cattle; his companions in the Cyclops' cave were from one ship, so also the men who opened the bag of winds, whose folly nevertheless affected the whole fleet. The theme of heedlessness now extends to the eleven ships which enter a long, cliff-fronted, waveless bay while Odysseus keeps his ship outside. It is not clear how he knows that in this country an in-driving can greet an out-driving shepherd and a sleepless man might have earned two wages because the paths of night and day are close. The deathly adventure is short: he climbs a cliff, sees smoke, sends three scouts; they meet the king's daughter at the spring who guides them to her frightening mother, as big as a mountain. She summons her husband Antiphates who devours one of them, the other two escaping to report. Myriad Laestrygonians gather to hurl rocks on the ships and spear the men like fish; Odysseus cuts his cable, and the one ship flees (10.100–127). The name Laestrygonians connotes devouring, Antiphates killing, and the city Telepylos remoteness. The six days' journey thither from Aeolus' floating island takes them beyond common space; on next reaching Circe's island they no longer know where is east or west. Frame's linguistic argument for a journey to death has been cited. The still recess of the enclosing bay, the far-gated city at the end, the country where in cognate passages day and night alternately start their travels, and the gigantic, consuming king and people carry this tone. Odysseus' tricks which availed with the Cyclops fall away; he keeps only prudence and the kind of fear-struck speed that later gets him from the Underworld when Persephone rouses the myriad dead with, as here, terrifying noise (11.633). Whether or not by mixture with tales of other travel and, if so, in what ways is uncertain, but with Aeolus the atmosphere of return from Troy falls away. Nor has homecoming approached; the mid-journey divides them from past and future by experience of interior cast. The adventure with the Cicones nearly repeated raids at Troy; at the Lotuseaters doubt unfitting a warrior did not cross Odysseus' mind; confident cleverness saved him from the Cyclops; he told Aeolus of Troy; the former code of action sufficed. The enormity of loss to the Laestrygonians coincides with change of common daylight; diminution and estrangement bring inward-turning; they no longer travel so much in space as in states of mind.

Sexuality haunts margins, is crepuscular, sings its clearest spell when the noise of action has fallen away. No part of the *Odyssey* is righter than the sequence that leads from the silence of the lone shore to Circe's glade-hidden house. The increment of lament for dead companions that marks their onward course like the increment of battle in the *Iliad* has grown heavy. Death precedes as the journey to the Underworld follows stay with Circe; for two days they lie on the shore in grief and fatigue. Odysseus, though not his companions, then sufficiently revives to climb a headland, spy smoke from behind distant woods, shoot a stag, and bring it to the others still lying wrapped in their cloaks on the beach (10.179). He had lain in the boat thus wrapped when the winds blew them back to Aeolus (10.53); the word connotes the name Calypso, his stay with whom carries something like the men's present lassitude. The earlier-quoted speech then follows, "Friends, we know not whither is the nether dark nor whither dawn" (10.185–197); but he reports seeing the smoke, and the men are terrified remembering the Cyclops and Laestrygonian Antiphates. He divides the crew half under himself, half under Eurylochus; lot chooses the latter, and the twenty-three (10.208) leave weeping to reach in a clearing of the forest a house where wolves and lions wander. These fawn on them like dogs on a food-bringing master; they hear Circe singing at her weaving. Polites, an honorable companion whom Odysseus liked best (10.224), urges calling to her, and all except Eurylochus follow when she bids them enter. She mixes cheese, barley, honey, and Pramnian wine with drugs that bring forgetfulness of home; with touch of her staff transforms them in head, voice, hair, and form but not in mind into swine; shuts them in a pen, and throws them acorns and cornel-berries. Returning shaken, Eurylochus can report only their disappearance into the house; he refuses to go again. The swine into which the men are changed are kin to the wild boars that appear bravely at bay in similes of the *Iliad* and in the tale of Odysseus' scar. They are as powerful creatures as the wolves and lions; the change does not imply indignity. The men remain former fighters; the drug simply brings forgetfulness but from an erotic impulse that distinguishes them from the men who would have stayed with the Lotuseaters. Odysseus, though spared transformation because he gets from Hermes the saving plant *moly*, feels the same spell. Circe's drug, like Helen's, coexists with and describes her beauty. The plant moly, as Page notes,[7] is not mentioned when he meets Circe, but it partly describes Odysseus, in two ways: he keeps some sense of self that the men lose, and this sense shows divine protection. At crucial turns, such as Leucothea's appearance to him on his raft or Athene's at Scheria as a little girl, he survives by the gods' grace; his strength and their favor are reciprocal. His yielding to Circe distinguishes her from Calypso as sexual enchantment differs from the ageless beauty of nature. The latter includes sexual attraction—Calypso is beautiful —but their love exists within an outer natural continuity. The hollow caves where Calypso would have had him live with her forever young give on bird-filled trees and flowering meadows. Circe's forest-hidden house, though tended by four nymphs of springs, groves, and sea-flowing rivers (10.348–351), looks inward toward her. Its delectation as much describes her as her drug. She is the world's inner, as Calypso is its outer oblivion, and the movement of the episode is from the company's lostness on the remote beach to that interior.

Eurylochus having refused to return, Odysseus sets out alone armed with sword and bow, marks of persisting strength, and meets Hermes as a handsome young man. Athene will meet him at the Bay of Phorkys in much this guise of fresh hope, but it was Hermes who sought him on Ogygia. He is a divinity of wild places as is Athene of civilization, is also resourceful and amorous, as in Demodocus' song of Ares and Aphrodite, and a guide to the dead, as in the Second Nekyia. The latter two attributes are not alien here, but in this wild setting he chiefly carries the divine grace without which Odysseus would be lost but which describes him. "Whither go you on, wretched man, over the highlands ignorant of the place? Your companions yonder are penned in Circe's house like swine on thick beds. Go you thither to free them? I tell you that you yourself will not return but will stay where the others are" (10.281–285). In the plant that the gods call moly—what men call it is not said—which has a black root and white flower and which is hard or, as Stanford says, dangerous for mortals to uproot (10.304–306), he gives him an antidote to the drug. When she will have him drink and will strike him with her long staff but will not

---

7. *Folktales in Homer's Odyssey* 55.

change him, he shall threaten her with his sword; shall sleep with her in order to free his companions and gain help onward, but shall exact from her a great oath by the gods that she will devise no other evil, lest naked he become feeble and unmanned. This is divine foresight, and Odysseus not surprisingly knows the youth for Hermes, of whom Circe soon speaks. The god fares off along the wooded isle for high Olympus.

All follows as he said: Odysseus reaches the house, Circe opens shining doors, has him enter, sits him on a deviously wrought chair, gives him the drugged cup, touches him with her staff, and bids him to the swine-pen, but when he darts at her with his sword, she evades with a cry and grasps his knees. "Who, whence are you of men? Where are your city and parents? Marvel takes me that drinking these drugs you were not at all bewitched. Never, never did another resist the drugs who would once drink and they pass his teeth's fence. In your breast is some unswayed intelligence. Are you Odysseus of many turns who the god of the gold staff, the slayer of Argus, ever said would come from Troy returning on his swift black ship?" (10.325–332). What started as Hermes' protection has become to her Odysseus' uniqueness. His attraction for her is his invincibility or what begins as such. Her attraction for him will lie not in her drug but in the love that keeps him for a year; the element of magic falls away. He sleeps with her and in the morning the four nymphs supernally array bath, clothing, chair, table, wine, and food, but he sits brooding; how can he eat, he says, before recovering his companions? She anoints them with a second drug and the swine-shape falls away leaving them handsomer and younger than before (10.395–396). She has him summon the men at the ship, who greet his return as skipping calves greet their dams at evening; even Eurylochus, after refusing and with memory of what he calls Odysseus' outrageousness that caused the men's death by the Cyclops, finally comes. When, though nobly bathed and feasted, they still weep remembering the past, she makes her gentlest speech: she knows, she says, their toils on the fishy sea and their sufferings on land from violent men. But they shall eat and drink "until you recover such spirit in your breasts as when you first left your fatherland in rough Ithaca. You are withered now and spiritless from memory of hard wandering. Your hearts are never in delight because truly you have suffered very much" (10.456–465). Her spell includes her sympathy, much as Helen's for the sad company in Sparta and the Sirens' later for

Odysseus. The mood of feminine enchantment somehow extends to all; the men changed back from swine to become handsomer and younger convey the response almost as does Odysseus in his year's stay. Elpenor, the youngest, neither spirited in war nor firmly fixed in wits, who on the night before they leave for the Underworld had sought cool on the roof after drinking but broke his neck when he woke to the clatter of leaving and missed the stairs down, is the final figure of oblivion. But Odysseus verges toward him as an idle Achilles to a frailer Patroclus; the later meeting in the Underworld is with one who shared only too self-forgettingly.

The men's rousing of Odysseus after a year (10.469) brings Circe's hard revelation that they must learn their farther way from dead Teiresias and her direction how to reach the Underworld and what to do there. Her island where they could not tell east from west, itself beyond the Laestrygonian long daylight, has been the place of love, unconnected with common reality yet in the world, beautiful but near death in apartness. Even so, it is Circe from whom now and later comes benign guidance. The optimism of the poem, that experience of the world, for all its danger, finally enhances, speaks in her help as in the men's rejuvenation. There is no implication for Odysseus' love of Penelope; Circe is a goddess, daughter of Helius, granddaughter of Oceanus, but beyond that the travels are a journey in reality. As the Sirens sing of knowledge and Calypso inhabits nature, Circe tells of love. The oath that Hermes advised lest she make him feeble and unmanned becomes minor. The danger to a mortal from love of a goddess, though prominent in other myths, shows here in the next journey, which for all its terror is beneficial. The poet keeps sequences but for his own illustrative purpose; the knowledge of the world with which Odysseus will return includes love. The explanatory, latently analytical function of myth that to Lévi-Strauss outweighs its bond with cult shows in this vision of cognate states of life.

Journeys to the Underworld evoke comparisons. Gilgamesh's vain journey to recover his dead companion Enkidu, which starts from passionate resistance alike to loss of his friend and to his own necessary death, ends in the privacy of half-acceptance. The snake that eats the thorny plant of second life that he got from under water ends hope of living again, and his conversation with Utnapishtim, who with his wife had survived the flood to live beyond the world only with memory, contains the inwardness of old age. Gilgamesh is forced back upon a quiet that he had not known was implied beneath his former outlooking strength and vast loyalty. In a tablet that is thought added to the first poem,[8] Enkidu rises like a puff of wind through a hole of the nether world to tell of his nothingness. The ghost of Patroclus thus floats like smoke from Achilles' grasp (*Il.*23.100–191), and in his huge power, friendship, loss, and final sorrow that is also acknowledgment, Achilles resembles Gilgamesh. But such overpowering emotion is absent from the *Odyssey,* where Odysseus sees and learns.

Aeneas descends into his past from which he finds his future. First Misenus, then Palinurus, then Dido, then Deiphobus take him backward in time through recent loss to loss at Troy. His final descent to his father Anchises brings him to his origin from which in turn rises his and Rome's future. The scheme of the journey is vertical, downward and by revelation upward. Odysseus both goes horizontally beyond the stream of Oceanus and sees stable relationships. Though in Teiresias' prophecy these show his future and in his mother Anticleia touch his past in Ithaca and the present there, they state persistent bonds: mother to son, wife to husband, father to son, son to father, community to king. The heroines who lay with gods and bore demigods reveal how greatness entered the world; companions at Troy tell of an evil wife, inquire of a son, show a friend who became an enemy. The sinners balance the heroines, showing not the origin but the limits of mortal greatness. Heracles at the end states endurance. This is not personal insight in the sense of inner response drawing meaning from the world; it is the reverse, stable reality imparting itself to a person and drawing him to itself.

In his Thomistic union of Aristotelian categories with Christian faith, Dante descends and ascends through existent and intelligible states of being. He sees the divinely ordained scheme, yet by traversing the immense route himself lives it inwardly. In this personal nature of the journey Virgil is his fit guide through the first two parts. Though to Dante an explanatory mental guide, he keeps for him the assumption of inner response that speaks in Aeneas. The poem shares the verticality of *Aeneid* 6. The horizontality of *Odyssey* 11 reflects Homer's relative lack of language for experi-

8. J. B. Pritchard, *Ancient Near Eastern Texts*[3] 97.

ence as privately conceived—not that heroic experience is not true and powerful but that it accompanies events. These illustrate an order existent behind human actions; to respond like the heroes is to exhibit the order's nobility but also its transience for mortals, and greatest actions by their transience beget understanding. The scheme of things that Odysseus sees in the Underworld indeed concerns him—he learns of his return and his future—but the outcome will occur within a natural frame. In perception of the frame he resembles Dante. As the Florentine at the height of the mountain of Purgatory recovers Eden, Ithaca will flower under a good king. Oedipus from formerly infected Thebes thus reaches flowering Colonus and, like Dante at Eden (*Purg.*27), at the end walks unguided forward. The existence of the latent but finally acknowledged scheme permits travel and emergence. In their mental sight, though not in the inwardness from which it issues nor in its otherworldly goal, the travelers Odysseus and Dante have some bond. But that is to say that the huge emotion from which Achilles and Gilgamesh rise to understanding of mortal loss is absent from the *Odyssey*. Achilles' final understanding yields to the labor of travel as frontal youth yields to the mature sight of consequences. But the perceived truth is similar; though in intensity Odysseus is less heroic than Achilles, he is as heroic in courage to perceive. Throughout the travels and in the Underworld what he meets and sees shows the reality. His travels are horizontal in space rather than vertically inward because outflung existence defines his knowledge.

Circe had described Persephone's grove beyond the stream of Oceanus on a headland thick with poplars and fruit-failing willows. The north wind will have sped them; on landing he is to advance toward Hades' habitation, toward a cliff where the sounding rivers Puriphlegethon and Cocytus fall into Acheron (10.507–515). The place and what he sees there have a certain vagueness and inconsistency, perhaps fittingly, the place being mysterious and the revelation uppermost. He is near but not in the world of the dead; the ghosts issue to him, and he sets sail in haste at the end when the myriad nations of the dead gather with an awful cry, from fear lest Persephone send up some Gorgon-headed monster. Yet his mother Anticleia's first words are of pity that he has voyaged alive beneath the nether gloom to see things hard for mortals to behold. The sheep-blood in the trench which the emerging ghosts first drink and which alone gives them force to speak gradually falls away, and he sees people for themselves. Agamemnon, who drinks of the blood (11.390), appears with those who died with him at Aegisthus' banquet. Achilles, who does not drink (11.467–472), has with him his friends Patroclus, Antilochus, and Ajax and at the end walks with great strides through the asphodel meadow (11.539). Minos as judge in Hades' broad-gated house and the famous sinners in their several torments follow. Odysseus' gaze follows Achilles toward the asphodel meadow. The circumstances of trench, blood, emergence, drinking, and speech that at first allow him knowledge progressively yield to the knowledge alone. Later addition has often been assumed, but the story carries two not easily reconcilable assumptions: that as a mortal he not enter Hades but that as traveler he behold it. The latter part of the account recalls Achilles' shield; the described actions are carried out: on the shield, the cattle-ravagers leaping on the unsuspecting herd and herdsmen, help for them soon coming, then the battle (*Il.*18.520–533); here Sisyphus pushing the rock toward a summit, the rock falling back, he pushing again (11.595–600). But chiefly the journey exhibits the next world as the shield exhibits this world. It is needless at this stage to rehearse the inconsistencies of Odysseus' narrative or the poem as a whole—for example, his companions' belief that Aeolus' bag held gifts "from people whose city and land he reaches" (10.39), though before Aeolus they had reached only the Cicones, Lotuseaters, and Cyclops. The story may have been familiar to Homer as told of, not by Odysseus. The formulaic language does not suggest addition. The voyage to the Underworld is central not only to his return but to his knowledge. The Homeric method of dividing what he sees from how he sees it—for example, the elaborate beginning at Scheria before he tells his travels or the description of the Cyclopes (9.106–115) before he ventures to the cave—operates here. The hero detailedly tells how he summoned the dead, then describes them in themselves.

The burned as well as the buried dead remain images of what they were; primitives believed that of animals. It is a short step to the presence of the dead among the living—ghosts returned in Athens on the day of Choes; as great ghost and sacral hero, buried Oedipus will guard the city—and a short further step to *nekuomanteia*, invocation of the dead as Herodotus (5.92) describes Periander invoking his wife Melissa. What Circe called Persephone's grove and shore is mysteriously further termed the sunless land of the Cimmerians; there may be later confusion with a known remote people.[9] The landing in any case takes place at the end of a day's sail (11.12), and the local and actual night coincide. Blind Teiresias of Theban legend is a greater prophet than Calchas of Trojan legend whose death and burial in Asia Minor was part of the tale of return. The war at Thebes took place a generation earlier, and Teiresias fitly begins a revelation that includes the past. He is further distinguished by Persephone's gift only to him of a mind unchanged: he in fact addresses Odysseus before drinking the sheep-blood but drinks before his prophecy (11.90–99). He digs the trench, pours the triple libation of melicrete (honey and milk), wine, and water that is not offered to Olympians but to chthonic powers; vows on reaching Ithaca a sacrifice to all the dead and a black lamb to Teiresias; then kills the ram and black ewe that Circe gave him and collects the blood in the trench. Ancient critics athetized the marvelous following lines on the ghosts' outcrying arrival (11.38–43)—brides, youths, burdened elders, quick girls with hearts new to grief, spear-wounded warriors clad in sullied armor—but in method the lines repeat the proleptic description of the Cyclopes and in spirit recall the previously cited opening of *Iliad* 12, on the flooding Trojan rivers beside which the breed of the demigods once fought. Like Virgil and Dante, the poet could hardly approach the other life without sense of its multitude. Companions are bidden sacrifice the sheep with prayer to Hades and Persephone; Odysseus with drawn sword keeps the ghosts from the blood until he shall inquire of Teiresias.

The revelation falls into two parts, concerning himself and concerning heroic life. The former begins with Elpenor, whose ghost had flown faster than their ship from Circe's house but can speak without drinking the blood because he is still unwept and unburied. Like Patroclus to Achilles, he bids Odysseus not forget him; his plea by Odysseus' wife, father, and son looks to the return and contrasts to the wandering; he wants his grave marked by the oar with which alive he rowed with his companions (11.60–73). Their death follows from conscious fault; his marks his frailty. Of the many such who left home, he remains the figure of insufficiency. Odysseus had left his mother alive in Ithaca; he weeps to

9. See above, p. 58 n. 3.

see her shade but, as in the firelit scene at sight of Penelope's tears, resists until Teiresias shall have drunk. The prophet's great speech (11.100–137), among the most memorable in literature, compressedly tells the future action of the poem, then goes beyond it. In function it resembles Zeus's speech at the start of *Iliad* 15 (64–71), when after restraining the gods from battle he foretells Patroclus' death, Achilles' rise, Hector's death, and the doom of Troy; his anger will then cease. Teiresias likewise omits details to relate Poseidon's anger and its placation. It was noted that in order to reach home Menelaus had first to consult the wise man of the sea, who would tell "the course and measures of your journey, and your return, how you will pass over the fishy sea" (4.389–390), the same words with which Circe directed Odysseus to Teiresias. She herself on his return to Aeaea will tell the immediate next steps. Like Proteus to Menelaus, Teiresias tells the essential condition, evading divine anger, then goes on to what Odysseus will find at home and to his end of life. Minor revelations do not befit great wizards.

Thus he starts from Poseidon's anger for the blinding of Polyphemus which, it is only implied, will keep them on Thrinacia among the sun-god's cattle; they will be held there by adverse winds. If they spare the cattle, they will reach home from their sufferings. Harm to the cattle will be doom for ship and companions; if Odysseus escapes, "you will come late and ill after losing all your companions, on an alien ship, and find sorrows in the house," the words of the Cyclops' prayer to Poseidon (9.534–535). The sun-god and the sea-god will jointly cause the others' death but, now instructed, Odysseus will escape Helius' anger. The first storm that met them after Troy involved them all; the second storm off Thrinacia distinguishes among them; the third storm between Ogygia and Scheria shows Poseidon's continuing anger but Odysseus survives; he will have learned the price of survival. The fact of divine anger outweighs its source; it is first Athene's and Poseidon's, then Poseidon's, Helius', and Zeus's, then Poseidon's only, then subsidingly Poseidon's. For a seafarer the seagod dominates—even Odysseus' death will come from the sea—but Zeus both ratifies the anger and sets limits to it. Insofar as the travels, though at sea, are travels in mortal possibility, Zeus finally determines.

Teiresias then describes the suitors' wasteful wooing in Ithaca and predicts Odysseus' vengeance, though without specifying whether it will be done openly or by guile, the option that Athene-

Mentes raised to Telemachus and that she decides for Odysseus at the Bay of Phorkys. The great passage follows. "But when you have killed the suitors in your hall by guile or openly with sharp bronze, then take your well-fitted oar and go until you reach people who know not the sea nor eat food mixed with salt nor know ruddle-cheeked ships nor fitted oars that are wings to ships. A clearest sign I shall tell and it will not fail you: whensoever another wayfarer falling in with you says that you carry on your bright shoulder a winnowing-fan, then after planting your fitted oar in earth and making due sacrifice to the lord Poseidon—ram, bull, and boar, mounter of sows—go home and do holy hecatombs to the deathless gods who hold the wide sky, all in sequence. Death will come to yourself out of the sea, most gentle, which will slay you attained of a shining old age. A prospering people will surround you. This I tell you true" (11.119–137). As a pre-Greek god of all waters, not of the sea only, Poseidon was worshipped in inland places. Though by later attestation, Odysseus was associated with cults of the god in Arcadia and Thesprotia.[10] If he too goes back to a pre-Greek figure and had early bonds with the god, these became chiefly famous on sea. The legend of the inland altar, whatever its origin, passes into poetry. As a runner at the end of a long race does not abruptly stop but slowly jogs intensity away, Odysseus must journey to quiet. Elpenor's oar will mark his grave; Odysseus' oar will also leave the sea; but its inland journey will be calm, and the stranger who thinks it a winnowing-fan will convert it from the barren wave to the fertile threshing-floor. It will be the hero's transit to land. Poseidon's abated anger asserts travel become home, sea become land, but—most magical part of the prophecy—not utterly, since Odysseus' gentle death will come from the sea.

The lines express the sea-god's final mercy. "But when in the circling seasons," the invocation of Book 1 concludes, "the year came when the gods had spun for him to fare homeward to Ithaca, even then he was not clear of trials and with his kindred. All the gods pitied him, save Poseidon. He ceaselessly raged against godlike Odysseus before he reached his fatherland." The before implies an after. The words "from the sea" that here describe his death are used three times in the *Iliad* of Poseidon's emergence (*Il.* 13.15, 44,

---

10. Albert Hartmann, *Untersuchungen über die Sagen vom Tod des Odysseus.*

20.14). Other than in this prophecy and Odysseus' repetition of it to Penelope, they recur six times in this poem; twice of Proteus' rising (4.401, 450), once of his seals (4.448), once of Amphitrite's great sea-creatures (5.422), twice of Thetis' emergence with her sister Nereids and the Muses to lament Achilles (24.47, 55). The poetic tone is preternatural. The rare word "gentle," *ablechros,* that will describe Odysseus' death elsewhere appears only twice, in the *Iliad* (5.337, 8.178): of Aphrodite's hand which Diomedes wounds, and of the newly built Achaean wall which, confident in Zeus's delusive bolts, Hector cries will fall away. This usage too has only divine associations. Odysseus' inland altar will have worked full placation, and Poseidon will share his fellow Olympians' mercy toward the sea-farer. The gentle death, the reverse of Hippolytus' death from the sea, will be Poseidon's doing, though, as in the storm after Troy, Athene will have wished and Zeus decreed it. The brevity of the beautiful lines expresses the mystery. The sea in some way marked Odysseus to the end—that is part of the mystery—but not in the unappeased restlessness that his figure was later to express, rather by another attribute of the sea, its horizons. The poet saw the beauty and privilege of the travels as the home-seeker could not, but these will return to him as memory and knowledge. That is asserted in the gentleness of his death and the people's happiness. The king's return will bring general good but also inward good. The theme is echoed in Arete's healing presence among the Phaeacians, in the beggar's praise of Penelope as good king under whom land and sea burgeon and the people flourishes, in Agamemnon's ghostly praise of Penelope as a theme of poets, and in the joy of reunion. The gods finally allow the calm of mental possession. It is not dissociated from its sea-origin but not identical with that; carries attainment of what was implied but hidden at the start, at last understood almost with the gods' eyes: a place vouchsafed, yet because that place has been seen in its great setting, possession of it as token of all mortal places. Place and horizons finally join. That is the theme of the poem of wise Odysseus, the content and sum of his wisdom.

On drinking the blood, Anticleia marvels that he has journeyed alive beneath the nether gloom. She assumes him to be returning from Troy but is not certain that he has not reached Ithaca; she evidently knows Ithaca as she left it, not as it is. After relating his errand and travels, he asks of her manner of death, of Laertes and

Telemachus, and of Penelope's mind, whether she stays with their son and keeps the house intact or has married—to all of which Anticleia answers in reverse order. It is not said when she died, perhaps a few years after he left since she knows nothing of the suitors, now at their fourth year of wooing. Eumaeus later describes her pining for her son, and adds that Laertes lives in double grief (15.353–360). Anticleia, perhaps inconsistently, knows his life almost of a farm-laborer, though he took to it after her death. Penelope, she says, lives nights and days of sorrow; Telemachus keeps his property, giving and receiving wide hospitality. That may be another inconsistency, but if her memory is from years ago, Achilles too as a child is pictured by Phoenix dining abroad, evidently a role of boyish heirs (*Il.*9.486–487). Laertes is her chief concern; he sleeps of winters by the fire on ashes in foul clothes, of summers on leaves in the vineyard. He has come on a hard age as, she concludes, she too did. Artemis did not slay her with gentle arrows nor wasting illness carry her off, "but your missing, your counsels, bright Odysseus, your gentle-mindedness took away my honey-sweet spirit" (11.202–203).

If he is to reach final calm of mind, to his mother at least it was never alien to him. Helen thus praises Hector's gentle-mindedness; Penelope's memory of her and Odysseus' first happiness says the same. But the call of the world and men's response to it from other parts of their nature make home and happiness fragile; Odysseus will have regained by a circuitous route what Hector could not keep. Homer's feeling for Hector—the *Iliad* ends with him—finds fulfillment in Odysseus; Achilles too remembers home, but the other two more fully express the obverse of heroism which is family. Yet when Odysseus thrice tries to embrace his mother's shade and it flutters from his arms like a shadow or dream, the difference from the *Iliad* appears smaller. Persephone does not cheat you, she replies, "but this is the edict for mortals when one dies. Sinews no longer hold flesh and bones, but the masterful power of blazing fire conquers them once life has left the white bones, and on wings like a dream the spirit flies away. Seek the light fast. Know all this to tell hereafter to your wife" (11.218–224). Homecoming will be less than immortality; Anticleia's final mindfulness of Penelope conveys the mood but also the duration of the return; she comes near echoing Teiresias' prophecy of a gentle death. In this awareness of death the *Iliad* and the *Odyssey* are at one; Odysseus' inability to grasp his mother's shade repeats that of Achilles in his dream of Patroclus. What was called the horizontality of the portrayal of the Underworld asserts stable relationships, so far suggested of three generations, which give the frame of life. Its beauty and desirability and the affirmation of human response are unquestioned; these state the gods' presence in the beautiful world and, within the given scheme, their solicitude for mortals. It is in this sense that the *Odyssey* is a half-divine comedy, yet not generically distinct from the *Iliad*. The poems show heroic possibility within a vouchsafed scheme.

Home and kinship, the condition of identity, have now been stated; whatever may later befall a man, these determine him and will show in his end. But destinies meanwhile crowd, on the great especially; whether in themselves or in their fates or in the union of these, the great become illustrative. Their dimension for good or ill also operates, one mark of which is divine descent. In the heroines who lay with gods and bore the storied heroes, Odysseus sees a greatness that anteceded Troy but continued there; it is Homer's assumption and theme. Nestor in *Iliad* 1 (260–272) recalls a mightier breed than now surrounds him; Sthenelus, Diomedes' charioteer, contrasts their fathers' failure to take Thebes to their own success (*Il.*4.404–410). The list of Myrmidon chiefs who accompany Patroclus to battle resembles the present list of heroines in describing unions with gods (*Il.*16.170–197). Phoenix, who of the three main elders of the *Iliad* expresses the wisdom of age as Nestor expresses its retrospection and Priam its mounting loss, knows the traditions of both catalogue and heroic story. He first in Hesiodic manner cites to Achilles the divine spirits *Ate* and *Litae*, Madness and Prayers, then the heroic tale of Meleager (*Il.*9.502–599). The Greek poetry of catalogue first known to us in Hesiod was familiar to Homer; its middle-Eastern origins that M. L. West traces attest to its antiquity.[11] The Hesiodic *Catalogue of Women*,[12] which was later added to the *Theogony* to explain the origin of races and cities as the *Theogony* explains that of the world, has been seen as behind the present catalogue, which has therefore also been thought late, but the difference of the Hesiodic from the Odyssean catalogue is striking. Even in its fragmentary

11. Prolegomena to his edition of the *Theogony*.
12. Merkelbach and West, *Fragmenta Hesiodea*.

state it shows an interest alien to Homer's in exotic myth, women's dress and beauty, and elaborated detail. The present heroines of the Underworld are simply presented; they emerge to Odysseus to explain the glint of divinity in the great past. They in turn lead to the so-called intermezzo, when he suggests stopping but for the first time wins Arete's wholehearted praise, is promised further gifts, and agrees to finish his story by postponing departure to the third night (11.330–376). His account of women, in Anticleia's feeling for him and mindfulness of Penelope, then in the heroines, touches Arete. As the return joins the one side of him which is family and origin with his other side which is Troy and travel, so the heroines join his intimate visions to public, exemplary visions which in turn evoke Troy.

Further, the heroines set one side of a frame that surrounds his former companions at Troy, the other side consisting of the famous sinners. If the gods by mortal union give brilliance to the world, they also stand apart from it. Gigantic strength, rape of a goddess, attempted theft of immortality, attempted escape from Hades, all collide with final limits. The frame constates a greatness that, being mortal, can affect but not keep the world. Understanding of Troy as within this frame is part of his instruction; the travels assert it, but as central experience the Underworld exhibits the truth schematically. The horizontal design of this part of the adventure comprises, as it were, two lines encasing a central scene, the Trojan figures. Brilliance carries over to them from the heroines, but the overreaching sinners finish the comment. As the last episode of the Trojan story, the *Odyssey* keeps evoking past events. In the heroines the poet extends this mood of summary to set the tale of Troy among other great tales; his resort to the tradition of catalogue is historical and synoptic.

The Minyan line that in Pelias and Neleus settled Iolcus and Pylos descends from Tyro's union with Poseidon behind uprisen waves at the outpourings of the river Enipeus (235–259). In *Iliad* 16 (173–178), the Myrmidon Menesthius was fathered by the river Spercheius, but Tyro who loved the Enipeus and wandered by his banks met a greater god. Antiope bore to Zeus the wall-builders of Thebes, Amphion and Zethus; Alcmene there bore Heracles to Zeus; in mortal union with her son Oedipodes Epicaste gave rise to the harshest cycle of Theban history. Similarly the last three Myrmidons of *Iliad* 16, notably Phoenix, do not derive

from gods but in themselves show their troublous fame. The onward line of Pylos speaks in Chloris, Neleus' wife and the mother,
among others, of Nestor and Pero, whom the seer Melampus won
for his brother from hard Neleus. The history is later continued in
Melampus' great-grandson the seer Theoclymenus (15.223–255),
who as a fugitive meets Telemachus at Pylos, accompanies him to
Ithaca, and makes crucial prophecies of Odysseus' return and the
suitors' death. Leda, mother of Castor and Polydeuces to whom
Zeus gave alternate immortality, relates Spartan legend; a line
echoes Helen's memory at Troy of her brothers (11.301, *Il.*3.243).
Iphimedeia bore the handsome and gigantic Otos and Ephialtes
who would have stormed heaven by piling Pelion on Ossa had not
Apollo killed them early. In the *Iliad* (5.385–387) they are said to
have imprisoned Ares for thirteen months in a bronze pot; the
overreacher Orion, whom Odysseus later sees, is here linked with
them. Crete appears in Phaedra, Procris, and Ariadne; Mycenae in
Myra, Clymene, and Eriphyle, the evil wife who for a gold necklace lured her husband Amphiaraus against his will to join the attack on Thebes. She resembles Clytemnestra and contrasts to
Penelope. After Tyro, whose offspring Poseidon directly prophe-
sies, the heroines' words to Odysseus are merely described, ellipti-
cally and with progressive crowding.

As often, the poet alludes rather than narrates, here seemingly
from sense of the multitude of human histories. Unlike Anticleia,
the great women speak little of death; they tell what befell them
and their progeny alive. But their histories, though touched by
gods, are famous rather than happy; as was evident at Troy, involvement with immortals chiefly states magnitude. Coming after
the prophecy of Odysseus' shining age and gentle death, the scene
raises contrasts of mortals to demigods. Achilles and Helen in the
Iliad have a power and brilliance that differentiate them from Hector and Andromache; as half-children of gods, they carry into the
world a dimension beyond common humanity. Odysseus and Penelope resemble Hector and Andromache. The *Odyssey* contrasts to
the *Iliad* as relating not the brief life of a demigod on whom love of
a friend forced human choice but the finally instructed life of a
mortal pair. The greatness, yet the sorrow and error that followed
on the heroines' divine unions are part of Odysseus' vision in the
Underworld. Much the same emerges from his next conversation
with his former friends at Troy and from the summary of the Second Nekyia.

The intermezzo follows, after which he meets and talks with his greatest former companions Agamemnon and Achilles. The third, Ajax, who after Achilles' death killed himself because Odysseus rather than he received from the Achaeans the prize of the supreme hero's armor, turns away in silence. It is often said that Homer's interest is in this life. The evident fact relates to his lack of language for the isolated mind or soul, a subject that since Snell has been much discussed.[13] *Psuché* means the frail replica that flies away at death; it is these that Odysseus sees and that get brief power of speech from the sheep's blood. Similarly other mental faculties,— the mind, spirit, and heart, *nous, thumos, ker, phrenes, kardie*— are quasi-bodily attributes almost in the class of eyes, arms, and legs; a living person operates by all of them. Yet the Minoans were concerned for the next life; some of their sacral implements, and presumptively their beliefs, persisted in the Eleusinian Mysteries.[14] Mycenaean tombs show a like concern; the twelve Trojans, four horses, and two dogs that Achilles offers at Patroclus' pyre (*Il.*23.171–176), if expressive of grief and revenge, also suggest service in the next world. Portrayals of another life are partly matters of vocabulary; response to this life is the sole effective guide. Dante's anger, love, and spirituality and his words for these dictate what he sees. The present Underworld echoes the rest of the poems. The love and enmity, the setting of nature, the physical vigor and sensed interworking of mind and body, yet the shock of death and pain of parting that mark the living show in the dead. If Homer lacked words to isolate the mind or soul as the root of identity, he knew identity. Later attempts to isolate it as, so to speak, self-subsistent collapse in the mystery of a person's debt to myriad outer and inner responses. The further mystery of the emergent self is added. Whether, in Homer's manner, the mystery takes language from divine and human events, from experience of land and sea, and from innumerable human ties or, by contrast, is expressed in the lone soul's response makes little final difference. Death supervening on vivid life remains the same. The shadowy state of the souls that Odysseus meets tells the one side; the mutuality of recognition tells the other side. Homer's lack of language for the isolated and directing mind is of relatively minor importance; the parting from known people—and theirs from once-present com-

13. *Die Entdeckung des Geistes,* translated by T. G. Rosenmeyer, *The Discovery of the Mind* Ch. 1.

14. M. P. Nilsson, *The Minoan-Mycenaean Religion* Ch. 14.

panions—from the visible world, and from distant but sensed former generations speaks more clearly. Odysseus' inability to embrace his mother is one fact, their lasting love is the other fact. Similarly in the coming scene, Achilles' vain wish for even the humblest life on earth contrasts to his great strides across the asphodel meadow. The dead are and are not; Homer's sense of them states the simple fact that they once had identity and, as known, still have it but that what they are is shadowy. Their missing the world partly says that memory of them gives it meaning.

Proteus told Menelaus of Aegisthus' murder, in his own house at a welcoming feast, of Agamemnon and his followers on the day of their return (4.530–537), which the dead king now relates. Much is the same—his murdered companions surround him, he was killed like a bull at the stall (11.411)—but as told by him and to the home-seeker, the terrible tale takes another color. Clytemnestra, whose part was muted in the other account, emerges the implacable welcomer. As the king's return will contrast to his hearer's, so do their wives. "You have been present at many men's death singly slain or in tumultuous battle, but at that sight would most have grieved in heart, how beside drinking-bowl and laden tables we lay in the hall and the whole floor ran with blood. Most piteous I heard the cry of Priam's daughter Cassandra, whom guile-minded Clytemnestra killed beside me. I raised my arms, then dropped them dying on the sword, but as I fared to Hades she turned away; she did not bear to close my eyes with her hands and press my mouth together. Nothing is thus direr and more shameless than a wife who puts in her mind such acts, the scandalous act that she conceived in hatching death for her wedded husband. I thought to return home welcome to my children and servants, but in her mind's extreme cruelty she poured disgrace on herself and on women who will live hereafter, even if a woman be honest" (11.416–434). The poem turns on women; Penelope fulfills a return that Athene initiates and Circe, Calypso, Nausicaa, and Arete help effect. Relatively absent though women are from the *Iliad,* it follows not only or perhaps chiefly from Helen as cause of the war but from Chryseis and Briseis as causes of the quarrel. Clytemnestra here is the mirror of Agamemnon in *Iliad* 1 but exceeds him in intransigeance as Penelope exceeds Odysseus in steadiness of mind. Comment thus returns to Agamemnon in Cassandra, whose presence effectually repeats his statement of *Iliad* 1 (113) that he prefers Chryseis to his wife. He becomes, as in Aeschylus' portrayal, a figure of the army to the exclusion of home. The balance between Troy and home that Odysseus achieves is as beyond the king as keeping home was beyond Hector. Characters are fixed, so to speak, proleptically in myth; travel and not least the revelation of the Underworld enhance Odysseus' understanding of home, but in the *Iliad* (2.260, 4.354) he speaks of himself as Telemachus' father. The statement as much describes him there as does Agamemnon's preference for Chryseis. But the king is weaker than his wife, as shows not only in his change of mind at Troy after his first obduracy about Chryseis and Briseis but in his expectation here that he would return welcome. The fates of Achilles and Hector carry sense of what might have been another outcome; Agamemnon's blindness to contesting loyalties, his taking home for granted, predicts his end. As Odysseus and Penelope emerge much alike, so do the king and queen. Beneath Agamemnon's lurid emotionality, his self-identification with the army shows in the alarm for it that he pours out at the start of *Iliad* 9 and 14, in his dream of *Iliad* 2 and his wakefulness of *Iliad* 10. Clytemnestra is the more single-minded as her world is narrower. He goes on to warn Odysseus to test even Penelope, steady in mind though he admits her to be, by returning secretly (11.455); he in effect resolves the option that Teiresias left open. In Penelope's final speech of recognition, Helen, though impelled by gods, is the dangerous exemplar that she strove to avoid (23.215–224). The three wives, Clytemnestra, Helen, and Penelope, make a spectrum of fidelity, and Agamemnon's praise of Penelope in the Second Nekyia, following closely as it does her fearful but firm self-contrast to Helen, comes near to closing the poem with the triple comparison.

If dead Agamemnon is as he was, so is Achilles. Devotion to him shows in the accompanying figures of Patroclus, Antilochus, and Ajax. When Odysseus calls him supreme among the dead as once among the living and bids him not repine, he answers with his old bluntness: "Do not gloze death to me, glorious Odysseus. I had rather be a soil-bound serf to another man, a landless man who lacks much substance, than rule over the perished dead entire" (11.488–491). The famous lines are sometimes wrongly taken to show in the *Odyssey* a changed estimate of heroism. On the contrary, Achilles is the same man who in *Iliad* 9 (309–313) blankly refuses Odysseus' vast offers from the king: "I must speak my mind unheeding, as I intend and as will come to pass, so that you not sit about cooing at me. I hate like Hades' gates a man who hides one thing in his heart and speaks another." His heroic clarity is unchanged. The like structure of the two poems shows, among other ways, in their close. As at the games for Patroclus and in the meeting with Priam Achilles stands half-removed from an action then decided by him, so Odysseus' home-coming brings retrospection and review. The Second Nekyia puts the past in a longer light, and the opening exchange between Agamemnon and Achilles gives comment on the present meeting. Agamemnon is the same there as here: his royal greatness was canceled in his end. But the Nereids who rise from the sea with Thetis to lament Achilles and dress him in immortal clothes and the nine Muses who sing of him (24.58–62) declare his endless fame. The death of a young man far from home has only this reward. In the future song that it is said the Muses will inspire of faithful Penelope (24.196–198) the reunited pair will have both a different and a like fame, as durable but of another destiny. But Odysseus is now in mid-passage; the Underworld asserts his mortality which this meeting supremely shows. No rejection of heroism but the incompleteness of young death speaks in Achilles' wish for even the humblest life on earth. Teiresias' prophecy to Odysseus of a gentle death in bright old age among a flourishing people promises only a longer time. Achilles goes on to ask of his son Neoptolemus, and on hearing of his arrival at Troy, his beauty second only to Memnon's, son of the Dawn, his bravery inside the wooden horse when others paled and trembled, and his safe embarkation, "he strode with great steps down the asphodel meadow, rejoiced that I declared his son glorious" (11.539–540). Other legend had him carried after death to the Leuke Nesos, the Shining Island.[15] If the pale fields of asphodel here partly fit the realm of shades, they are a more beautiful place than has been described of others, a kind of disembodied Trojan plain where he still masterfully strides. Here most of all the dead figure both is and is not. For the older and still living man, his matchlessness attests to both similarity and difference, similarity in their mortal lot, difference in their lives and characters. To Odysseus at this turn toward home the encounter is not wholly forbidding; it foreshadows the continuity of a son and the longer continuity of poetry.

15. Proclus' outline of the *Aethiopis*; T. W. Allen, *Homeri Opera* V 106.15.

As in *Iliad* 9 (624–642), a further difference shows in Ajax. He had no understanding there of Achilles' complexity of feeling, still less regard for Odysseus' oratory and Phoenix's meditation; to him Achilles' refusal was simple neglect of friends. He characteristically makes his two greatest speeches of the *Iliad* in battle, at the beleaguered wall and over Patroclus' body (*Il.*15.733–741, 17.629–647). Odysseus here vainly wishes that he had not won the armor for loss of which Ajax died; he repeats the Iliadic characterization of him as the greatest warrior after only Achilles and says that the army mourned them equally. Zeus's anger, he says, was on the army and caused his death (11.553–562). He pleads for a reply but gets none; Ajax turns toward Erebus. "Even then," Odysseus concludes, "though angry he might have addressed me or I him, but the heart in my breast wished to behold the souls of other dead" (11.565–567). The contrast of Odysseus' mental nature, apparent toward Achilles, is still clearer; even his wish to hear the Sirens' song shows it no more patently. Does it say that after the death of Achilles, at once a speaker of words and a doer of deeds (*Il.*9.443), choice arose as between words and deeds and that in this choice Homer, like the myth, declared for Odysseus? His regret for the past is presented as genuine; war, travel, and not least the Underworld have touched him. He has had cause in his own life to know Zeus's anger against the army; what in him can show as words shows more deeply as understanding. Ajax's inflexibility contains a sense of form, the form of the self, without which a man is unrecognizable. Greek regard for the limit of form is continually expressed, not least in statuary. Yet intelligence that sees and learns from the world is more generically human; fidelity to form is shared, also in Greek art, with animals. That the poet sees limit in Odysseus is clear from the tale of homecoming; he ends where he began, yet after seeing the cities of men and knowing their minds. Ajax's changelessness toward a changed Odysseus expresses the poet's sense of the mental demand of travel as necessary to one who will find final peace. The Underworld adds intellection to homeward guidance, and Homer's regard for Odysseus as of like, though different, dimension with Achilles speaks in the contrast to Ajax.

Achilles and Ajax do not drink of the blood; other spirits, perhaps Patroclus and Antilochus, are said to have told their sorrows. Sight of the asphodel meadows was not suggested of the place where Odysseus first invoked the dead but opens after departing

Achilles. The narrative moves from the circumstances of vision to vision itself. The *Theogony* describes the habitation of Night's children Sleep and Death in a place, as in the *Odyssey,* ungazed on by the rising or setting sun (11.16–17, *Theog.*76–761). It is near the great bronze threshold where Night and Day alternately greet each other (*Theog.*748–757), the place that seems cryptically echoed of the country of the Laestrygonians (10.82–86). Mighty Hades and dread Persephone, also as in the *Odyssey,* rule in the land of Death (11.47, *Theog.*768). The former is called the chthonic god (*Theog.*767, *Erg.*465); the term appears in the *Iliad* in Phoenix's account of his father's curse of him by chthonic Zeus (*Il.*9.457). Cerberus who fauns on those who come devours those who would leave. In the *Works and Days* (140–142) the violent and irreverent people of the Silver Age to whom Zeus put an end nevertheless have place beneath the earth. The men of his Fourth Age, the demigods who fought at Thebes and Troy, live in the isles of the blessed beside deep-eddying Oceanus (*Erg.*157–173). All this has small specific connection with the present Underworld, but distinct as is Hesiod's purpose—in the *Theogony,* the emergence of the divine order, in the *Works and Days* its dictates on earth— Hesiod is aware of a realm of the dead, of its inescapability, of the power of the chthonic god, and of the differing fates of righteous and unrighteous generations. Prometheus, Epimetheus, and Pandora have for him an illustrative purpose, though that again differs.

Over and above the guidance to his future that Odysseus gains in the Underworld, the poet intends it to show the nature of things, which the travels also show but less schematically. Judgment of the dead can hardly be absent. The sinners are not common men; their affront was against that Olympian rule the origin and existence of which Hesiod celebrates. Minos, a son of Zeus, is here the judge from whom souls hear their portion (11.568–571). The giant huntsman Orion, mentioned earlier with the sons of the heroine Iphimedeia who would have piled Pelion on Ossa, named also by Calypso among the mortal lovers whom the gods will not let goddesses keep—he was loved by the Dawn and killed by chaste Artemis on Ortygia (5.121–124)—still hunts in the asphodel meadow. His fate refutes Calypso's offer to Odysseus of agelessness and immortality. The still huger Tityus, son of Earth, lies outstretched, his liver feasted on by vultures as in the *Theogony*

(523–524) is Prometheus' liver by an eagle, because he laid hands on Leto. The liver is the seat of the passions; the eagle that afflicts Prometheus more directly expresses Zeus's anger, but Tityus attacked a bride of Zeus and, like Typhoeus the last rebel of the *Theogony,* is a son of Earth. Only the punishments of Tantalus and Sisyphus are described, their offenses being evidently taken as known. Tantalus stands in a pond, but the water dries and bare earth shows when he bends to drink; pears, pomegranates, apples, figs, and olives hang above him, but winds blow them skyward when he reaches to eat (11.582–592). Later myth had the gods share with him their nectar and ambrosia, which he stole to give to mortals (Pindar, *Ol.* 1.59–64). Sisyphus strains with arms and feet pushing a great rock toward a summit, just as it reaches which the shameless rock falls back and he repeats; sweat pours from him and dust is on his head (11.593–600). To Theognis (699–718) he is the clever man who tried to escape Hades; his cleverness is mentioned in the *Iliad* (6.153). These sinners, it was argued, finish the frame around the Trojan figures which the heroines initiate. The two groups jointly set the recent between the long past and shed example on it. There seems further tie to Hesiod in his distinguishing the beneficent earth-abiding spirits of the Golden Age from the flagitious subterranean spirits of the Silver Age and both from the demigods on the blessed isles. The tie is not of substance but of method and purpose. Though the sinners and the heroines have been thought later additions, they enlarge Odysseus' sight by the epic method of exemplary categories.

Heracles at the end like Anticleia at the start marvels at his mortal fate of gazing on the dead; the adventure rounds to a close. He too, he says, by fated service to a lesser man lived a life of endless labor, the extreme of which was descent to capture Cerberus. Yet, as with Odysseus, Hermes' and Athene's guidance let him do even that (11.625–626). The poem and the speech at Scheria start as tales of toil; the endurance that underlies the hero's many traits has its prototype in Heracles. He is such in *Iliad* 19 (95–125), though less for his labors than for the blindness by which Zeus himself was tricked by Hera to subjugate him to his inferior half-brother Eurystheus. Odysseus has now seen and endured more than fits a mortal, and the cry of the innumerable dead will soon speed him away. But his labors will end well, and that too is shown in Heracles, only whose shade appears in Hades while he himself takes joy among the gods with Hebe for wife (11.602–604). The explanation resembles that by which Odysseus later knows of Helius' anger for his slaughtered cattle. The motive is evident. Heracles was beyond others dear to his father Zeus; in the *Theogony* (529–531) he is for that reason given the fame of shooting the eagle and freeing Prometheus. Though his final translation to Olympus is first mentioned in the *Odyssey,* it is in the spirit of the poem as showing both release from toil and Zeus's final justice. His baldric, adorned with pictured animals and battles, resembles the crown that in the *Theogony* Hephaestus makes for Pandora (11.610–612, *Theog.*581–582). The themes by which the poet shows Odysseus can change fast; thus just earlier he told Alcinous that he would stay a year for greater gain, yet on the next afternoon he yearns like a tired laborer for sunset. The labor of his journey shows in Heracles, yet as the great ghost leaves and Persephone is about to rouse the screaming nations of the dead, Odysseus says that he waited in hope of speaking with other heroes. Labor and knowledge, the two themes that mark him at the start continue to describe him. Their interworking will make possible the return and peaceful end of which he learns in the Underworld, even as he learns the nature of the longer human history within which his famous life takes place. The travels chiefly show the natural world, Hades chiefly the world of history and example. The poet chose the story over many possible others, and it may tell something of him that, though possessed of these two forms of knowledge, the hero reaches home a beggar.

They saw the Underworld at night and return to Circe's island at dawn. The time inspires the description of "the isle Aeaea where are early-born Heos' dwelling and dancing-places and Helius' risings" (12.304). The homeward half of the journey awaits, and as at the radiant start of the *Purgatorio,* dawn greets the fresh arrival. Yet the nether gloom, the *zophos,* that shrouds the Underworld is in the west. Stesichorus (fr.6) has the sun round from his journey in a golden cup to the depths of night to mother, wife, and children whence he will rise, but if Homer conceived travel by world-encircling Oceanus to and from a western shore beyond, he does not say so. His concern is for the present and seen. In the Underworld he did not explain how Odysseus from the shore saw shades within Hades; in the *Iliad* the phrase "on the left," used seven times of the fight at the wall and ambiguously of attackers and attacked, is vivid rather than descriptive. Circe was earlier called sister of Aeetes and now warns of clashing rocks fast enough to trap a dove, through which only the Argo, "all men's concern" (12.70), by Hera's aid safely passed; that journey also echoes in the eastern island. But the homeward turn is uppermost, the more because its last two stages at Ogygia and Scheria are past and the hero's speech lengthens. Circe detailedly lists the next dangers, ending with Teiresias' warning not to harm the seven herds each of fifty cattle and the like herds of sheep, immortal and without issue, Helius' delight. In warning of Scylla, she describes the monster's cave "turned toward the nether dusk to Erebus" (12.81). The six men who will die there will not long have escaped Erebus, nor the rest of the company who in spite of Odysseus' efforts will kill and eat the cattle. The shining day that dawned for them all on Aeaea will keep its hope only for him.

Their first concern is to bury Elpenor with his weapons, mark the grave with a stone, and plant his oar on it; Circe then foretells the next hazards to Odysseus alone. It has been supposed that Teiresias should have done so and that the Underworld shows a variant, perhaps an interpolated, sketch of the future. But Circe's more detailed account has its separate purpose, in two main ways. First, the Underworld, central among the thirteen adventures, is crowning, not directly practical. Odysseus, like Menelaus from Proteus, learns the precondition of his return, avoidance of Helius' wrath, but chiefly sees the boundaries of life, his own and others'. The king who will right Ithaca will have seen the world both spatially and mentally. Teiresias warns about Helius' cattle because restraint toward them summarizes the gain of Odysseus' wanderings. The cattle are, so to speak, Troy repeated, and peace will come from moderated desire. The Underworld is the apex of the travels. Second, Circe's foresight speeds to an end a speech that has now passed its height; foresight beseems an enchantress and daughter of all-seeing Helius, but for the purpose of the poem. The *Iliad* gets clarity by accumulation, but many prophecies—Zeus's initial plan to honor Achilles, vision of the erased Achaean wall, Zeus's temporary restraint of the gods, his granting half Achilles' prayer for Patroclus' glory and safety, his pity for Hector's blindness, Hera's statement that Achilles shall be invincible for a day—these and much else give further guidance. The *Odyssey* too advances by near-repetition—gigantic Cyclops and Laestrygonians, deflecting Lotuseaters, Circe, Sirens, and Calypso, mistake made or shunned with the Cyclops, Aeolus, and on Thrinacia—but the episodes are more various than battles, and prophecy serves. Brief account of the Lotuseaters sufficed when much would follow, but at this stage the tale of the Sirens and even of Scylla would be thin without repetition. In function Circe's foresight resembles Odysseus' and Penelope's review of their trials on the night of reunion (23.310–343). Both accounts collect the narrative after a climax. Nothing remains now of Circe's allurement. Nausicaa reappeared for a moment of farewell and Calypso guided to the place of raft-building, but the narrative was slower then; it now accelerates to Odysseus' final division from his men.

Mythical events differ from those of common daylight, set in myth though these may be, and one expects him to emerge changed from the Underworld. Doubtless he is changed; he spares Helius' cattle and at Scheria and Ithaca shows more than a kingly mind, much more than Agamemnon, more than Nestor and Menelaus in the first Books. The margin of his life has kept widening. But daylight revives his old traits, and his impulse to hear the Sirens and, though Circe warned against it (12.116–126), to resist Scylla shows him the same man. It may be said, rightly, that these episodes simply carry forward familiar themes and formulae, but a riddle of the poetry is its counterpoint between the myth and the characters. The thematically fixed characters are who they are, but the myth stretches outward carrying them with it, with the result that they are at once themselves and more than themselves, figures in an immense design. Odysseus nowhere inwardly summarizes or meditates on the travels; rather they summarize him. As the poem advances, the counterpoint tips toward the myth but not entirely. Outcomes describe but do not utterly change the characters. The power of the poetry is partly in this sober estimate of human identity; life keeps recognizable constants. But its growing dimension also describes the characters, partly in their actions, increasingly as figures in the myth. The poet's language is the formulae, but his mind is toward the myth; the mystery of his power is partly in the interplay.

Odysseus' wish to hear the Sirens' song, which Circe assumed and for which she instructed him, illustrates the point. His curiosity might have been thought satisfied in the Underworld. But that revelation surrounded or concerned his own past and future; the Siren song has no tie with him. The one gave him personal knowledge, the other promises universal knowledge. "Hither faring, greatly-praised Odysseus, the Achaeans' large boast, halt your boat to heed our voice. No man has yet passed here in his black ship before hearing the honey-voiced speech of our lips but in delight and with more knowledge sails away. We know all that in broad Troy the Argives and Trojans painfully did by the gods' will. We know whatsoever comes into existence on the much-nourishing earth" (12.184–191). It was noted that Phoenix in *Iliad* 9 (502–599) invokes both the, to us, Hesiodic and Homeric traditions, those of genetic catalogue and of heroic story, and both appeared in the Underworld. It is these two traditions that the Sirens offer entire. The sweetness of their song is the allure of total knowledge; this is the Faustian adventure. He will reach home by what he learned in the Underworld; this other complete, impersonal song ends a man's hope of wife and children (12.42–43). The labor that was elsewhere the price of knowledge falls away; more than among the Phaeacians the windless pause is nearly godlike. Though the Sirens add flattery and sympathy, the full tale of Troy, surrogate of total history, and the song of all origins are the temptation. Homer seems to contemplate and reject that impossible poetry. Bones and dry skin attest to past listeners, song-drunk Elpenors. Even so, as Circe instructed, Odysseus stops his men's ears with wax, has them tie him to the mast-box, and bids them tie him harder if, as he does, he grimaces for release (12.192–193). The prophecies of the Underworld told his future, but fixed in identity though he is, some part of his mind remains unsatisfied. Did he hear all or only part of the song? Surely only part, since others died listening but the Sirens sing on; their song is endless. Benign as his prophesied end will be, an impulse to totality, the mind's desire, still prompts him and he responds. The famous song expresses one side of a myth of which homecoming expresses the other; the two sides are not quite compatible.

His activism too continues. Circe foretold alternate routes through the clashing rocks or between Scylla and Charybdis, and he chooses the great but lesser hazard. He exhorts the men recalling his resourcefulness in the Cyclops' cave and giving hope that they will live to look back on this new danger (12.208–221). It is the third reminiscence of the Cyclops. The first was in their hope-

lessness on Circe's shore, the second when Eurylochus refused to
go to Circe's house blaming the deaths in the cave on Odysseus'
recklessness, the fourth will be on the night before the suitor-slaying when, as here, he takes comfort that courage and presence of
mind then saved him. The sequence illustrates the slow effect of the
myth. Eurylochus was right about his first recklessness; their sorrows followed from it. No more than then will he now save all the
men, but he no longer acts from curiosity and hope of gain. Even
so he remains his impulsive self. As in the firelit scene with Penelope his eagerness to appear different from other taletellers
prompts him to accept foot-washing only by some old servant,
which nearly ruins his plans by producing Eurycleia, so he now
forgets Circe's warning. Eagerness causes most of his errors: sleep
after continuous steering from Aeolus' island, sleep again on
Thrinacia when he leaves to pray for means of escaping the island,
more vaguely his year's stay with Circe, perhaps even his final testing of his father, as if he felt compelled to finish his inquisitory
plan. Eagerness is the fault of his imagined Cretan; Penelope's sudden laughter when she imagines appearing in beauty before the suitors shows something like it. It is natural brother to vitality;
much-tried people could hardly have lived without it, at least in the
immortal setting of the myth. He dons armor, plants himself at the
bow, peers toward the high cave on the misty cliff, meanwhile eye-
ing hollow Charybdis on the other side. He sees the six-necked and
six-jawed monster only as, like a fisherman, Scylla hauls as many
men gasping aloft. Their arms and legs show above his head; they
cry out and stretch their arms to him as she devours them, "the
most piteous thing that my eyes beheld, in all my toil searching the
paths of the sea" (12.258–259). On Aeaea the crew was divided
into two groups of twenty-two under himself and Eurylochus,
forty-six men (10.208). The Cicones had killed six from each ship;
Polyphemus had eaten six, Antiphates one; Elpenor then died, now
these six. Thucydides (1.10.4) judged biggest the complement of a
hundred and twenty listed in the Catalogue for the Boeotian ships,
smallest the complement of fifty listed of the ships of Philoctetes. If
the poet still takes account of such matters, the original fifty-nine
are now thirty-nine.

At sea again and near enough Thrinacia to hear lowing and
bleating, they are told by Odysseus, not quite exactly, that Teiresias and Circe warned him to pass by the island; what they said

was not to harm the animals. The poet may make the change unconsciously; his theme was then the precondition of return, it is
now the hero's mounting anxiety. This is the one adventure mentioned in the prologue; progressive diminution has led to it; more
than any other it connects the halves of the poem. His old critic
Eurylochus also grows to the moment; he contrasts Odysseus' iron
to their fatigue, paints the risks of night at sea, and urges stopping
just for the night (12.279–293). The others side with him, and
Odysseus says, not to them but to the Phaeacians, that he then saw
fate's intention (12.295). He makes them swear not in recklessness, the word used in the prologue, to kill any animal. Eurylochus
used the same word of Odysseus' rashness in the Cyclops' cave
(10.437). The repetitions make a kind of triangle from the prologue: the men's folly mounts as his abates. As often before, they
lament the recent dead, and when the night is a third past, Zeus
sends a great storm. He is the sky-god, but naming him evokes his
first astonished speech of the poem, how mortals unjustly blame
gods for the result of their own faults, also his ratification of the
Cyclops' prayer for vengeance. The view that causation in the *Odyssey* is more humanistic than in the *Iliad* hardly holds; a double,
coinciding causation persists. In Ithaca Odysseus warns Amphinomus to leave the house as he warns the crew here; the prophet
Theoclymenus' dire vision of night on the suitors' faces and blood
on the walls (20.351–357) is in the spirit of the cattle's flesh
squirming and lowing on the spits when the crew sits down to eat.
Granted that the battles of the *Iliad* show death's abrupter face,
the link between rash act and death is identical. Gods are the link
because life is not random. The travels are a reciprocal testing,
Odysseus' of the world and its of him; in that he emerges, the gods
are benign but limitedly, he being mortal, and severely, the world
being big. Consequence comes less fast in travel or common life
than in war, but it comes, and gods bring it.

   In the beautiful pseudo-Theocritus 25 the herds of Augeas,
Helius' son, return at evening like innumerable clouds, and the
most powerful of them, sacred to Helius, are as white as swans.
Apollonius (4.977–978) has the returning Argonauts see the pres-
ent herds on Thrinacia, which he calls white with golden horns.
Helius' daughters Phaethousa and Lampetie who here tend the
herds and flocks show a like radiance. The cattle of Indic and
Greek myth which harmful gods steal or hide in caves and benig-

nant gods or Heracles release may signify the rays of day or water-
bringing clouds; the cycle of the year has been seen in the seven
herds of fifty. If in adding equivalent flocks of sheep Homer seems
heedless of old myth, he again keeps something of its spirit. The
animals are immortal and without issue (12.130–132), evidently
not in the sense that they cannot be killed, rather as fonts of life
and abundance that can be spoiled. It is in this sense that the adventure is the reverse of Troy. The river Scamander clogged and
defiled by corpses rose against Achilles (*Il.*21.305–323), but the
war also concerned Paris's defilement of a marriage. Even so the
gods who approved the Achaeans turned hostile at the end; the
heroes severally paid, and Odysseus' payment is his journey. The
various traits that have supported him converge in this act of moderation; in deriving from the Underworld it is a mental act. Danger, labor, and accumulating deaths blind the crew, but he too
knows the drain of time, which cannot be escaped but only reme-
died by mental sight. Thus in Scheria his first words to Alcinous are
about the shameless belly; in Ithaca he challenges Eurymachus to a
contest of labor in the fields. He has been reduced but not mentally. It may be replied that he alone sleeps with Circe, speaks with
the dead, and hears the Sirens. But the travels are finally characterization; had the others been he, they might have done the same.
This last of the joint adventures shows by contrast what in his nature has survived and profited.

The fateful storm that keeps them a month on Thrinacia may be
slightly more enigmatic. Focke, seeing in it a fatality different from
the error stressed at the start of the poem, argued a later outlook in
the Telemacheia. But the delay evidently follows from the Cyclops'
approved prayer that, if Odysseus is to return, he shall come late
and ill, alone on an alien ship. Neither here nor in the prophecies is
Poseidon named as cause of the storm; yet it is a mischance of sail-
ing. Zeus fulfilled Poseidon's approval of the Cyclops' prayer; at
the start of the poem, when asked by Athene why he remains angry
at Odysseus, he protests that the anger is Poseidon's (1.64–75).
The return becomes a compromise between the two gods; the
myth, like others, is proleptic in the sense that Odysseus alone is
fated to return. Fate can be simply the future seen backwards but is
more; it is the likelihood of certain kinds of things happening, if
not today then sometime, to certain kinds of people. In the original
North American woods some trees clearly outlived others that died

at the height at which present trees of the same species commonly die. The old-growth trees survived by individual strength, falsely suggesting that in that heroic forest all were as mighty. Odysseus' stamina of mind lets him resist when the others yield. The outcomes are their different fates.

They all exist for a while on Circe's provisions, then rove the island fishing and hunting birds. He at length seeks a quiet place, washes his hands and prays for means of leaving, then has the second of his fateful sleeps that supervene on strain. They resemble Penelope's and prove as important. As on the way from Aeolus, the men talk among themselves; Eurylochus calls starvation the grimmest possible death and proposes killing the best cattle with present sacrifice to the gods and vow of a shrine to Helius if they reach Ithaca. Better, he prophetically ends, to die from the god's wrath in a single stroke at sea than by long torture on a lone island (12.340–351). They do as he says, at the sacrifice scattering oak leaves for lack of sacral barley and with libations of water instead of wine. Among much else, their fixity in former habits distinguishes them from the learner. He wakes to smell the savor and cries to Zeus and the gods that they lulled him into ruin in a cruel sleep (12.371–373). He grants that the others planned the act but identifies with them; his emotion repeats the statement of the prologue that he strove for his comrades' homecoming. As after the Cyclops' prayer and on the return of the Phaeacian ship from Ithaca, conversation on Olympus follows. He knows it because Hermes told Calypso; it is not explained how he knew the response to the Cyclops' prayer, and Homer tells the Phaeacian decision—proof, if any were needed, how thin a line divides the speech from the narrative. He will no longer shine on earth, Helius tells Zeus, but on the dead beneath the earth unless Odysseus' companions pay for the cattle in which he would take joy on entering the starry sky (12.377–383). The earlier-mentioned sheep fall away leaving the ancient myth of cattle on which the sun-god gazes at daybreak. "Helius," the king of gods replies, "shine among immortals and mortal men over the wheat-giving ploughland. Soon but touching their swift ship with my flashing bolt I will wreck it in the wine-visaged sea." All is decided, but in eerie portent as before the suitor-slaying, as also in the bloody dew with which Zeus portends Sarpedon's death by Patroclus, the future is foreshadowed in the creeping and lowing cattle-flesh (12.396–397). Though the men recriminate each other, they for six days continue killing and eating, when the storm clears.

The description of the crowning storm at sea partly recurs in the beggar's Cretan tale to Eumaeus (14.301–309). It there follows the trickery of the false Phoenician who promised to carry from Phoenicia the enriched Cretan but intended selling him as a slave in Libya. Patroclus in *Iliad* 16 (384–388) advances like the hurricane with which angry Zeus visits givers of crooked judgments and expellers of right, men mindless of the gods' gaze. This storm has a like intention. Dark blue cloud hides the sea; raging Zephyrus snaps the foreropes and the falling mast kills the steersman. Lightning spreads the smell of sulphur; men overboard surround the shattered ship like shearwaters; a god denies their home-returning (12.403–419). Sulphur reappears after the suitor-slaying when Odysseus cleans the house with it (22.493–494), and Achilles so cleans the cup with which he makes libation to Zeus before praying for Patroclus' safe return (*Il.*16.228). Here and in the Cretan story it has this cleansing function toward the men's impiety and the alleged Phoenician's deception. If this seems simple moralism, it concludes for the men a widest journey. Unless the world is unintelligible, such experience should lend understanding. The myth and poet are clear that it does, seemingly in two main ways: first, strength being transient and loss universal, a final equity behooves humans (Achilles' fable of the jars of Zeus) and, second, the earth's beauty and abundance (the sun's cattle) being essentially what is vouchsafed, they call for respect. Courage and vitality are necessary even for these actions, so necessary as to seem the basic human merits. But comprehension is an equal if different necessity. Like Achilles on his day of supreme strength, Odysseus hearing the Siren Song and perhaps elsewhere reaches a godlike moment. Merits necessary to life spin upward as ends in themselves. But the limits remain and it is these that, in spite or because of the greatness of their outward flight, the supreme heroes perceive. Moral implication issuing from intensity of life ends in clarity of sight. If there were nothing to understand, the crew's cattle-killing and the suitors' spoliation and attempted murder would be simple acts of self-betterment, but if there is a latent order, hard as it is to see—in short, if Zeus exists—morality is its recognition. The *Iliad* and *Odyssey* are here at one; the *Odyssey* differs in the hero's opportunity of longer sight, therefore in the fuller peace of his end.

In the water he finds the detached keel and broken mast with a thong still on it by which he binds them together and rides out the storm. Borne again to the strait he this time cannot clear the more terrible Charybdis but, as she sucks down the keel and mast, grasps a wild fig-tree growing out and down from the cliff just above; Circe mentioned it. Charybdis retracts thrice daily; he cannot climb the sloping tree but clings to it like a bat until at evening, the time when after judging many disputes a man leaves the market-place for supper, he drops beside the emerging timbers (12.431–444). Four trees mark and protect his journey: this wild fig-tree, then the half-wild, half-cultivated olive under which he safely sleeps at Scheria in fallen leaves, then the lone cultivated olive at the head of the Bay of Phorkys where the Phaeacian seamen leave him asleep with his treasure, finally the olive from which he long ago made his marriage bed. The fruit trees of his youth identify him at the end to Laertes. Traditional sequences that guide the poet could hardly have extended to these trees, which in their way stand witness to his genius—which may be to say, to his immersion in the movement of the poem. Wildness changes at Scheria to part-wild, that to cultivated, that to old use: progressive tokens of the whole. The opposite speaks in the staff that Achilles says will never again grow leaves and twigs having left its place of cutting on the mountain, also in the wind-blown wild fig-tree at the watching-place outside Troy by which Hector runs in flight from Achilles (*Il.*22.145). Earth and place which trees keep are lost or regained, and Odysseus' succoring fortune in them resembles his aid from gods. Still borne on, he says, he reached Ogygia, Calypso's dwelling, on the tenth night, but though he has not told the assembled Phaeacians how he thence reached Scheria, correctly says that he yesterday told the king and queen and dislikes repeating.

To look back is to see the adventures unfolding in the common light of visible nature. Even the fruit for which dead Tantalus reaches is blown by the wind toward shadowing clouds. But coasts or landfalls on a continuous sea more than unite the travels; they put them, however disparate, within a man's physical response. In this respect Scylla and Charybdis as outer perils do not differ from love of Circe and speech with the dead. A living being collects the world to his experience, and though reason may distinguish the origin and character of what he sees, it all touches him. Homer's power speaks in this lack of differentiation. If every life mingledly draws from outer sight and inner impulse, distinction between them is finally impossible. All poetry states the amalgam. But by allying formulaically fixed people and places with wide myth, this poetry leaves the point of junction between the mind and the world quite open. Imagination equally accepts common hunger and desire to see the dead. The dead recur in dreams and memory; they are as much a part of life as hunger. The sensateness of the adventures mirrors the living consciousness. The journeys include experience of societies with that of nature and of inner promptings. The primitive Cyclopes and graceful, lightly-living Phaeacians touch opposite sides of common life; they extend the ordinary and clarify it by difference. The undiluted extremes define the mean. Desires that in masked form haunt the ordinary also show in pure form; they comprise chief travels. The Lotuseaters' harmless and dreamy idleness, the lone shore beyond which is Circe's love, Calypso's ageless at-homeness in the green of nature, cessation of time and loosing of all ties in the Sirens' song, reunion with the dead and intimation of one's life from it: these inward journeys transport from the ordinary and having done so carry back. The common plane that these share with Aeolus' winds, the waveless Laestrygonian bay, alternative Scylla and Charybdis, and Helius' bright cattle puts all the adventures on the same earth beneath the same sequence of day and night. They are a mortal's possible knowledge. It is a knowledge touched by gods but finally a mortal's. The sleep from which Odysseus wakes on the shore at home in retrospect nearly changes the journeys into dreams. Whether of nature or societies or desires, they are the intimations that shape the mind.

6. Telemachus

If tragic irony means blindness to coming evil, comic irony means blindness to coming good. If the evil or good is later seen to have emerged in the course of nature, it will have implied an order that the gods grasped from the first but mortals only slowly. A happy outcome will not be such for all, but those who are shocked by it, in this poem the suitors and unfaithful servants, will have lived in delusion, moths at a brief flame. Those who kept faith in a better scheme and eagerly seek its confirmation, in the first Books Mentor, Haliserthes, Eurycleia, Menelaus, and especially Nestor, in the later Books the faithful servants and supremely but sceptically Penelope, inhabit a kind of twilight as forerunners. Telemachus' development is debatable. He moves from shadow into light, yet less by his own efforts than in the reflection of words and events that others plumb more presciently. He throws himself into the outcome and to an extent advances it but largely by tutelage, and at the end awaits a future for which inheritance and example fit him but which is yet to become fully his. The smile of the *Odyssey* draws not least from this emergence of a better possibility than seemed credible yet, if gods exist, should be credible. It is not a random or accidental possibility but got from the successful treading of a granted path. Odysseus' travels are in this sense not in phantasy. Though in regions beyond the inhabited world, they show the circumference of the near world, the conditions that should be understood if one is to grasp it sanely and reach its genuine if limited promise. In early Greek, revelation of an operative law commonly accompanies its working. In the *Odyssey* at least, what is won by the intelligent and enduring pair, and for their son and in Ithaca, shows what is given, perhaps the best that is given, hard-pressed mankind. Comic irony is the latent promise.

It initially shows in two main ways: in what happens to Telemachus and, on the poet's part, in a tone of narrative that feelingly asserts the inherent, though at first clouded, desirability and beauty of the world, a credible invitation.

We have traced the gods' planned rousing of Telemachus and Odysseus and, though the plan was not stated, of Penelope, whom on the day of the five hopeful signs and prophecies Athene at last stirs to her necessary step toward remarriage. Athene-Mentes' first encouragement of Telemachus turns on paternity; he looks, the stranger says, like his father before he left for Troy (1.208–209). So his mother says, the youth inertly answers, but no one knows his own begetting; better to have a rich father who ages in his property; I am called son of the worst-fated of men (1.214–220). But when Mentes has sketched to him a plan of action—visit Pylos and Sparta, learn whether Odysseus is alive or dead, and cope with either outcome—he intensely thanks him for advice like a father's (1.308). He sees Mentes leave, then sees a sea-eagle. The goddess, it is said, has given him vitality and confidence and has put his father in his mind more than before (1.320–322). He marvels and suspects a god and with these thoughts join the suitors.

This first scene reaches its full contrast in the last scene when beside his father and grandfather he prepares to fight the dead suitors' kinsmen (24.502–515). As Mentor, Athene is again present. "Telemachus," Odysseus says, "you stand at last where it is shown who are best of warring men, and will know how to bring no shame on us your forebears' breed who in the past have excelled over all the earth in toughness and courage." There is impatience in the reply (which echoes Odysseus' reply to Agamemnon, *Il*.4.353), "you will see me if you wish in this spirit of mine not shaming, as you say, our breed." Old Laertes makes the fit comment, "What is this day to me, dear gods. Greatly I rejoice. My son and grandson vie for virtue." Strengthened by Athene, the old man strikes with his spear and kills Eupeithes, father of Antinous whom Odysseus shot first the day before. The initial divine decision that Odysseus shall return rounds to the final decision that bloodshed in Ithaca shall stop. If he will not stop, Athene warns of the continuing anger of Zeus at which she expressed surprise at the start. The poem ends with feeling praise of her, still as Mentor in whose guise she had cheered but tested him during the suitor-slaying and chiefly had encouraged and instructed Telemachus. The peaceful Ithaca to which, Teiresias prophesied, Odysseus will return from placating Poseidon unites the three generations of the frugal and prudent family that in each generation produced one son (Hesiod recommends a single son unless a man is rich, *Erg.*376–380). As at the suitor-slaying, Telemachus has stood beside a father whom he had assumed dead and whose paternity he had doubted. Penelope's fixed notion that her son wished her to remarry reflected his low hope of saving even a little for himself. But the reality proved far brighter, and its gradual opening is his education in what the world can become for the kind of merits that the gods approve.

Themes that surround mistreated Achilles mark Telemachus' first plight, but brighteningly. On rejoining the suitors after Athene-Mentes' strange departure he shows his new confidence by rebuking Penelope, perhaps for the first time. Let Phemius continue singing, he tells her, of the doom that angry Athene gave the Achaeans after Troy; Odysseus was not the only man that died (1.346–350). The tone of young self-assertion that persists toward his father in the last scene contrasts to Odysseus' gentleness at main moments but also to his own better moods. He is on his way toward a final poise that is never quite his father's. But, as Mentes advised, he gives notice to the suitors that he will call an assembly the next day to protest their spoliation; he will invoke divine vengeance on their evil acts. Calling an assembly implies kingship, and when Antinous questions that he will go on to become king in Ithaca, he replies that he will at least rule in his own house (1.389–398). Achilles on spurning Agamemnon's gifts says much the same; he will enjoy his father's wealth in Phthia (*Il.*9.394–400). The question for both is whether in a violent world such early ease is likely. When Eurymachus, as usual following Antinous placatingly but treacherously, assures him that he will keep his house and goes on to inquire of the recent stranger, he dissembles calling

Mentes merely a former friend of his father. The next day's assembly follows. With good omen old Aegyptius hails the revival of the lapsed custom. Though sadly denying news, Telemachus recalls Odysseus' old beneficence, states his incapacity against the many suitors, appeals for public support, and invokes divine vindication, ending like Achilles at the assembly at Troy by throwing down the speaker's staff (2.80, *Il.* 1.245). His gesture is weak and desperate, he weeps as he throws; that of Achilles is violent, but both are young and isolated. With native harshness Antinous proceeds to blame Penelope by telling, for the first of the three times in the poem, the tale of the web; no fabled Achaean lady, he concludes, not even Tyro, Alcmene or fair-crowned Mycene had her charms or wiles; her delay makes her fame but your loss. When Telemachus protests that he cannot return her to her father Icarius against her will—for revealingly mixed reasons, his loss in repaying her bridal wealth but also the uncertainty of Odysseus' death, a mother's curse, and the people's anger (2.130–137)—and again invokes the gods' vindication, a second clearer sign is given, Zeus-sent eagles from the right bloodily fighting above the agora. Old Haliserthes who at the end similarly grasps Athene's presence sees the import, which Eurymachus with threat to him doubts. For less good reason than Hector at a like moment (*Il.* 12.237–240), he questions finding signs in any bird that flies. Telemachus states his plan of seeking news abroad; Mentor, still Odysseus' old friend and not yet Athene, repeats Odysseus' beneficence and chides the slack people; but the suitor Leocritus thinks that it will be long before Telemachus gets a ship. The futile assembly dissolves, and like Achilles Telemachus walks alone by the gray sea (2.260, *Il.* 1.350). Both invoke goddesses, Achilles his mother, Telemachus the goddess who came yesterday. His first uncertain sense of her as a sea-eagle has stayed with him, and his prayer will have, not in fame but in achieved good, fuller outcome than Achilles' prayer to Thetis.

The next days inculcate much: piety, manners, sense of a greater past, hope of an opener future and, by implication, inkling of what is asked of heroes. His adlection into that world is vicarious. Even its present exemplars, Nestor, Helen, and Menelaus, will have lacked the width of knowledge with which Odysseus returns, and Nestor's sense of the storied dead—Achilles, Ajax, Patroclus, his son Antilochus (3.108–112)—conveys a nobler price than he, Menelaus, and the avenged king Agamemnon paid. In this sense

Telemachus' travels share the retrospection of Odysseus' tale at Scheria. A last stage or reunion and recovery awaits, but as the Phaeacian ship turned to stone closes the farther world, so for Telemachus the Trojan past survives as story. In the economy of the poem, over and above his prime need by show of independence to bring Penelope to the decision for remarriage that will give Odysseus success, his young sight of survivors at home puts him in the position of all later hearers of the great story, even Homer. The glint of the past becomes key to the future, a mental inheritance that gives life profundity.

Inheritance at least is Telemachus' start. Right instinct had made him receive Athene-Mentes politely when the suitors neglected the stranger. Now at his prayer to the god who came yesterday, Athene as Mentor offers to raise a ship and crew and bids him get provisions at home. You will prove yourself Odysseus' and Penelope's son, she says: "few sons are their father's equals; most are worse, few better" (2.274–277). Antinous obtusely meets him on the way and offers his hand. He tears his hand away swearing that he will somehow get a ship and prove the suitors' ruin, but it is darkly remarked that, if he goes, he may not return. In a wonderful passage (2.337–348) he enters his father's storechamber at home which Eurycleia watches day and night against her master's return; it is as if he had never before seen it. Gold and bronze, clothes stored in chests, and casks of old wine line the walls awaiting the homecoming. The wealth, the antiquity, the order declare the inheritance on which he at last seeks to enter. He nicely asks for twelve amphorae of the best wine except only that which is being kept for Odysseus, also for skins of flour. To the old woman's keening for his youth and loneness and to her fear that the suitors will kill him, he asserts a divine hand in his errand and swears her to eleven or twelve days' silence from Penelope. His concern that his mother not weep, like that for his father's best wine, states something deeper in him than contentiousness, and this glad innocence of hope shines at the end of the day when on the speeding ship with Zephyrus astern and Athene as Mentor among them they pour libations to the unknown present goddess (2.420–434). Lines recur from Odysseus' idyllic return of Chryseis in *Iliad* 1 (430–483) but, as with the themes that marked Achilles' isolation, the youth's hope is firmer.

The splendid manifold enlargement of his day and night with

Nestor culminates in piety. The patriarch's festive clan gives him first and glad companionship. He is welcomed in plain politeness, then warmly as his father's son, proves abler than he feared to address the great man, learns of heroes famous at Troy and not least of Odysseus, and in the account of Orestes' vengeance for Agamemnon hears again the recent model, only three years past, that bears on himself. But Nestor has changed from the oaken exemplar and respository of fixed practice that he was in the *Iliad*. He is lost in the wonder of the past, in both its cost and sorrow and its revelation of gods. As Odysseus has moved toward Achilles' crowning vision of Zeus's law at the end of the *Iliad*, Nestor has lost his former certainty to become a kind of surviving Priam, still a king among his numerous breed but with the loss of his best son, companion of the great dead. Odysseus as a relatively poor king from rocky Ithaca always differed from the rich kings and returning as a beggar will differ still more. Though both know sorrow, Nestor in his palace thus contrasts to Laertes on his farm. Addressing such memory-sunken old men has problems even for Odysseus at the end, and Telemachus doubts his capacity. But the goddess encourages him—"you will yourself devise some things in your mind, and a divinity will prompt others. Not without gods' favor, I think, were you born and reared"—and he rises to the fit address, "Nestor son of Neleus, the Achaeans' great vaunt" (3.26–28, 79).

Homer's sparkling gaze toward the young hardly shows more brightly in Nausicaa's dream of marriage and girlish deception of her father about the mulecart than now toward Peisistratus, Nestor's youngest son, Telemachus' contemporary. On guiding the strangers to seats he properly first offers Athene-Mentor as the elder wine in a gold cup urging prayer to Poseidon, at whose feast they have come. "All mankind has need of gods," he youthfully explains (3.48). He has his father's piety, and pleased by his mind and manners the goddess prays the sea-god for prosperity in Pylos and success for Telemachus. The poem began with Poseidon's hostility to Odysseus, and this conciliatory prayer carries the tone of the outcome. But if she approves Peisistratus, she rebukes Telemachus. Told who he is and on what errand, Nestor at some length— he has not lost that old trait—elegiacally evokes the famous dead, recalls his joint enterprises with Odysseus and their rare disagreement on Tenedos on the angry night after the sack when Odysseus left him and Menelaus to rejoin Agamemnon at Troy, dwells on the vanity of the king's hope of placating Athene, relates his own and others' voyages home, and concludes with the fame of Orestes' vengeance which Telemachus should emulate. But as Peisistratus has learned piety, Telemachus inherits scepticism. "Gods have woven no such bliss for me," he replies (3.208–209), "for my father and me. I must endure." The old king lives with the mystery of things; to his mind all that gods wish is possible. "Who knows," he raptly continues (3.216–224), "whether returning he will someday repay those men's outrage, alone or Achaeans with him? If grey-eyed Athene might consent so to be his friend as she once favored bright Odysseus in the Trojans' land where we Achaeans suffered—never yet have I seen gods so visibly befriending as Pallas Athene visibly stood by him—if she thus might be his friend and felt concern of heart, then any one of them would forget marriage." Telemachus is unconvinced. "Old man," he persists, "I think your assertion will never come to pass. It is too vast. Awe possesses me. It could never befall my hope even if gods so wished." Unknown Athene herself corrects him: "Telemachus, what a word has escaped your teeth's fence. Lightly if a god wished could he save a man even from far. I should myself prefer to reach home and see my day of return, though after great pains, than returning die at my hearth as Agamemnon died by Aegisthus' and his wife's guile" (3.230–235). The lines look to Odysseus' prudence at the Bay of Phorkys, to his hard-won instinct to test the household which the goddess approves; her mind is the reciprocal instinct. Nestor remembers Odysseus' capacity at Troy and has faith that it may have carried him through Troy's required sequel. The two men will each have paid, but the traveler will excel in knowledge even the reverent and experienced king, nor will he have lost his son, who now from narrow Ithaca begins to see both the dangers and the possible opportuneness of the great world.

The plan that Telemachus visit Pylos and Sparta showed both Mentes' and the poet's foreknowledge that, for all his memories of Troy, Nestor would know nothing further of Odysseus. But the old king pointedly leaves to Menelaus the account of Agamemnon's death which he knows about (3.254–312), and the tactic duplicates in small the relationship between the two poems. Parts of the total tale take their fit places, fixed to characters; presentness dominates. The *Iliad* is constantly implied in this poem. Close parallels exist of duration and structure, but the time has changed; Odysseus is called in the second line the sacker of Troy. Near-repetition by pairs—Mentes and Mentor, Cyclops and Laestrygonians, Helen's and Circe's potions, many others—marks the *Odyssey*. In the outflung scenes of the poem the method seems counterpart to the intensifying battles of the *Iliad;* both methods subsume while carrying ahead. Thus now at Pylos Athene's second departure as a sea-eagle looks both forward and back. In his high propriety and extreme contrast to the suitors, Nestor will not hear of Telemachus sleeping on shipboard; he must be entertained at the palace. But having proposed his next day's overland journey to Sparta, Mentor pleads concern for the ship and a later errand. The goddess's purpose for Telemachus is launched; in mood and mind he has entered another world and will need further help only on his perilous return. Her departure assumes his entrance into Menelaus' and Helen's still wider world of remembered travel, a dimension nearer his father's. But the sign that two days before roused the half-believing youth intensely moves the memory-laden king; at sight of the sea-eagle all his piety pours out. He marvels and seizes Telemachus' hand. "O friend," he exclaims (3.375–381), "I foresee you not destined to become low and defenseless if gods are your guides thus young. This can be no other of the dwellers on Olympus than Zeus's daughter, most glorious, trito-born, who honored your excellent father too among the Argives. Lady, be merciful and grant me good fame, me and my children and my revered wife."

The famous detailed description, in spirit prophetic of the frieze of the Parthenon, sets forth the next morning's sacrifice: the getting of the heifer, the gilding of its horns, the ritual water, the barley, the prayer to Athene, the blow, the women's cry, the offering and libation, the feast. The poet lingers in manifest summary of the golden sunset of the king's life. His wife, a daughter who bathes Telemachus, and several sons are named; a tone exists almost as of the storied heroines of Book 11. With sceptre in hand Nestor sits as did his father Neleus on polished stones before the palace and orders each detail; there is a large propriety. In the near world this is the closest counterpart to the Phaeacian ease, though recovered after pain and still touched by the loss of Antilochus. The mysterious reference in the *Iliad* (5.397) to Heracles wounding Hades "in Pylos among the dead" might suggest a continuing sacral tradition concerning Pylos, with Nestor a kind of second Rhadamanthys whom the Phaecians mentioned carrying from Elysium to Euboea, but if so, Homer characteristically keeps his humane color. On this human plane more seems described than wealth and visionary age; Odysseus at least is hardly to be imagined ever settling to Nestor's prolix calm. The old king's kind of wisdom, here and at Troy, evidently seems to Homer lacking in intensity, expressive of neither Achilles' ardor nor Odysseus' search.

But this is Telemachus' journey, and if Nestor's retrospection, though enlarging, in mood or substance fails to meet his need, neither—prospectively at least in the example of Odysseus and Penelope—does the tone of incompleteness and surviving sorrow that surrounds Menelaus and Helen. Not that the narrative is put from his point of view; as with Odysseus, what he meets appears as event, yet in a sequence that implies a mind's formation. Family dominated at Pylos; love speaks at Sparta: in the marriage of Menelaus' natural son Megapenthes at which the youths arrive (4.10–13), in Helen's beauty and potion resembling Circe's, in her rueful but interested statements about her past and in that context her protestation of happiness with the excellent Menelaus (4.263–264), in his eerie account of the night inside the Trojan horse when she from outside summoned each man in the voice of his wife, and before Telemachus' departure in Book 15 his dream of Penelope's imminent marriage, then Helen's gift to him of a peplos, the work of her own hands, to keep in memory of her for his future bride (15.123–127). The son in Jugoslav epic who seeks but does not retrieve his father characteristically finds a girl; if Telemachus does not, he moves in that direction toward maturity. As in the contrast of Circe's enclosing house to the journeys before and after, the rich house at Sparta at first imposes, soon to open to the sad accounts of adventures from which it was regained. Peisistratus accompanied Telemachus on the two days' journey in what has been thought a Mycenaean war-chariot (3.481–482)[1]—if so, with epic enhancement akin to the location of Ithaca farthest toward the nether dusk. Busy with the present marriage, a servant questions admitting them, but like Alcinous Menelaus resents hint of inhospitality. A sober man, he further overhears Telemachus' provincial amazement at the glitter of bronze, gold, electrum, silver, and

1. H. L. Lorimer, *Homer and the Monuments* 503–504.

ivory and his exclamation that the house equals Zeus's. Mortals
may or may not, he says, surpass him in wealth; no mortal vies
with Zeus (4.71–78). The wealth, he goes on, came to him in the
course of his seven years' wandering after Troy to Cyprus, Phoe-
nike, the Egyptians, Ethiopians, Sidonians, Eremboi, and Libya, but
his brother was meanwhile murdered and he lost excellent friends
at Troy, not least the toiling Odysseus. A third of his wealth would
suffice if he could reclaim them, especially the now vanished Odysseus whom Laertes, Penelope, and Telemachus mourn in Ithaca
(4.97–112). His humanly acquired wealth contrasts to that which
Odysseus brings back as gift from magic people, his kingly ease to
the return as beggar, his melancholy to the other joy. Helen enters
soon after his mention of Penelope, and the difference is clearly in
her.

Penelope in her speech of recognition expressly denies blaming
Helen, who resisted her unseemly act until a god impelled her, nor
does Priam blame her in the *Iliad* (3.164). In spite of the wish of
the old councilors on the Trojan wall that she not stay as a sorrow
to them and their children, and in spite of her regret, indignity, and
isolation, she remains, as the councilors say, terrifyingly like the
immortals in beauty (*Il.*3.156–160). Her sense of Paris's instability
(*Il.*6.352–353), awareness of the storied fate that the gods have
given them, and final praise of Hector's gentleness show her mind.
This mixture of transporting beauty with sentience and sorrow
persists now but with a subtle change partly from the years, chiefly
from the implied contrast to Penelope. Among the hither characters, Helen alone keeps in this poem an Iliadic dimension of
powers beyond human coping. Athene's impulse to Penelope to
announce remarriage and seek wedding-gifts, though mysterious,
finally fits a controlled and mental nature; so also Athene's care for
Odysseus and Telemachus. By contrast, her presence beside
Achilles in his encounter with Hector less explains than describes
the hero's meteoric power; he is invincible for a day, Hera said,
and burning Hephaestus at his side wasted the life-giving Scamander. But the *Odyssey* concerns a purely human pair, and if
Odysseus sees more than will be granted another mortal, the sight
amends the violence of Troy and gives final quiet.

Some such contrast now unfolds in the sequence of Helen's radiant entrance, her instant recognition of Telemachus (4.138–146),
the sorrow-dispelling potion by which she brightens the sad com-

pany (4.220–226), but then her cruel tale of Odysseus entering Troy as a disfigured spy, of her recognition of him and her pleasure in the deaths and sorrows that he caused (4.259–262), and finally Menelaus' unearthly tale of her outside the Trojan horse, now after Paris's death and with Deiphobus as husband, summoning each Achaean in the voice of his wife (4.277–279). What starts as supreme beauty (Circe has four servants, Penelope two, Helen has three, also a golden distaff and a wheeled silver wool-basket with golden rim, gifts of an Egyptian queen) and continues with sure awareness of Telemachus (like Arete, she is quicker than her husband) soon with the drug takes on near-magic and with the Trojan stories ends with her sorrow and hard mood at Troy even when she kept her witching powers. As at Penelope's gift-soliciting several strands intertwine. Her radiance is unchanged, and her statement that she missed her child at home and the excellent husband that she left by Aphrodite's power repeats her self-condemnation of the *Iliad* (4.261–264, *Il*.3.173–176), but the present melancholy in the house and her and Menelaus' absorption with the past show small joy of return. As with Achilles and the heroines of the Underworld, half-divine parentage gives intensity but not peace. Telemachus' meeting with her nearly reproduces Odysseus' meeting with goddesses; son and father will both have seen the world's unattainable allurement. The *Iliad* fiercely rises to that flash; the *Odyssey* sees it more mentally, without impulse to possess, more fully as sight alone. The suitors' desire for Penelope states her beauty, which Athene enhances before the gift-getting; in her own mind she too has less joy than she gives others, and she has her secret plans. But the kindness that is stressed of her and her final statement that she was continually on guard against strangers (23.216–217) show her desire to keep her mortal station, her fear of vast intrusion. She feared such outcomes as drove Helen to her cruel moods at Troy; she shrank even from her dream of dead geese. Intrusion of gods into famous lives is what Telemachus now sees but, in his sight of Helen, with sense also of the irridescence.

The next day belongs to Menelaus, whose tale of wanderings complexly foreshadoes that of Odysseus but differs in outcome. Held like Odysseus at sea, he had first to learn from a wise old man, the sea-god Proteus, his means of return, what he will find at home, and his end of life. He will find not suitors but dead Agamemnon, yet by his marriage to Zeus-begotten Helen, Proteus says, in death will attain the Elysian fields. Whatever their earthly sorrows, their more-than-human fate speaks in that. He returned three years ago just after Orestes' vengeance, and in addition to relating Agamemnon's death and that of the violent Ajax Oileus, Proteus told of seeing Odysseus on Calypso's island (4.556–560). Knowledge that his father is or lately was alive is for Telemachus the glad, though still uncertain, outcome of his errand, and the reaches of the world that Menelaus unfolds further intimate of the traveler. Odysseus' hope as regards the afterlife does not equal that of Menelaus and Helen—the visit to the Underworld says the same —but is firmer for this life. As Nagler well writes, Achilles at the end of the *Iliad* returns from his huge isolation to a mortal order that by humanity softens death.[2] The yearning for life that he expresses in the Underworld states something left over, his youth's never quenched response, but his great strides through the asphodel meadow convey his other side, his immortal fame. Heracles in the Underworld shows the same duality; his shade relates its earthly labors but is simultaneously on Olympus. Proteus' prophecy to Menelaus of his and Helen's end thus contrasts to their present incompleteness. But old Nestor's golden piety says something different, closer to Teiresias' prophecy of Odysseus' old age among a glad people. Laertes' final joy is similar. In the two poems Homer sees both a transit and an arrival. Telemachus' sight first of Nestor, then of Menelaus and Helen reverses the stages, arrival preceding journey. As such it repeats the plan of the poem whereby Odysseus' return is foretold at the start; the fact gives rise to the comic irony. But the hard passage from the one to the other state meanwhile intervenes and it is of this that Telemachus gains inkling from Menelaus. Nestor in *Iliad* 1 (275–284) vainly urges reconciliation between Agamemnon and Achilles, but the whole poem is needed to tell the price, which proves immensely deeper. In his movement from Nestor to Helen and Menelaus Telemachus mentally broaches a process from which Odysseus is on the point of emerging.

Menelaus' tale of wanderings starts near the end. In the story, his wide and lucrative travels are past; like Odysseus and his men on Thrinacia, he with his five ships was held by hard winds on the island of Pharos, a day's sail off Egypt. The ships are those that

2. *Spontaneity and Tradition* 186–198.

had survived the storm after Troy from which Odysseus and Agamemnon suffered; he had recouped only these at Phaestus on
southern Crete and moved thence to his travels in the known but
still fabled south. Homer's disposal of materials shows again in the
fact that Nestor had related this start (3.286–300) which Menelaus is thus spared telling, even while he omitted Agamemnon's
death which gives the shattering climax to Proteus' tale. Nestor
added that birds could not cross in a year the seas that Menelaus
traversed. The island of Pharos, which was in fact so close to shore
that Ptolemy II attached it for the famous lighthouse, is put a day's
sail off; in the poetry southern seas and peoples, presumably by
Mycenaean tradition, nearly share the dawning light of the western. For twenty days, Menelaus says, the hungry company wandered the island; like Odysseus' men they were reduced to fishing,
and like Odysseus Menelaus finally went off alone. In Proteus'
daughter the sea-nymph Eidothea he meets one who in saving
impulse resembles raft-encountering Leucothea and in guidance
Circe. He must, she says (4.383–424), lay hold of her father Proteus, "who will tell your route and the measure of your journey
and your return, how you will traverse the fishy sea," Circe's
words in directing Odysseus to Teiresias. The resemblance then
lapses in a magical passage. The meridian calm that Aeschylus describes of windless noons at Troy (*Agam.565–566*), when in the
Hymn to Pan (*H.H.* 19.10–14) the wild god from the mountains
surveys the silent world, is here the time of Proteus' sleep among
his seals. Menelaus and three companions, she says, must lie down
among them; she provides seal-skins and, in the spirit of Hermes
with his moly, kindly gives an antidote to the smell. When Proteus
emerges from the sea, counts his flock, and himself lies down to
sleep, Menelaus and his men must seize him. The wise god will
take many forms, nature's forms—lion, snake, pard, boar, water,
tree—but if you cling, will resume his shape and tell the good and
ill of your return and your hard route. Menelaus does as she says.
The god rises in a nooning shiver of the calm; counts his seals but,
wise as he is, misses the men. The four fall on him; he takes his
foretold shapes, then reverting tells the past and future. Odysseus
in the Underworld goes on to see a wider past but similarly learns
of the present at home and of his future. Homecoming for both
hangs on placation of gods: Menelaus must return to Egypt to
complete his omitted sacrifice, Odysseus must spare Helius' cattle

and build an inland altar to Poseidon. The sea for both carries two corrections: loneness after crowded enterprise and the inner sight that loneness gives.

As Odysseus wept at Circe's hard instruction but finally accepted it, so now does Menelaus, then asks of others' return from Troy. Proteus warns against such knowledge; in the Underworld Odysseus learns as hard truths. Better, he says, not to know a god's full mind (4.492–494), but he finally tells of the three men, Ajax Oileus, Agamemnon, and Odysseus. In the *Iliou Persis* the lesser Ajax violates Cassandra at Athene's altar, alienating the goddess who with Hera and Poseidon had been the Achaeans' chief stay.[3] But this and other outrages of the sack are muted in the *Odyssey;* Athene's wrath has become her revulsion from violence. Her storm bore on the Atreidae as leaders of the expedition; Odysseus was implicated by reason of his closeness to them and chief part in the capture; his movement over ten years from cleverness to understanding has won her back; his instruction has become her restored favor. Not that she has not been and cannot again be a wargoddess but, as intelligent goddess unlike berserk Ares, she sees the purpose beneath violence; in that spirit supports Odysseus against the willfully blind suitors and at the end intends and produces peace. Thus Ajax Oileus, Proteus says, would have survived the storm, had he not boasted to have done so in spite of gods. Athene's hostility to him, mentioned in half a line (4.502), is the sole clear allusion to the legendary cause of her anger.[4] He drowns when Poseidon shatters the Euboean cliff to which he clings. Among the chiefs, he is the arch-contrast to those evoked in Pylos, here, and in the Underworld. Home-staying Aegisthus, in one sense his opposite, in another his analogue, and both as greater exemplars of the suitors, appears in the next account of Agamemnon, as by implication does Clytemnestra, who with Penelope and Helen completes a like spectrum of women.

Nestor had further prepared for this account by telling how Clytemnestra long resisted Aegisthus' fetching words (3.263–275). But he was not quite Paris, and Clytemnestra finally yielded not as, Penelope says, Helen did by Aphrodite's power (23.218–222). Agamemnon was evidently less confident of her, in that on depar-

---

3. Proclus' summary, T. W. Allen, *Homeri Opera* V 108.
4. There is a vaguer allusion at 5.108.

ture he had a bard keep watch of her, and when Aegisthus set the bard on a lone island to die, he took her home to their mutual joy. Resistance is the theme of the three wives: wise Penelope achieved it; as is shown in *Iliad* 3 and said in *Iliad* 24 (30) and by Penelope, in her minion Paris Aphrodite swayed Helen; after delay Clytemnestra simply consented. Nestor's view of her initially good wits describes rather the king's large mood than hers; Athene thinks differently (3.232–235), and to Agamemnon in the Underworld she was moved by pure hate. Menelaus, Nestor went on, returned just after Orestes' vengeance, and Proteus now describes the murder. In the outcome, the storm that drove Odysseus and Menelaus took a strange and fated turn for Agamemnon. About to be swept beyond Cape Malea, he was suddenly borne northward to the edge of the Argolid where he might have landed safely, then to his joy reached Mycenae (4.514–523). But though he kissed his native earth, Aegisthus had learned his arrival from a year-long watcher; set armed men in the palace, accompanied home the triumphant king and, as Agamemnon bitterly repeats in the Underworld, killed him "like a bull at the crib." The followers of both died. The wind is not the only curious part of the story; nothing is said of his other ships, nor is Agamemnon surprised that Aegisthus should be at Mycenae. Minor points evidently fade. So also with Clytemnestra, who here plays no part. As Nestor told of her yielding, the ghost of Agamemnon will describe her pitilessness to him in death and the lorn cry of Cassandra. He being the spokesman of the Second Nekyia, her treachery still embitters him but, at that stage of the poem, in her contrast to wise Penelope of whom singers will tell. This varied treatment puts neatly the Homeric method. The portrayed moment dictates, and people speak as it commends. The moment of course follows from who they are; they speak as themselves; but it is peremptory, showing not a whole character, the speaker or the person described, but the character in that circumstance. Intensest moments elicit profoundest views. Thus Clytemnestra's queenly delay fits Nestor's large mind and narrative; she emerges implacable in dead Agamemnon's memory; at the end stands in radiant Penelope's shadow. She appears at varied moments and by people's then emergent views and, though a minor character, is not in that respect differently known from the major figures. As regards characters, this is the style of mountingly refracted portrayal.

Proteus tells, as last of the three leaders, of Odysseus held on Calypso's island yearning for return. He ends with Helen's and Menelaus' remove after death to the Elysian plain and limits of earth, "where blond Rhadamanthys is and life is lightest for mortals. Neither snow, nor heavy winter, nor rain is there, but Oceanus forever sends clear-breathing airs to revive mankind" (4.564–568). He then disappears below the sea. Menelaus returns to Egypt, does a hecatomb to all the gods, and like Odysseus for Elpenor, builds a cairn to Agamemnon. The three fates of dead Ajax, dead Agamemnon, and living Odysseus are at this stage as illustrative as, in the summary of the Second Nekyia, are the fates of Agamemnon, Achilles, and Odysseus. Telemachus' great but still incomplete instruction finishes in these examples. Menelaus urges him to linger in Sparta and promises as a parting gift three horses and a chariot, and like Odysseus at Scheria, the youth says that he would gladly stay a year (4.595). The polite reply seems conventional but, franker than his father, he pleads need of return and calls horses unsuitable tȯ rocky Ithaca. In the linear Homeric manner he in fact stays for the thirty days of the following narrative—Hermes' arrival on Ogygia, Odysseus' four days of raft-building, seventeen days at sea, three days of swimming, three on Scheria, his night-return to Ithaca and day and night with Eumaeus, then Telemachus' departure on the next morning. Menelaus approves his realistic young guest and promises instead his most precious possession, a silver mixing-bowl with golden rim, a work of Hephaestus given him by the king of Sidon. It summarizes Menelaus' travels and Telemachus' enlargement, and the poem returns to Ithaca in the discovery of his absence. Penelope's reassuring dream, though silent about Odysseus, affirms Athene's guidance of her son, and his brilliant days at Pylos and Sparta have prepared him, though hardly for the beggar.

In this opening narrative the poet's tone is as operative as the events. The world's stable beauty shines through both poems but in the *Iliad* in mounting contrast to mortal brevity. The power of the *Iliad* partly draws from this contrast. Achilles' huge outpouring is his response to loss of friend, home, and future, of the shine of life itself, and the night-scene with Priam renounces long daylight. Homer can only have lived with this style-embedded antithesis of the bright world to human fates, and the *Odyssey* is the obverse of the *Iliad* in the differing proportion. The sea gives widest language to the earthly frame; Achilles walks beside it in the moment of his first repulse and summons his mother the sea-goddess; it gives Odysseus his dimension. It conveys possibility; is cooler, less immediate than land; offers hope but hides actuality. The length of Odysseus' stay with Eumaeus, through parts of four Books, fits the gradualness of the transition. Landscape opens a nearly like width. The Iliadic similes that introduce the Catalogue of Ships imply distance: the flash of troops resembles a fire on a far mountain, their movement the progress of flocking birds across a meadow, their number the flowers of spring and clouding flies at a sheepfold, their gradual order the separation of intermingled flocks (*Il.*2.455– 483). All give total view from the outside; the poet sees the army outstretched before his mind. When Agamemnon at the end stands in head like Zeus, in girth like Ares, in chest like Poseidon, like the bull in the herd, the perspective shortens. The separate contingents of the Catalogue follow; spaces soon grow close and dangerous. Gods, similes, memories, and descriptions—Odysseus returning Chryseis, Poseidon's golden chariot parting the waves, Zeus gazing toward the distant Hippomolgoi and Abioi, the farther hill Batieia and nearer hot and cold springs outside the Trojan walls, old Priam in the plain at night—keep giving perspective until at the end it merges with Achilles' interior sight. But the relationship of the action to the surrounding frame is largely reversed in the *Odyssey*. Closed Ithaca soon opens to Telemachus' journey, and in his Cretan tales and disguise as battered traveler Odysseus brings back distance with him. Laborious as are his travels, horizons keep opening to him; his curiosity vies with his desire for home. The opposites of the framing world and the self-impelled, self-revealing, humanly necessary act both issue from the style, and their differing weight reflects its double impulse. It is the supreme style of mortal life in an earthly setting. The two sides are reciprocal; self-fidelity would be less searching were the world less beautiful. Yet on both mental and moral grounds dualism lacks profundity; a life is finally one. Powerful as is either pole of the contrast, the two sides must somehow merge, and different as is the weight of outer and inner in the two poems, both claims draw the protagonists to a single reality.

The first scenes in Ithaca follow not only the divine meeting but description of Calypso's hollow caves. "It is a wooded isle," says Athene, "and a goddess has her dwellings there, daughter of baleful-minded Atlas who knows the depths of all the seas and himself holds earth and sky apart. His daughter keeps back the ill-fated man lamenting, and ever with soft and subtle words weaves spells that he forget Ithaca. But pining to see even smoke upleaping from his native land he yearns to die" (1.51–59). As in the first scene on Ogygia, beauty and deprivation vie. The same holds for Ithaca. Nagler expounds the motif of the veil as mark of chastity;[5] veiled Penelope thus appears with two servants before the suitors. As applied to a city, the veil of the walls when broken destroys chastity, and the suitors threaten that. But her sad and beautiful reserve still protects her; the same elements apply in reverse as with Odysseus and Calypso; the beauty that fails to move Odysseus shows beneath Penelope's sorrow. So also with the motif of assembly. Both poems start with assemblies that fail, but the fresh description of Telemachus going to bed at home before the next day's meeting carries a deeper safety than he understands. "Where his high chamber stood within the perspicuous court, Telemachus went off to bed brooding much in heart, and Eurycleia, daughter of Ops son of Peisander, carried blazing torches for him, whom still in first youth Laertes once bought with his possessions, and he gave twenty cattle for her and honored her in the halls equally with his wife, but never had union with her and forewent his wife's wrath. She bore the blazing torches, and of the servants he most revered her; she reared him as a child. She opened the doors of the well-made chamber, and he took off his chiton and put it in the wise old woman's hands. Having folded and tended it and hung it on a peg beside the bored bed, she left the chamber and fastened the door with a silver hook and by a thong drew the bar into place. All night long swathed in a sheep's fleece he pondered in his heart the journey that Athene had spoken" (1.425–444). Antinous had laughed at him; the assembly will prove vain; but the beautiful security of boyhood still protects. The poet's pleasure in his going to bed speaks a deeper assurance than the youth can know.

His rising is as detailed. At rose-fingered dawn he gets up, pulls on his clothes, hangs a sword from his shoulder, ties handsome shoes on his bright feet, and leaves the chamber in looks like a god. Having bid heralds summon the assembly, he enters, bronze spear in hand and followed not by servants but by two white-footed

5. *Spontaneity and Tradition* 45–63.

dogs. Athene pours marvelous grace on him; the people admire his coming; he sits in his father's seat, and elders yield place to him (2.1–14). As Nagler further writes, early wakefulness, formal accompaniment, and imposing presence are normal to the theme of assembly.[6] But the detail of Telemachus' dressing and the contrast of his manly sword and spear to the two dogs, substitutes for grown-people's followers and in his fresh company obviously of different age and looks from the old dog Argus who dies on seeing Odysseus, again show his youth and the poet's pleasure in contemplating it. The failed assembly repeats that of the start of the *Iliad*, but its sequel—his prayer by the shore to yesterday's god, entrance into the ancient storechamber at home, and libation at evening to Athene present unknown aboard the running ship—conveys a fuller hope than he can understand. As with Nausicaa, the poet smilingly sees the unconscious perfection of the young. The comparison of Nausicaa to a young palm tree speaks the naturalness of right growth; in *Iliad* 6 (401) Astyanax shines like a star from his nurse's arms. Whatever their future, their present is complete, and in this poem Athene is the force, almost the process, of right continued unfolding. In both poems Homer knows more of gods than mortals can know, and the knowledge here translates itself into scenes in which the Ithacan family acts partly consciously, as in Penelope's device of the web and Telemachus' polite reception of Mentes, but largely unconsciously with perfect grace. To their own minds they are unfortunate, but their latent fortune speaks in their beauty of looks and movement.

The spacious scene that greets Telemachus at Pylos prepares all his enlargement. The sun has risen bearing light to gods and men. A great company of nine perhaps tribal groups, each of five hundred people, is gathered on the shore to sacrifice black bulls to the blue-locked earth-shaker. The ship puts in and Athene steps first ashore. "Telemachus," she says, "you need no backwardness, even a little. You have sailed the very sea for a purpose, to inquire of your father, where earth hides him and on what fate he has fallen. Come, make straight for horse-taming Nestor. Let us learn what counsel he harbors in mind. Yourself beg him to tell the truth. He will not speak falsehood; he is exceedingly wise" (3.14–20). The youth's self-doubt, the goddess's encouragement, the propriety of

6. *Ibid.* 86–111.

his address to the formidable patriarch, Nestor's comment that he speaks like his father and his surprise that a young man speaks so fittingly, all follow. Young Peisistratus' piety gives a model that Telemachus at first fails to heed. The old king tacitly, Athene-Mentor expressly correct him, and her second departure as a sea-eagle completes the assurance. Though he remains at Sparta the provincial youth that he started, he proves sufficiently at home in the great house to speak his mind about Menelaus' suggested gift. Helen instantly knows him; he has seen her beauty, heard her and Menelaus' tales, and chiefly has gained assurance that his father, three years ago at least, was alive. All this is by incident, yet also by tone. His inbred scepticism, which continues in his appraisiveness toward Menelaus' gift and in his later dream of his mother's remarriage, shows him in one sense his parents' son, in another simply growing up. The freshness of his boyish hope that marked the first two Books changes in the manner of Ion's in Euripides' play. Homer traces him by both tone and incident. These coalesce, and the scope that in Menelaus' story extends to distant seas and peoples was first, in the divine council, set about Ithaca. The style-fixed duality surrounds the waiting wife and son with a beauty that is itself in part the narrative.

7. The Beggar

Whence comes calm of mind? To judge by Odysseus, from a triple source: identity, act, and understanding. His epithets Ithacan and son of Laertes, his self-reference in the *Iliad* as father of Telemachus, and his stated wish to Calypso for his mortal wife Penelope show him quite certain who he is. No ghost was to drink at the trench before Teiresias, but he first spied his mother there. Abilities go back to his youth: he built his marriage-bed, builds his raft, challenges Eurymachus to a day's ploughing, and as token to his father names the fruit-trees that Laertes gave him as a child. His stringing the bow that he left at home shows among much else these youth-fixed powers. The narrowness of Ithaca says the same. Whatever a man may later do and become, life began limitedly; the later limit does not chiefly lie ahead but behind, in first bonds and assumptions. But beyond even the mandates of the so-called shame-society, finished youth takes a man into the world. Nestor's memory in the *Iliad* of Achilles' intense curiosity about the coming expedition states the outward impulse; the poetry traces the consequences. Act is the necessary but not the sufficient result; it is insufficient because action takes place in a world that has its own imperatives. An amalgam must follow between what the world asks and what a man offers. If merely experienced rather than understood, the outcome can be blind death. Homer keeps seeing the interaction more fully than can most characters. Agamemnon's abrupt death, here as in Aeschylus, is not accidental; the king's ghost understands what the living king did not. But greatest figures themselves come to perceive the nature of their lives, Hector both prophetically in his parting from his wife and expressly in his recognition of his god-willed final loneness (*Il*.22.297–305), Achilles in his meeting with Priam. They share, Achilles most fully, the poet's comprehension of them.

But that is to say that action, if fully human, leads to comprehension. Mind is the finally human trait. The animal-similes of the *Iliad* convey intense strength and spirit but identify humans with boars and lions, not with the seeing gods. If Homer comes near sharing the divine sight, it is what he expects of his greatest characters. Achilles and Odysseus differently rise to this perception but are at one in reaching it. Odysseus' travels and return extendedly trace what Achilles sees in a moment, at the end of an analogous remove. The human mystery may be deeper: the quite definite self is the precondition of this enlargement and persists through it, because, if weaker, it would have been trapped into any one of the many byways that it has entered. Odysseus' delay with Circe and more generally with the sea is in this respect analogous to Achilles' near-entrapment by the river Scamander. But vision gradually returns, for Odysseus mountingly after the central episode of the Underworld. He has been and in the suitor-slaying will still be tied to action, but simple Ithaca, a place much narrower not merely than Troy but than Pylos and Sparta, defines a first identity that alone can issue into knowledge. The mind's healing function, persistent in Greek thought, is dominant in Homer but intertwinedly with the self. Homer in this respect shares Sophocles' vision of granitic people reaching illumination and Plato's vision of the life and death of Socrates. He does not share Hesiod's assumption, in the *Theogony,* of objective and impersonal knowledge, nor that of Parmenides, Heraclitus, or Aristotle. To him sight is the identifyingly human goal without which life approaches that of vivid animals, and it is reached by a lone person on the other side of action.

This intertwinedness of knowledge with the self compels the two parts of the poem; the mortal traveler would be incomplete without return. As C. H. Whitman writes, his progressive recognitions by son, dog, nurse, workingmen, suitors, wife, and father carry him back to his origins.[1] His life before Troy had lain with the first five of these, but his wife and father inwardly declare him to himself. The fruit-trees that identify him to Laertes go back to his boyhood. This is one side. The other side speaks in the misty cave by the Bay of Phorkys, where on rocky looms the naiads weave their sea-purple robes, where bees make honey, and which has two entrances for men and for gods (13.103–112). With Athene's help he hides his riches there. The Phaeacian ship bore home "the man of thoughts like the gods who formerly endured in heart innumerable pains making proof of men's wars and bitter waves but then slept motionless forgetful of his sufferings" (13.89–92). This side at once of endurance and knowledge persists in his disguise as old man, his late-night retrospection with Eumaeus, his words to Amphinomus "such is the life of mortal men as the father of gods and men brings on their day," his tears on seeing son, dog, wife, and father, his gentleness in Penelope's delay, and their account together of the long years. From among the many themes that surround him, that of test grows uppermost, both his of others and theirs of him. But scepticism too is an upshot of experience; it is what the goddess commends and what Agamemnon lacked. Penelope, as finally the more sceptical, ends by testing him. If the return lacks the scope of the wanderings, it presupposes them. The poet's event-fixed art shows ends in the actualities from which they emerge; Odysseus' knowledge is quite simply the travels and return, with Troy before. That fact too shows the inextricability of knowledge from the self; the movement is what counts. Many died at Troy surprised by death; so also Odysseus' companions. Nestor, Menelaus, and Helen, though at home, lack his completeness. But that in turn asks homecoming as the last step; the near-disembodiment of his seven years with Calypso states the difference. Travel and return, knowledge and identity, are finally one.

The comic irony that for Telemachus shows the possibility of a bright future shows the same for Odysseus, but since he consciously shares his purpose with Athene, he acts almost as a god. The Phaeacians said that gods sometimes dined with them, and when Antinous throws a footstool at the beggar, the others object because gods walk the earth observing men's violence or propriety

1. *Homer and the Heroic Tradition* 301.

(17.483–487). But like his son, Odysseus too needs unguessed favors, chiefly Penelope's inspiration toward the bow and axes of which Athene at the bay said nothing. His meeting with Telemachus at Eumaeus' hut is a further favor, in this case directed by the goddess. Nor is he quite sure of himself in the suitor-slaying; he doubted his capacity the night before and in the event does not, like Achilles against Hector, enjoy Athene's full presence but only as a swallow on a beam. His position resembles that of Diomedes in *Iliad* 5 (778) whom Hera and Athene support against wild Ares, but in the shape of doves. Odysseus is confident but not sure; uncertain act will continue to involve him until the unknown wayfarer will call his oar a winnowing-fan.

Both poems turn on the reception of intruders. Agamemnon's rejection of Chryseis starts the *Iliad;* Achilles' acceptance of Priam ends it; the central and crucial turn is Achilles' rejection of the embassy which, if made up of friends, finds him estranged. In simplest terms the structure is two rejections producing an acceptance. People define themselves by their setting, which an alien presence disturbs; other lives force their way in; the world proves larger than was supposed, and the question of relation to it is raised. A god's possible arrival as a stranger puts the question most widely. Zeus wills and gods prepare Achilles' final acceptance of Priam; his privacy opens to their mercy and comprehension. The *Odyssey* is a series of arrivals; Telemachus' rejection at home but acceptance by Athene-Mentes and abroad introduce the possibilities. Harsh Cyclops and Laestrygonians, alluring but imperative Circe, dangerous Sirens, forbidden cattle, and forgetfulness-urging Calypso prepare Odysseus' two final stages. At Scheria as at Ithaca he first speculates whether he has again reached wild people; Nausicaa would have kept him as her husband. He starts, to his own mind, as a shipwrecked traveler and only slowly recovers, partly by insult, partly by Demodocus' songs, the identity that emerges in his tale. On his first evening at the palace Alcinous prematurely—the king's one lapse—asked him whether he was a god, but he pled the belly's need (7.199–206). The Phaeacians, though not without hint of menace, prove kinder than the suitors, to whom he can tell only false tales. The bow that he tests as a bard strings a lyre replaces his Phaeacian tale.

As in the *Iliad,* the intruder imports a larger world that must be let in. The suitors share with less cause Agamemnon's self-boundedness, they too from mingledly erotic and self-advancing motives, but cannot finally maintain it. Who wants strange beggars, marrers of dining, exclaims Antinous on Odysseus' appearance in the house (17.375–379). While agreeing, Eumaeus lists four kinds of strangers who are accepted and even sought from abroad: the seer, the healer, the craftsman, and the bard (17.384–386). Theoclymenus in the *Odyssey* exemplifies the seer; in the Hippocratic *Concerning Airs, Waters, and Places* the traveling physician wins acceptance by knowledge of the diseases natural to various sites and exposures; the Megarian Eupalinus who, Herodotus says (3.60), tunneled the mountain in Samos may illustrate the progressively large and mobile class of craftsmen; Homer was presumably a traveling singer, or so the *Hymn to Apollo* represents (165–175). The poet's sympathy for such gifted but relatively poor people has been seen in the beggar's maltreatment by the rich and idle suitors,[2] but in the poem the beggar is specifically not classed among these; it is true that he can verge toward a seer and bard. Thersites in the *Iliad* (2.225–242) reviles the kings for preempting spoils, ransoms, and women, and Odysseus' men open Aeolus' bag to spy the booty and gifts with which he, not they, returns. But they hardly express social protest. Thersites is malformed, bitter, and boastful; he is cheated, he claims, of ransom for some Trojan's son "whom I or another Achaean have bound and brought in," he who physically could not have been a fighter; he calls Achilles slack for not stabbing Agamemnon. He is simply the anti-hero. Even Hesiod in the *Works and Days* has no quarrel with wealth but with idleness and crooked judgments; he is not interested in foreigners and dislikes travel (*Erg.* 649–651). Odysseus appeals to a basic Greek simplicity of life. Nausicaa helps wash her five brothers' clothes; queens weave and look out for households; the munificence of epic dining presumably argues its rarity; Argus lies on the dung-heap before Odysseus' house. In a later age Herodotus (7.102) famously has the exiled Spartan king Demaratus tell Xerxes "poverty is native to Greece, virtue acquired"; after the battle of Plataea Pausanias unfavorably contrasted in two banquets the Persian opulence to the Spartan frugality (Herod.9.82); the mighty Pericles, Plutarch says (*Pericles* 16), lived sparely with an eye to accounts. Granted that Mycenaean kings and later ty-

2. P. W. Rose, "Class Ambivalence in the *Odyssey*."

rants could live splendidly and granted the epic breadth with which Eumaeus lists his absent master's flocks and herds, Odysseus returns as a man recovering origins. Nor presumably would auditors have heard any other meaning. Life estranges, people are self-absorbed, the seeming outsider imports the world's chanciness, which he has coped with but not they. Limit is seen from opposite sides, by them as complete, by him as completing. The role of stranger and beggar repeats Odysseus' position toward the sea; it asserts a mortal smallness that yet by stamina achieves meaning. This human condition, not social comment on the behavior of rich to poor, is the main burden of the poem.

Which Books are the most beautiful is hard to know, but the thirteenth is surely one of them. At the changeless Phaeacian banquet his yearning like a tired laborer's for sunset, his feeling farewell to the queen and motionless sleep aboard, the quiet bay in Ithaca with lone olive tree at the head and near the naiads' cave where he is laid ashore with his treasure, then the returning ship turned to stone but doubt whether a mountain shall be set about the town (since gods fulfill their plans, perhaps yes, as further bar to convoy, 13.180–184): all this turns his past into memory. It has been thought inconsistent that the mist which Athene casts about him in order to keep him unknown until the vengeance makes not him but the island strange (13.187–196). But the poetic transfer perfectly puts the twentieth-year arrival; pasts do not survive intact, through their and the mind's change. His first sense of having been tricked by the Phaeacians and fear that he had again reached wild people, though soon amended by sight of his treasure, are in a sense correct; the treasure will not be his as beggar and, though he characteristically counts it, takes on the sea-cave's dimness, and the suitors will be wild. The Neoplatonist Porphyry saw in the sea-cave an allegory of the soul, obviously wrongly in that Homer is not an allegorist, yet rightly to the extent that what is brought back is hidden in a mysterious place accessible to gods and men, memory's place. His change from sea to land follows when Athene clears his sight. She points to the Bay of Phorkys, the olive, and the cave, and he feelingly vows new sacrifice to the naiads if Athene will let him live and his son grow. After his transformation as old beggar he familiarly climbs the steep path from the bay along wooded heights (14.1–2). The excavated cave has yielded a long line of votive offerings to Odysseus.[3] Though higher above the bay than is represented in the poem and thus, like the position of the island itself, transformed in the poetry, it evidently draws from Mycenaean tradition. If his first strangeness and fear of wild people prepare the future action, Athene's self-disclosure does so more fully. As he says, not quite correctly, since she had invisibly helped him at Scheria, she had been absent from him since an angry god scattered the returning Achaeans (13.316–319).

The stages of the recognition were cited: her arrival as a handsome young shepherd, his question what the place is, her reply praising Ithaca, his first false tale of himself as a once rich but now unlucky Cretan, then her queenly change and raillery: "Scamp, devious-witted, insatiate of wiles, even in your own land you would not give up trickery and cunning words, which are dear to you from the ground" (13.291–295). She calls herself likewise the cleverest of gods; that is part of their bond. The movement from insult to fond recognition foreshadows his final meeting with his father. Why in both cases the abuse? Obviously not from lack of feeling. Dejection when good is about to break may prompt a certain god-like smile—human blindness can look absurd—but from wish to heighten the coming good. Abuse also delays an emotion too great for first show; it protects both people, gives them time. In this and the final scene son and father equally need this interval; there can be humanity in insult. But whatever the explanation, both disclosures quickly bring change. The goddess's protest, "I cannot desert you in misfortune because you are controlled and close-witted and mind-keeping" (13.331–332) tells her affection. She feels it because he already intends what she has in mind for him: namely, not to rush home before testing the household, even Penelope. Agamemnon in the Underworld so advised but Odysseus' present caution, quite different from that which he showed toward the Cyclops, draws from his whole travel. He approached the Phaeacians with notable reserve; he and the sage goddess have mentally drawn together. Hence his lively gratitude for her express plan; he might otherwise, he says, have died like Agamemnon (13.383–385). The mention of Troy and Agamemnon in this scene makes clear the poet's assumption why the man who had notably

3. S. Benton, "The Cave of Polis."

enjoyed Athene's favor at Troy had more to learn, therefore why she left him for nearly ten years, yet evidently watching from a distance, finally to weave the nexus of his return. She now bids him to the swineherd's hut, explaining Telemachus' absence in Sparta and promising the youth's safe passage through the suitors' ships. "With these words Athene touched him with her wand. She withered the fair skin on his curved limbs, cast the light locks from his head, and on all his limbs set an old man's skin. She blurred his two once fairest eyes and cast on him a different mean cloth and chiton, torn, foul, and stained with base smoke. She covered him with a swift deer's great hairless hide and gave him a staff and contemptible torn wallet; a woven string carried it" (13.429–438). On retransformation to Telemachus, he has a black beard, blue-black like Poseidon's (16.176); transformed for Nausicaa, he had hair like a hyacinth (6.231), perhaps curling hair. But whether Homer lapsed or the combination of heroic auburn hair with a black beard seemed to him to fit the man of varied devices, the change is both disguise and description; Odysseus is both worn and enhanced by the twenty years.

It may at first seem odd that he is more fully known by travel than at home. But he himself made the long speech at Scheria, and the narrative, itself primary, traced his response, the more because landscape kept hinting what he would find. The seen world subtly merged with his discovery of it. But his near-completeness on reaching home puts the weight on others; the splendid turning-point at Books 18 and 19 is largely Penelope's. These events too complete him, but since he is more than he was on leaving, the question becomes what others have meanwhile done. The distinction comes into play between what is expected of well-born men and what of women and the ill-born. It was just said that the poem, or this part of it, is not chiefly a social commentary on the behavior of rich to poor. Yet the great war is past and the question of settled life emerges. Homer's presumably life-long absorption with heroes colors the answer, which has to do with memory. Penelope bitterly chides Antinous for forgetting that Odysseus once saved his father, a fugitive (16.424–433); Eurymachus falsely claims to remember Odysseus' kindness to him as a child (16.442–444). More broadly, a singer is taught by the Muses; Demodocus, Odysseus said, sang of Troy as if he had been present there, and he himself has like praise from Alcinous and Eumaeus; the past is made alive to Telemachus. But the figures of the Underworld showed the sorrows and errors that accompanied the great past; knowledge of it alone seems not enough or at least leaves both ennobling and sobering examples that the future must accommodate. Doing so asks a profundity of mind that includes, yet transcends the humanity of rich to poor. In these latter books the problems of peace can appear harder than those of war because localism enters. Imagination, kin to poetry and capable of becoming it, seems Homer's answer, profundity of vision. To his own mind, his first auditors must have gained that from him, and it is what is asked in Ithaca. The weight is on others' response to the man who seeks peace.

The wide art of the *Iliad* includes private scenes: Hector meeting Andromache at the Scaean gate where he intends leaving; in *Iliad* 10 (74–80) Menelaus finding Nestor asleep beside his shield, two spears, helmet, and belt and the old man rousing to rest his head from his elbow; Achilles singing to the lyre as the embassy arrives (*Il.*9.186–189); at the end sitting alone while two companions work and the supper table is still not taken away when Priam enters (*Il.*24.472–476). Small momentary acts then replace the crowded doings of battle or assembly, and in the nature of the story such acts now mountingly recur. If Athene's raillery foreshadows Odysseus' final meeting with his father, so does Eumaeus' humble occupation as the beggar approaches. The hut, the yard with thorn-topped stone fence, and the twelve swine-pens that Eumaeus himself built are described in the manner of Laertes' farmhouse, farther vineyard, and orchard (14.5–17, 24.205–212). An old Sicilian woman looks out for Laertes; both men have absent male slaves who later come in. Arrivals surprise; someone was doing something (imperfect tense) when the newcomer appeared (aorist tense). The point is important because two unique usages at 24.386 and 388 have been used to cast doubt on the genuineness of the last scene:[4] in the imperfect tense "they were putting hand to dinner" instead of the usual "they laid hands on the ready-lying food," and the slave Dolius and his sons coming in "from the fields hasting," incorrectly taken to mean "from labors weary." In 24 as in 14, doings expressed in the imperfect tense are interrupted by an arrival expressed in the aorist. Laertes thus gloomily kept spading

4. The scene is discussed in Appendix II.

his vines when Odysseus addressed him (24.242). The returner's test of the swineherd's generosity by his false tale of how at Troy Odysseus got him a cloak matches his test of his father. Detailed sight of small circumstances, abrupt arrival, and shrewd but trusting test connect Odysseus' first human meeting in Ithaca with his last; the intimacy of scene is the same.

Eumaeus was cutting himself shoes from an ox-skin when the clamor of his four savage dogs announced the stranger (14.23–24). Odysseus' response may also go back to his youth; he dropped to the ground and let fall his staff until the swineherd scattered the dogs with shouts and stones. The staff, *skeptron,* has been thought a sign of hidden royalty, and staffs in fact mark kings and speakers, but the lame Hephaestus uses one (*Il.*18.416), and after the fight with Irus the beggar mockingly replaces his opponent's staff in his limp hand (18.103). The staff seems to fit him as beggar, not as latent king. As trees progressively mark his return, so do dogs: first, the handsome dogs that accompany Telemachus to the assembly, then Eumaeùs' wild creatures, then their fond greeting of Telemachus (16.9–10), then their cowering when Athene invisibly enters (16.162–163), then old Argus who raises his ears and wags his tail, to die on the dung-heap, the first to have greeted Odysseus in his own house (17.291–327). Argus contrasts to the dogs that Priam darkly foresees rending his dead body (*Il.*22.66–71). Odysseus secretly weeps to see Argus but does not approach or touch him, rather asks whether he was, like most, an idle table dog and takes joy in the foreseen reply: he was first to track and meet great beasts in the woods. Table dogs resemble the suitors; Argus has a hero's praise; the heroic style shines toward him. But the present wild dogs mark Odysseus' descent from his Phaeacian height; he can go no lower than the ground, unless it was to the Underworld.

The swineherd is as full as Nestor of piety and memory. Had the dogs killed the stranger, he says, the desecration would only have crowned his sorrow in the loss of his good master and the suitors' thinning of his herds. But let him enter; "strangers and beggars are from Zeus. Our gift is small and fond, as is the rule for servants, ever fearful when the new lords command" (14.57–61). The deliberate following scene starts the retarding movement of this half of the poem, for evident reasons: the importance of detail, the emphasis on others, the poet's recapitulation and lingering before the climax. But a further purpose now exists, of relating the many false reports of Odysseus that mercenary people have kept bringing, with the result that neither the swineherd nor Penelope any longer believes them and the suitors think him surely dead. Her incredulity in the night scene is prepared. More politely than Alcinous the swineherd has him eat and drink before guessing who he is, meanwhile dilating on the change in Ithaca. Even cattle raiders, he says, heed Zeus's gaze; the suitors must have some oracular word of Odysseus' death, so reckless is their feasting, more than one or two animals a day and wine to match (14.89–95). But Odysseus was very rich. He lists the diminishing cattle, sheep, swine, and goats on Ithaca and the mainland; they fit Odysseus' origin as does the Phaeacian treasure his gain; nothing less would epically describe him. Who was this man who, you say, went off to Troy, the beggar asks; I may have heard of him in my wanderings. The reply is absolute: no one could persuade Penelope, Telemachus, or me that he is alive. But seeking cloak and chiton people keep trying, as you likely will, and in a wife's way she questions and weeps. "But dogs and quick birds will already have torn the skin from his bones, and his spirit is gone, or fish have eaten him in the sea and his bones lie on a headland rolled in much sand" (14.133–136). He shrinks even from speaking the name Odysseus, whom he yearns for more than his lost parents.

But the beggar is as firm. It is the dark of the moon, a fact that appears when Eumaeus goes out to sleep among his swine. I will take no cloak or chiton, the beggar says, until the hero comes. He partly repeats Achilles' words of *Iliad* 9 (312) that he hates like Hades' gates a man who lies for gain, and swears by Zeus, this hospitality, and Odysseus' hearth that the king will come "in this same light-passing . . . as one moon fades and another rises" (14.161–163). But the swineherd only bids him continue eating and drinking and gloomily turns to Telemachus' imminent death in the suitors' ambush; then changes the subject to the beggar, who tells his Cretan tale, full of resemblances to the travels, ending with the Thesprotian report of Odysseus' imminent return with riches—which in 17 becomes to Penelope one of the five signs of that rousing day and which the beggar exactly repeats to her in the night scene (19.306–307). His future need of deviousness to his wife has become very clear, and the weight of the scene returns to Eumaeus. Your tale of sufferings moves me, he says, but why continue lying about Odysseus? Gods were hostile to him; otherwise, after weav-

ing war's skein (as in *Il*.14.85–86 he says he does) he would have
got glorious burial at Troy (as he wished when the storm struck his
raft and as at the end the ghost of Achilles wishes that Agamemnon
might have had). For myself, I no longer go to town unless Penelope calls me to hear another false report; an Aetolian who claimed
to have seen Odysseus in Crete on his way home lied to me and I
now believe no one. The beggar bids him throw him off a cliff if his
report proves false (14.399). Zeus the god of hospitality would approve that, Eumaeus sardonically replies. As with Laertes, the
other slaves come in and, as with Nestor, careful if simpler sacrifice
precedes the meal. It is a stormy night (14.457), and alike from
chill and for crowning test the beggar tells of the cloak that Odysseus cannily got him at Troy. The swineherd comes off faultlessly,
alike in surrendering his own cloak and in his ironic comment,
"old man, your tale is perfect. No word of yours has been excessive or unconsidered" (14.508–509). He is unconvinced but interested, and his duty to guests extends to his swine, by which
under Boreas he sleeps warmly in a fleece beneath a cliff.

The interweaving of the action, at the end of Book 4, now in 15
and 16, and notably in 24, in degree at least seems novel to this
poem. The *Iliad* foreshadows it, in scenes of shifting battle, in Hector's setting fire to Protesilaus' ship, his farthest success, at the end
of 15, which on Patroclus' return Achilles sees in 16, and in the
final movement between Olympus, Troy, and Achilles' hut. But the
Iliad is largely linear. The *Odyssey* comes nearer Sophocles' or-
ganic structures; Aeschylus' obliviousness to lapse of time in the
Oresteia shows the problem. Now as later, presentness dominates;
the ring-composition by which after Ogygia and Scheria Odysseus
retraces the action to that point makes clear the poet's linear habit.
The divine scenes of the *Iliad* help give direction, and they are not
absent here; as was noted, the Olympian councils of 1 and 5 repeat
the scheme whereby in *Iliad* 15 and 24 two gods are in each case
dispatched by Zeus but on sufficiently brief errands that the scene
meanwhile returns to him and the results follow nearly simultaneously, whereas in the *Odyssey* six days intervene between
Athene's descent to Ithaca and Hermes' to Ogygia, though both
errands were planned in the first council. Telemachus in 4, while
politely saying that he would gladly stay a year in Sparta, pled immediate need of return to his ship, yet in fact stays to the thirtieth
day of the intervening narrative of Odysseus. Eumaeus tells Penel-

ope that the beggar enchanted him like a bard for three days and nights (17.515), but the poem gives four days: first the beggar's arrival and night at the hut, then Telemachus' goddess-sent dream at Sparta, his departure, night at Pherae, and second evening at Pylos whence he promptly sails; then his fourth day's arrival at the hut, Eumaeus then leaving to report his safety to Penelope. The great day of 17 through 19 is Odysseus' fifth in Ithaca, and Eumaeus means the three days that he spent alone with the beggar. The suitors' first response to Telemachus' absence, of which Penelope learns from the herald Medon, and their frustration on his safe return and further debate about killing him at home, of which she is similarly told, mark the end of 4 and 16. But such calculation is idle. The significant point is what, in our ignorance, seems Homer's structural originality. Greatest works mark historical change. Relatively to Ennius' *Annales,* the *Aeneid* expresses change from Roman conquest to Roman inwardness; the *Divine Comedy,* though judged a summary of the Middle Ages, yet in its Italian as contrasted to Latin and its advocacy of secular as contrasted to Papal government looks to a coming age; Shakespeare's tragedies reflect a lost sense of the divine right of kings and of the fixity of morals.[5] Homer's sense of human actuality, marked in the *Iliad* by dominant heroes acting alone or jointly with gods, marks the *Odyssey,* but structurally also. His concern for actuality, though in a god-filled world that keeps auras of sacral travel, fixes at the start and end on Ithaca. The resulting complication dictates what seems the epochal novelty of his structure.

The four human strands of the poem appear separately in 15 and 16: Odysseus is at the hut, Telemachus returns, the suitors discuss killing him, lone Penelope upbraids them. But the strands start intertwining; father and son join in 16 or, since Odysseus has yet to grasp his means of success which Telemachus grasps only when the bow is about to be strung, they begin to join. As on Scheria, all starts from a dream about marriage, then Nausicaa's, now Telemachus' dream about his mother's remarriage. Gods send dreams for their own purposes; to honor Achilles, Zeus in *Iliad* 2 gives Agamemnon false visions of winning by himself, and these Athene-sent dreams are similar. But as in most human interchanges with gods, the mortal is also described. Telemachus' self-assertion against his

5. Theodore Spencer, *Shakespeare and the Nature of Man* 29.

mother and partly mercenary chafing at her delay, though he has better moods also, rise in his dream of her diminishing the house to benefit a new husband (15.20–23). She continues to criticize what she thinks his young heedlessness (18.215–225), as he does her final delay in accepting Odysseus, but in the scene when the bow is produced his praise of her, if now genial since he knows his father, as surpassing all women in Pylos, Argos or Mycenae helps make up. He will keep her by him, he says, if he himself proves able to string the bow (21.107–117). This affectionate side showed in Penelope too in her first Athene-sent dream in which her sister assured her of his safety. Her two other dreams, of the geese and eagle and of Odysseus as young man sleeping with her, are not sent by the goddess but follow the five hopeful signs and her god-given beautification.

Telemachus at Sparta wakes in thrilling anxiety; he kicks his sleeping friend Peisistratus, who tells him to wait for daylight. Menelaus, polite as always, will not keep a reluctant guest, though he would have liked, he says, to show him the cities of middle Argos, in one of which he wanted to settle Odysseus to have him near (4.174–180). He dares hope that the youth will find his father at home and report his stay, which in spite of the dream Telemachus thinks possible. A great meal is prepared even at this hour; Menelaus gives him the Sidonian mixing-bowl and Helen the peplos, work of her own hands, for his future bride (which Penelope shall meanwhile keep). As on their arrival the two youths were astonished by the glittering palace, Peisistratus admires the splendid gifts (15.132). Something like Hermes' marvel on seeing Ogygia has accrued to them; like his father, Telemachus leaves with gifts safely packed. The prophetic signs that showed at the Ithacan assembly now resume, and mountingly from here on, in the form of an eagle carrying off a goose, much the same sign that Penelope tells the beggar that she dreamed. Inspired Helen at once interprets it, and the youth replies in his father's words to Nausicaa, "so may Zeus, Hera's loud-crashing husband, bring it to pass; then there also I should pray to you as to a god" (15.180–181). She comes near comprising his Phaeacia. Reaching Pylos on the second evening, he prudently shuns the palace; Peisistratus agrees that Nestor would insist on entertaining him. He is about to sail when the fugitive seer Theoclymenus, who will give three crucial prophecies, to him, to Penelope, and to the suitors, asks to come aboard. He descends in the fourth generation from Melampus, whose feats in winning Neleus' daughter Pero for his brother Bias Odysseus learned among the heroines; Melampus later ruled in Argos, whence Theoclymenus is in flight for killing a man (11.287–297, 15.225–255). Telemachus accepts him, and Athene, who in his dream had directed his route home, guides him clear of the suitors' ships, though by what route is uncertain. Their ships are said to lie off the island Asteris in the channel between Ithaca and Same (4.844–847, 15.29), but there is no such two-harbored island between Ithaca and the modern Kephallenia. Yet if Eumaeus' hut by the Crow Cliff and the spring Arethusa which Odysseus reached by a wooded path over rocky headlands may be imagined at the south of the island, Telemachus should have landed nearby. Names for places rather than their location evidently lingered in the poetry. He in any case has the others sail to the town without him, directing Theoclymenus to Eurymachus' house, who he says will marry Penelope (15.17, 518–522). He may be testing the prophet by saying what he hopes will not happen. At sight of a hawk carrying off a dove Theoclymenus exclaims that no breed in Ithaca is more royal than his; the hawk fits him as do eagles his father. He changes his mind and bids the steersman Peiraius keep the guest until he shall bring him to the palace. Athene has effected his safe return, but the human tone of the narrative is evident.

The gods who dined with the Phaeacians will hardly have looked old, but those may who walk the earth surveying men's deeds. Demeter reaches Eleusis as a sorrowing old woman; as Mentes and Mentor, Athene is on in years. The beggar as tester is an old man because testing asks experience and experience age. He has learned of Penelope, Telemachus, and the suitors; only his parents remain, and time recedes as the swineherd tells of them and of his own parents. It is the night before Telemachus' return, and as final test, the beggar proposes leaving for the palace. Hermes, he says, has taught him a servant's arts of wood-splitting, butchering, roasting, and wine-pouring (15.319–324). But Eumaeus shudders for him; the suitors' violence, he says, strikes heaven; moreover, they have young and handsome servants. "Nothing is harder on mortals than wandering," the beggar agrees, "yet men endure misery for the belly's sake, if travel, pain, and sorrow reach a man" (15.344–345). He is repeating what he told Alcinous and will say in his own house. To his question about Odysseus' parents, the swineherd describes Laertes' lone and wretched age and Anticleia's death pining for her son. This too looks both back and forward, to the meeting in the Underworld and the final meeting at the farm; much prepares the last scene. Memory of Anticleia carries Eumaeus to his boyhood; she kindly reared him with her daughter Ctimene, at whose marriage and home-leaving for Same she established him in his present life. Gods enhanced his small plenty, for himself and to give strangers, but he misses in these years a mistress's gifts and the occasional light talk by which slaves set store (15.371–379).

He had mentioned his own lost parents, of whom the beggar goes on to ask. "Quietly hear and take pleasure," Eumaeus replies, "sit and drink your wine. These nights are endless. There is time for sleep and for the pleasure of listening. No need for you to lie down beforetime. Others whom heart and soul command may go out and sleep, then with showing dawn eat and follow the lords' swine. But drinking and dining in the hut let us take joy in each other's hard pains, recalling them. A man later delights even in sorrows, one who has borne very much and wandered much" (15.391–401). He was born, he tells, though Odysseus must know, the king's son in the abundant island Syria near Ortygia, perhaps Syros northwest of Delos. Phoenician merchants laid out their wares on a beach, and his nurse slept with one of them, a Sidonian. She had been taken from home and he swore to return her; she proposed stealing the child as price. The Phoenician brought to the palace a gold necklace strung with electrum and while the Queen and her women were admiring it nodded to her; she took the child's hand, passed among the men at their wine, stole a gold wine-pitcher, and brought him to the ship. They sailed at evening; on the seventh day Artemis struck her; she dropped like a tern into the hold, and they threw her to the seals and fish; on reaching Ithaca they sold him to Laertes (15.403–484). Even so he had a happy youth; royal birth as well as present change unites the two, and memory makes them appear older than they are. The long night suggests the winter solstice and, if so, tradition of the king's return not only on Apollo's first day of the month but at the dark of the year. His voyage to the dead and sparing Helius' cattle would fit. But such sacral tones, if credible, are nearly gone, and the long night takes on the poetry of the naiads' cave. Night and cave have become repositories. Eumaeus' true account matches the beggar's false but tonally true story; in length and vividness they resemble the account of how Odysseus got his scar. Auerbach saw in the latter the Greek absorption with present detail, but all these stories look to the past. In the sense that the setting of life on earth is constant, past and present may be interchangeable, but people's lives change and pasts carry to a new present. The two stories at the hut are counterparts of the tale at Scheria but now in the shadow of a closer reality. Age is the idiom of this survival of the past into the present.

The meeting of father and son recapitulates and prepares; 16 is the midpoint of the Ithacan narrative. It is the early morning of Telemachus' return; Eumaeus drops the casks from which he was mixing wine and with joyful tears kisses him as a father kisses a son returned from ten years' absence (16.12–19). The nearby father being the ten-year wanderer, this is one of those similes in which the myth gives substance to character, not vice versa. As at the Ithacan assembly, Telemachus carries a spear, the dogs familiarly fawn on him, and the old beggar yields him his seat, Telemachus nicely saying that he can find another. Are there still cobwebs on his mother's bed, he doubtingly asks; she spends days and nights in sorrow, Eumaeus replies in Athene's words at the bay. The question and reply perfectly resume the situation. Charles Segal notes the progressive thresholds of the poem:[6] at Scheria Odysseus crosses the threshold into the palace (7.135), recrosses it on leaving (13.63); he thus enters his house and sits there as beggar (17.339); he leaps to the threshold with his bow and shoots from there (22.2); at the recognition Penelope crosses the threshold to sit by the hearth (23.88); at Laertes' farm the slave Dolius spies from there the suitors' approaching kinsmen (24.493). Penelope at the recognition says that gods begrudged their taking joy of youth and reaching age's threshold together (23.212). This series of crossings now unites father and son (16.41). Told that the beggar intends going to the palace, Telemachus protests his inability to protect him. Are the people of Ithaca hostile or do you lack brothers to support you, the beggar asks; ardor nearly betrays him as he exclaims that, were he Odysseus or Odysseus' son, he would rather fight and die than see guests insulted and servant women mauled, acts not hitherto noted. No, Telemachus replies, Arcesius

6. "Transition and Ritual in Odysseus' Return."

had one son Laertes, he one son Odysseus, and he one son; he repeats his words to Mentes, Penelope neither rejects nor fulfills marriage, the suitors waste the house and soon will kill me. The roster
of the family is complete when Eumaeus carries the news of his return to Penelope but is told not to go on to Laertes, whom she can
notify.

The past has been elaborately reviewed when Athene enters. The
poet's desire for presentness is a great as in the battles of the *Iliad*
but under the burden now of uniting the narrative toward the climax. The goddess takes her second form at the Bay of Phorkys as a
woman fair, tall, and skilled in fine works. Telemachus does not
see her; "gods in no way show themselves visibly to all, but Odysseus and the dogs saw her. They did not bark but shrank whining
to the other side of the hut" (16.161–163). She nods Odysseus
outside, transforms his looks and clothes; on his return Telemachus thinks him a god. "I am no god. Why do you liken me to the
immortals?" he replies. "I am your father, sorrowing for whom
you bear great pains bent to men's violence." When the youth still
doubts, he calls this Athene's act; you will get no other Odysseus
than me, much afflicted, far wandered, returned in the twentieth
year; "lightly can gods who hold broad heaven exalt or debase a
man." Embracing they weep like taloned birds, ospreys or vultures, whose nest has been rifled; evening would have fallen on
their tears, had not Telemachus asked how he got back (16.220–
221). His emotion is less intense, understandably. Informed and to
a question about the suitors, he enumerates the 108 of them: 52
from Doulichium, 24 from Same, 20 from Zekynthos, 12 from
Ithaca, plus a herald and some servants. He asserts that, famous
fighter though Odysseus is, the two will not match them. But
Odysseus adds all-powerful Athene and father Zeus, and the youth
is at last ready to agree with old Nestor that gods suffice. He is told
to endure the beggar's maltreatment in the house and at a future
sign from him to clear the weapons from the wall, except two
swords, shields, and spears, with the pretext that smoke sullies
them and the drinking suitors might hurt one another; "iron itself
lures a man" (16.294). The famous substitution of iron for bronze
reflects the poet's, not the Mycenaean age but, more importantly
as regards the poem, nothing is said of the bow. Athene and Zeus
will bewitch the suitors; Penelope and Laertes are meanwhile to
know nothing; you will show whether you are truly of my blood.

This last statement and Telemachus' confident reply look to the final scene, and both with eye to it and in self-description, he amends his father's express plan of visiting all the scattered properties (16.309–321). Test only the household, he advises, especially the women servants; time would otherwise fly and the suitors continue their wasting. As Stanford notes, two sides of his mind are evident: his fixed concern with property and special abhorrence of the erotic women. The future is sketched except in one crucial respect, the means of victory.

We thus return to Penelope, from whom we started. Athene's initial plan has reunited father and son, the one after elaborate tuition following Troy, the other by the report and example of Troy. But place describes heroic women as leaving it describes men. The heroines of the Underworld all endured the mixed consequences of their birth and beauty, as did Helen, Clytemnestra, and Cassandra. If travel was Odysseus' test, home-staying was Penelope's, but the event-fixed style has less means of tracing her silent than his eventful years. She placated the suitors by hope and messages, meanwhile weaving Laertes' still-unfinished shroud; the weaving coincided with Telemachus' late youth, and its enforced end matched his maturity. The iteration of sleep and dreams, an intangible kind of weaving, further marked her life. If heroic action harbors hope of escape from common mortal limits, yet in the end only brief escape, her role may be the more rationally heroic. The heretical view has been held that she was flattered by the suitors' presence.[7] But as Odysseus epically has flocks and herds, a rich and beautiful queen is unimaginable in gray neglect. Her dreamed lament for the geese that the eagle killed is not for the suitors but for a changed, perhaps ruinously changed, way of life; she woke to see the geese as always taking grain from the basin. Papyrus fragments of the Hesiodic *Catalogue of Women* (frs.196–204) recount the great company that wooed Helen; as her sager counterpart, Penelope must cope with as many, though less famous, suitors. At Troy Helen wove in a web the deeds of Trojans and Achaeans done for her (*Il.*3.125–128); the webs contrast as do the weavers. The theme of endurance that marks Odysseus recurs in Penelope's unwillingness either to reject or to accept marriage; the one choice

7. See above, p. 19, n. 7.

would endanger her son's property and even his life, the other would end her hope. Odysseus' despondency in his seven years on Ogygia matches her fixed sorrow on which Telemachus first broke with the command that Phemius continue singing of the heroes' returns from Troy. Her rise from inertia is as crucial as her husband's and son's. It takes place on the great day of Books 17 through 19, with brief prelude and epilogue. Attention still stays with the beggar on his arrival at the palace in 17, but she is central even there. She had inveighed at Antinous for proposing to kill Telemachus (16.418–433), in the morning criticizes with familiar tears her son's neglect of her for Theoclymenus (17.101–106), but ends by laughing aloud at his well-omened sneeze. Her latent spiritedness grows, partly to her confusion and surprise, in Athene's enhancement of her beauty. She is intensely poised between fixed doubt and sudden hope, and the inwardness of the firelit scene frames her interior travel.

Suitors now take on or enhance their identity, though most remain names. Antinous, from the start the bluntest of them (his contrariness is in his name),[8] is also the clearest-minded. At the news that Telemachus' ship has returned he gathers the others and grants the youth's ability and the people's regard for him, in effect revising his earlier harshly stated doubt that Telemachus would go on to become king in Ithaca. He therefore expounds an option: either kill him before he can again summon the people or retire to their own places, thence severally woo Penelope, and leave the house to the fatedly successful man who offers most (16.364–392). Penelope thus refers to her possible future husband, and in the Hesiodic *Catalogue* (fr.204.87) Menelaus is Helen's richest suitor. But Amphinomus demurs: he will agree to the killing only if an oracle so commends, and his temporizing (also in his name) wins approval. Unlike Antinous who had proposed the ambush at sea and bitterly resents its failure, Amphinomus laughs to see the returning ship (16.354). His conversation, it is said, most pleased Penelope (16.397–398); the beggar addresses to him his famous words on mortal change and advises him to leave; he is troubled but does not leave—an indecisive man, mentally the Elpenor of the suitors. Informed of the meeting, Penelope sharply reproaches An-

8. The many so-called "speaking names" of the poem are discussed by W. B. Stanford in his edition, II lii–lv.

tinous for forgetting Odysseus' protection of his father, and Eurymachus smilingly replies in Achilles' words to Calchas that while he is alive and gazes on the earth no one shall harm her son. As in *Iliad* 2 (786–794) Iris in the likeness of a Trojan scout reports from the distant mound of Asyetes the advance of the Achaeans, Eumaeus sees the returning ship from the hill of Hermes outside the town, and Telemachus' smile at the report portends his mother's laugh (16.470–477).

He leaves for the palace at dawn of the great day, the swineherd and beggar soon to follow. The ragged beggar shuns the early frost, perhaps another vestige of the king's return at the dark of the year; Hesiod so describes winter dawns and with reference to clothes (17.24–25, *Erg.*547–549). Hermes had saved him on Aeaea and Ogygia and, so he told Eumaeus, had taught him menial arts. The clever god complained to Calypso of missing the hecatombs available in populous places (5.100–102), and the beggar pleads like reason for seeking the palace. Civilizing Athene is his main guide; the sparer of the sun-god's cattle will triumph on Apollo's day; but ingenious Hermes is not quite absent. The scene shifts as Telemachus with mind on his guest curtly gives his mother the first of the five good signs, that she sacrifice for future vengeance (17.51). He returns with Theoclymenus to bring the second and third signs: Menelaus' statement that Proteus saw Odysseus alive and the prophet's instant rejoinder that sitting or walking Odysseus is already in Ithaca beholding the evil acts (17.142–161). He swears in the beggar's words to Eumaeus, by Zeus, this hospitable board, and Odysseus' hearth, but she as usual simply wishes that it might be so, promising fit hospitality and gifts if it were.

As the scene shifts again, "Let us be off," says Eumaeus, "your day has surely come, but it will be chill for you be evening" (17.190–191). He is both right and wrong; the beggar will be taunted and abused and before sleeping will brood on the Cyclops and his present and future foes, but Athene will give him heart and he will know his means of victory. Abuse can scowl as well as smile; the difference reflects, among much else, space of mind. Localism speaks both in the goatherd Melanthius' sneers and kick and in Antinous' mockery and thrown footstool. Provinciality has two faces, angry and endearing; Theocritus, who remembers this scene (*Id.*7.10–20), knows the rural hardness (*Ids.*4 and 5). Zeus,

Eumaeus says, takes away half a man's merit when the day of slavery grips him (17.322). "So here is a scamp leading a scamp," cries Melanthius at sight of the two (17.217–218), "god always brings like to like. Miserable swineherd, where are you taking that glutton, hideous beggar, banquet-fouler?" This is Odysseus' first indignity at home, but he resists killing the goatherd, praying instead to the nymphs of the poplar-fringed spring where they meet. Like the spring beyond Alcinous' garden, it is the communal fountain anciently built by the eponymous Ithacus, Neritus, and rich Polyktor (17.207). The fresh waters express his future as did the naiads' salt cave his past. The subtle doublet repeats the poet's method. Oral practice does not quite explain; his weddedness to it is the further factor, his endless pleasure in near but progressive likenesses. Life never entirely changes, nevertheless does change. Years and wisdom allow the movement.

It is a great moment when he sees his house. Such a handsome place must be Odysseus' palace, he tells Eumaeus; savor and music announce feasting. Old Argus on the outer dung-heap is oblivious to the feasters inside; the tone of sunken memory that arose at the hut persists in him. He is a royal dog, not to be greeted sentimentally but praised, and his lone death on lowering his ears and wagging his tail to his master and after Odysseus has entered the house has a hero's isolation. His likeness to Laertes is evident; both persist neglected. Even fond raillery recurs in the knowing question, was he simply a table-dog; Laertes at the end likewise recalls his younger feats. The theme of the poem, salvation of common life by endurance, shines in Argus. The change is abrupt as the beggar takes a place near Telemachus, then prompted by Athene circles the tables asking food. The goddess shares his will to test the household but continues her ten-year test of him; to her mind his debasement is evidently his crowning instruction. The swineherd, seated by Telemachus as is the goatherd by Eurymachus, boldly answers in his speech about outsiders Antinous' objection to his bringing a beggar, but Telemachus silences him; be free with others' food, he tells Antinous. The beggar further reproaches Antinous' backwardness and he ends by throwing a footstool as his gift, which the others think dangerous because gods can come as strangers. The scene rounds to Penelope's prophetic wish that the bow-god Apollo might strike him. She most hates him because the beggar asked from poverty and the others gave; another dawn would not come for them, adds Eurycleia, if we had our wish (17.492–497). Eumaeus proceeds to give the fourth sign of this, to her, startling day by repeating the beggar's tale of having learned in Thesprotia of Odysseus' near return with riches (17.515–527). He further describes the beggar's bardlike powers but fails to repeat his exact prophecy that Odysseus will come at the new moon. She rises as always to such reports and has Eumaeus summon him. When she wishes that it were credible, Telemachus—fifth sign— sneezes, and she laughs aloud (17.541–542). The beggar is enhanced in her eyes—he is clearly a prudent man—by postponing conversation until evening when they will be alone. A report like many in the past impends, but crowding signs agitate her.

Books 18 and 19 both start with the beggar, then shift to her, the latter decisively. Abuse of him continues with the arrival of a big but vacuous local glutton whom the suitors call Irus because he runs messages, and when the two quarrel for place on the threshold, Antinous indecently proposes a formal fight. He more gleefully repeats Laodamas' challenge at Scheria, and Odysseus at first protests his age as he there did the sea's wear, then prudently and with Telemachus' support makes them swear not to help Irus. Nothing is now said of his transformation to his former strength; the event may be beneath Athene's notice. He simply hitches up his rags to show his mighty frame. The art that at first looks realistic can suddenly enlarge; Diomedes at the muster of *Iliad* 4 (412– 418) answers Agamemnon's taunt with perfect propriety but soon has fire blazing from his helmet (*Il.*5.4–7). Odysseus has had five upward or downward changes, to Nausicaa, at the Scherian games, at the Bay of Phorkys, and two at the hut; only the final change to Penelope at the recognition awaits. For the poetry he is already two people. Sudden rise from the common to the miraculous or half-miraculous and equal assumption that both are real is authentically Homeric, assertion of the margin surrounding common life. The beggar easily lays out his hollow opponent, leans him against the courtyard wall, and replaces his staff. His speech to Amphinomus on mortal change (18.130–137) and advice that he leave follow. Wilamowitz, who saw in the speech the later tone of elegists, judged it late.[9] Likeness to Mimnermus (fr.2) and Theognis (441–446, 1029–1036), also to late Pindar (*Py.*8.95–

---

9. *Die Heimkehr des Odysseus* 30.

97, *Ne.*11.43–49), and Sophocles (O.C.1211–1248), exists but equally to Glaucus' comparison in *Iliad* 6 (146–149) of the generations of men to the generations of leaves. Zeus contemplates in like words the divine horses weeping for dead Patroclus, "nothing is frailer than a man, of all things that on earth breathe and fare" (*Il.*17.446–447). The theme of mortal change runs through both poems. What is more present to the Underworld? But the beggar's success is brief and mockery resumes; the pretty servant Melantho, Antinous' girl, calls him drunk for presuming to light the torches at evening, and Eurymachus likens the shine of his bald head to a torch. When he replies with the previously cited challenge to a day's work in the fields and by saying that Eurymachus thinks himself great because he consorts with few and not brave people (18.366–386), he throws a second footstool. Telemachus condemns such riot, and the pliant Amphinomus gets them away to bed. The fight and these last insults frame the scene of Penelope's beautification. If nothing changes for the beggar, the day has brought drastic change for her.

It remains uncertain change, signs rather than promise. The slowing movement has so far kept resuming and repeating, and tangled themes now notably surround her. The reason is that Athene's express plan for Odysseus and Telemachus was not stated for her; it simply occurs. Divine plans and human acts being reciprocal, the mystery of the goddess's mind extends to hers. Her sudden impulse to appear before the suitors surprises the servant Eurynome, who merely comments that what she has long prayed for has come about: Telemachus is bearded. Nothing is then said of remarriage, but in addressing the suitors she soon recalls Odysseus' parting command that if he should fail to return, she remarry when their son is bearded. "A night will come when hated marriage will meet me, wretched that I am, from whom Zeus has taken joy" (18.272–273). She told Eurynome that she wished to warn Telemachus against the suitors—her previous knowledge of their plans to kill him speaks in that—but she in fact criticizes his failure to protect the beggar. To her mind she had kept them in hand as he does not; his young incapacity, she feels, should still have given her time. Antinous in the tale of the web described her hopeful words and messages to them but added "her mind intends other things," which the watching beggar now repeats (18.283). The strange laugh with which she greets Athene's impulse to her to

appear before the suitors and, after her beautifying sleep, her be-
mused gesture of passing her hands over her face are nearly som-
nambulistic. This second laugh shows further change from her old
sorrow; she is strangely spirited and beautiful, yet wishes that Artemis would strike her as softly as did her sleep. Odysseus is intensely vivid to her but as he once was; she dwells on his eminence
(18.204–205). She is responding to the day's signs but as the goddess, not she, fully understands. Yet in announcing marriage and
reproaching the suitors' failure to bring gifts, she has something in
mind. It is importantly but secondarily a thought of wealth rival-
ing her husband's and son's and lightly correcting the latter's fear
of impoverishment. The beggar smiles at her success, and she po-
etically deserves not less than he brought home. But she primarily
seeks delay. She had wished the suitors' death by the bow-god.
Though Eumaeus did not exactly repeat the beggar's prophecy
which he himself will tell that evening, that Odysseus will return
with the new moon, Telemachus sneezed. She later tells the beggar
that with the completion of the web her last device was taken from
her (19.157–158). But that proves not quite true; she now fixes no
date for the marriage. She gains time for the signs to declare themselves. Athene's inspiration is her final recourse, perfectly uniting
fidelity to Odysseus' old command with today's new hope.

As the thronging gods of *Iliad* 20 and 21 withdraw or nearly
withdraw before the climax, so now and at the suitor-slaying.
Though touched by gods, outcomes are human. Athene's lamp
wondrously lights the house as Telemachus takes the armor from
the walls, and she distracts Penelope when Eurycleia sees the scar
and lets the beggar's foot clatter into the basin, but husband and
wife become mountingly alone, Odysseus dismisses Telemachus,
"that I may further rouse the servants and your mother and she for
grief tell everything" (19.45–46); aroused feeling will show her
true mind. Servants are briefly shown in the pretty and again insulting Melantho whom Penelope rebukes and in the trusted
Eurynome, who now spreads a fleece on the beggar's chair and will
tomorrow light the couple to bed; Odysseus' old nurse Eurycleia
has been known from the first. His path into his wife's confidence
has been traced: his opening comparison of her to a good king
under whom the land burgeons and the people prospers—it echoes
Teiresias' prophecy and confounds king with queen—then his further Cretan tale, this time with the claim of having seen Odysseus

on his way to Troy, then his crowning description of Odysseus'
clothes, her own work, and his two-tubed clasp with image of dog
and fawn, and his swarthy, curling-haired, bent-shouldered herald
Eurybates (19.224–248). She had begun by saying that the completion of the web took away her last recourse against marriage,
but it is only after her tears and his citing of Odysseus' clothes that
he repeats his prophecy to Eumaeus of the return at the new moon
(19.306–307). He has so far been in command, but her statement
to Eurycleia that Odysseus would now be old shows her imagining
the return; all now rests with her secret mind. The foot-washing,
Eurycleia's recognition, and the tale of the scar intervene, but the
two night-tales bring back her interior life. The pause has prepared
her. The nightingale's changeful song, she says, phrases her nightly
quandary whether to leave or stay. In spite of his assurance that
the dream of the eagle and geese is true, she calls it issued from the
ivory gates of deceptive dreams. It is a "dire dream," though
"dearly would it be welcome to me and my son" (19.568–569).
Her waking to see the geese familiarly feeding at the basin tells
nothing changed (19.552–553). She had not said that she would
make her choice of husband tomorrow but, though she doubts the
beggar's prediction, she acts on it. "Who most lightly strings the
bow in his hands, him I will follow, quitting this house, the house
of my marriage, full of livelihood, which I think I shall remember
even in dreams." It is her inspired compromise between doubt and
hope, between her memory of Odysseus' old command and her
faith in today's signs, now enhanced by the beggar's credibility.
Her nightly thoughts and dreams oscillate between duty and desire, and she neglects neither. Her double fidelity, distantly
Athene's work but inwardly hers, gives the solution.

8. *Reunion*

War implies peace and home-leaving return. The *Iliad* keeps recalling people's origins, and the poetic tradition that took them to
Troy includes the survivors. The later *Nostoi* traced some of them,
and Nestor, Menelaus, and Helen carry to the *Odyssey*. The
suitor-slaying revives the former fighting but subsidingly and in another spirit. It is not, like Achilles' battle with the Scamander and
killing of Hector, the climax of a mounting fury but the end of
trials. It has been rightly said that Achilles' isolation does not
wholly reflect his quarrel with Agamemnon; with Book 9 it
emerges as itself the theme of the poem. The quarrel was, in Aristotle's language, the inciting, not the formal cause; with Patroclus'
death his isolation dominates. War enters into Achilles, and the fire
that flames from his head merges with the fire that sweeps the
once-fertile plain and will soon sweep Troy. The power of the
poem is not least in this incandescence. The suitor-slaying by contrast is a climax less to fury than to endurance. The heroic tradition doubtless arose from fighting and basically includes it; to that
extent the slaying describes Odysseus. But war is finally secondary
even in Achilles. His isolation is his predicament as mortal, and his
huge feats take on the character of protest, which in his final mercy

draws toward acceptance. His and Priam's joint weeping, the one for Patroclus and his father Peleus, the other for Hector, leaves them still alone, but the act acknowledges their human bond. If this is Homer's purpose in a poem of war, it is evidently such in a poem of peace. From among the many themes that the tradition offered, that of recovered mortal lot is peculiarly his. Nor is the change of subject wholly surprising, from the isolation of war to that of the world. People's loss of what they first assumed was to him a main but not the chief reality; their meeting it and revision of their former hopes carry them further. The violence of the suitor-slaying is less significant than its place at the end of a long recovery.

The violence is also differently seen, in the one case with inward passion, now more largely as narrative. But if tragedy sees the world from inside as suffering, comedy from outside as invitation, the difference is of genre. The term is anachronistic, but narratives carry their identifying tones. If Achilles is the more intimately known, the reason is that the terrible urgency of events echoes in him, enflaming his mind and becoming part of him, whereas Odysseus moves through adventures that describe the world. He of course responds but rather by act than reflection. That is not wholly true, since his exultation toward the Cyclops differs from his despondency on Ogygia; the steps of his travel change him, and his beggarly role in Ithaca crowns his endurance. Even so he returns as the man who has seen the world; it is described in his experience. This substitution of the thing felt by the thing done, of express response by visible act, of characters inwardly conceived by characters in a line of story, is the hallmark of myth. Even the tragic *Iliad* carries Achilles through actions manifesting loneness, loss, self-reproach, huge isolated sorrow, and shared sorrow rather than through these and other emotions in themselves. Characters live the story.

There results, for later minds at least, a basic difficulty in Odysseus as a character. The world that opens to his travels is beautiful; no poem more expresses the fortune of living and seeing. He occasionally responds delightedly, to Circe, the Sirens, and partly at Scheria, yet always with curiosity, even in the Underworld; his will to live attests to life's desirability. But he is also the suffering home-seeker; this side dominates the latter part of the poem. It follows that the poet sees the beauty and interest of things more steadily than can he, who is immersed in events. Calypso's island is the great example; its beauty moves even the god Hermes, but Odysseus languishes. So also at the start, the fresh charm of Telemachus' safe youth attends his going to bed and getting up, though he cannot think so. This counterpoint between the tone of the narrative and the characters' experience of it gives what was called the comic irony. The latent beauty keeps summoning and the main characters hear, but commonly against hazards. The antithesis is nowhere clearer than in the suitor-slaying, preceded as it is by Penelope's beautification and the firelit meeting and followed by her token of the bed and final outpoured self-explanation. The suitor-slaying revives Troy; the surrounding scenes carry the new feeling and goal. Odysseus has need to be his many-sided self thus to ally the scope of the world and the joy of home with the exigencies of both. One or another of his traits and epithets dominates one or another scene. The city-sacker rises in the slaying, yet, given the total narrative, in a context different from old triumphs. His mingled intransigeance and restraint describe him, by action, partly by the whole preceding action. The victor remains the journeyer and endurer. Like Achilles, he lives the poem, yet more outwardly because in him the *Odyssey* expounds the human lot of being at once nearly boundless, yet bounded. Optimistic though the myth is, it traces what is involved in uniting the extremes.

Penelope's crucial day ends with her late-night dream, her third and last, of Odysseus as young husband sleeping with her. But she cries that gods send her bad dreams and prays that Artemis strike her, that she may go below the earth with him in her eyes before delighting the mind of a lesser man (20.87–90). The direness of this as of the previous dream is her doubt of them. Yet unlike her first dream that fled by the door-bolt when she asked of Odysseus (4.836–839), they show him intensely in her mind. Such is the language of myth that, over and above the beggar's recollections and prophecy, his presence helps make Odysseus actual to her. At the start of the foot-washing Eurycleia said that no stranger ever so resembled him in form, voice, and legs (19.380–381). But he deflected the remark, and Penelope's rejection of the dreams makes clear that she has no inkling who he is. Such hope as she has follows from the day's signs and his persuasiveness and prophecy. Hint of him from his presence is in the myth, but as an overtone, almost inaudible.[1]

---

1. See above, p. 14, n. 6.

On the same night he sees women servants leaving to make love with the suitors, and his heart growls like a dog defending her litter (20.14–16). Changed sex again describes him; at Scheria he wept like a woman who has lost her husband in war, and at Aeaea the men at the ship greeted his return from Circe's house like calves skipping about their dams. The previous dogs have entered into him as keeper of the house, and the changed sex carries the feminine tones of home. Hence possibly Telemachus' special resentment against the love-making servants. He singled them out at Eumaeus' hut, and it is he who later hangs them. But in Melantho Odysseus too has reason for resentment and as tester shares his son's anger. Monogamy is central to the theme of home. In *Iliad* 6 (243–250) Priam's patriarchal house on Pergamus with fifty chambers for married sons and daughters seems intendedly alien. The war was fought for Helen, and Agamemnon's preference of Chryseis to Clytemnestra and plan to bring her back, as he in fact brings Cassandra, operate in his quarrel and death. Odysseus' feeling praise of marriage to Nausicaa is at once politic and thematic; the bed is his test of recovered Ithaca. This sexual theme extends to the household. He bids himself endure the women as he did the Cyclops (20.18–21). His soliloquy, which resembles Hector's before his final battle (*Il.*22.99–130), carries forward the night-mood of his meeting with Penelope, and though Athene cheers him before sleep, he at dawn prays Zeus for a sign. It becomes two signs, both thunder from the clouds and the prayer of the frailest of twelve corn-grinding women who had not finished her work when the others had (near sister of the careful weaving-woman of the simile of *Iliad* 12.433–435, who toils to support her children). May the thunder, she prays, portend the suitors' last day of dining and an end to her exhausting work. It is the dawn of the long-sought day, and the well-omened speech carries the recovery to the weakest member of the house. Elpenor died at the sexual moment of the travels, but this frail woman shares the better outcome.

Her difference from the love-making women extends to the male slaves. The intimacy of scene and retarding movement that began with Eumaeus culminates in the early hour before Penelope gets the bow and axes. The poet's purpose was partly to consolidate the action, but the slowing pace also reflects his detail-filled style. His interest in small acts is nowhere clearer than now; if they differ from acts of battle at Troy and those soon to follow, they have the same specificity. His genius is in part his utter weddedness to the oral style, which flames in war but glows to small events. Telemachus, again entering with spear and dogs, asks Eurycleia how the beggar spent the night; his mother, he thinks, cannot distinguish worthy from unworthy strangers. No, the old woman replies, he refused the offer of a soft bed and has so far refused food; he is quietly drinking his morning wine. Neither knows that the other knows the beggar's identity. It is Apollo's festival (20.156), and she has the servants beat and spread the chair-covers, clean the tables, and wash the mixing-bowls and cups. Eumaeus brings his three fattest swine, asks the beggar how he fares, but hears nothing of that, only of the suitors' recklessness. Melanthius likewise brings goats, with renewed abuse; the two contrast as do the servant women. But the forward movement shows in the new figure of the honest and meditative cowherd Philoitius, who sees in the beggar the misfortune of his lost master. He confides his dilemma (20.195–225): shall he continue transporting to the suitors Odysseus' mainland cattle or desert Telemachus by taking the herds to another lord? Odysseus gave him charge in youth of his herds in the country of the Kephallenians (in the Catalogue of Ships he commands these people as well as the islanders from Ithaca, Zakynthos, and Samos, here more often though not always called Same), and Philoitius is loyal but troubled. Last night's prophecy and the former oath by Zeus, this hospitality, and Odysseus' hearth recur with the emphasis of the day: Odysseus will come while you are here, the beggar swears, and with your own eyes you will see the suitors falling (20.232–234).

The early hour further concludes the suitors' debate whether to kill Telemachus; the favorable sign for which Amphinomus waited two days earlier is denied by a bad sign from the left, again of an eagle, this time clutching a dove. Telemachus asserts his authority when they return; this is not a public house, he says, but his. In the town heralds summon the people to Apollo's shaded grove (20.276–278). It will be the suitors' last meal in the house, and thoroughgoing Athene brings Odysseus new indignity, with unclear purpose whether to rouse or further to debase him, in the form of an ox-hoof thrown by the rich Ctesippus (the throwing matches Xenophon's banquet among the uncouth Thracians, *Anab.*7.3.22). But the beggar simply smiles grimly, and Telemachus inveighs against Ctesippus with what now amounts to a refrain (20.310, 2.313, 18.229, 19.19); "I was then still a child" but should kill you had you hit the beggar. He effectually repeats his words to Penelope at the time of her beautification; he has observed everything, he says, but lacks power against the great number. The mild suitor Agelaus grants that outrage is excessive and that mother and son have properly delayed, but since Odysseus is surely dead, she had best marry and Telemachus keep the house— to which he surprisingly agrees if she wishes, promising large gifts. The irony turns hectic in Theoclymenus' third prophecy. Surprised by Telemachus' mild answer but also by Athene's will, the suitors laugh wildly; blood is on the meat before them, and their tears of laughter are tears of grief, as the prophet, not they, sees. He cries that their heads and legs are wound with night, their tears are groans, the walls and reaches of the hall drip blood, ghosts hasting toward Erebus crowd the door and court, the sun has sunk, and a dire mist has fallen (20.345–357). Other traditions show parallels,[2] and at the turning moment of the travels Helius' cattle lowed from the spits. In *Iliad* 11 (53–55) Zeus opens with bloody dew the day of Hector's success, and again casts bloody dew about Sarpedon and night over his corpse (*Il.*16.459, 567). The river's superhuman pursuit of Achilles and Hephaestus' burning defense of him mark a like stage of the narrative (*Il.*21.263–271, 342–355). The ghosts that Theoclymenus sees speeding toward Erebus will be those that Agamemnon and Achilles will see at the end. Theoclymenus is dismissed by the suitors as raving, but Penelope from her upper room has heard.

She descends to the store-chamber that Telemachus entered at the start; bronze, gold, iron, and clothes in fragrant chests keep their antique order. With a bronze, ivory-handled key in her stout hand (21.6; Norman Austin well calls the formulaic adjective more emotional than physical)[3] she casts back the bolt, and the opening doors bellow like a bull in a field, from disuse and prophetically. How Odysseus got the bow from Iphitus son of Eurytus is related: during Laertes' kingship, he went still young to Messenia on a public mission to retrieve stolen flocks, met Iphitus and exchanged gifts with him but never, as he hoped, welcomed him in Ithaca because impious Heracles after a banquet in his own house killed him (21.27). The account repeats Heracles' violence at Pylos told in

2. Stanford at 20.351 gives parallels.
3. *Archery at the Dark of the Moon* 73.

Iliad 5 (395–397)—he wounded Hades there—but draws from his sack of the Euboean town Oechalia and killing of Eurytus in passion for his daughter Iole. The myth recurs in Sophocles' *Trachiniae*, which is to astonishing degree an anti-*Odyssey*. The waiting wife Deianeira is described by night and dreams; the son Hyllus leaves for news of his long-absent father; young Iole, whom Heracles brings home, contrasts to Deianeira as Nausicaa, whom Odysseus leaves, contrasts to Penelope; the passionate Heracles does not reach home; Hyllus is to show his breed (*Trach.*1158, *Od.*24.508) by bearing his dying father to the pyre on Oeta. Like themes end exactly oppositely, and the bow of Eurytus connects. Burkert sees in Creophylus' *Sack of Oechalia* poetic concentration on a regnant passion resembling Homer's on the wrath.[4] The passion is nearer that of Achilles, but the exactly opposite action shows in Odysseus. The reversed parallel classically illustrates the working of themes.

Penelope weeping sets the bow on her knees; in her emotion she tells the suitors that they only claimed to court her but preferred drinking and dining in the masterless house; their test has come. In youthful thought of Iphitus Odysseus used the bow at home and left it there (21.38–41). Eumaeus sets it and the axes before the suitors; Antinous abuses him in nearly Theocritean language, "silly countrymen with thoughts but of a day"; yet calls the test accursed; he remembers as a boy seeing Odysseus string the bow (21.94–95). It is unclear just when Telemachus grasps his father's purpose. He apologizes for laughing and praises his mother beyond Achaean ladies, asserting that if he himself can string the bow, he will keep her by him. He thrice tries in vain and would have succeeded at the fourth try, had not the beggar raised his head to stop him (21.128–129). That may be when he understands, but his laugh resembles hers at her plan of announcing remarriage. If he already understands, his effort variously conveys maturing, deception, amends to his mother, and emulousness of his father, as in his last speech of the poem before the fight with the kinsmen. As often, notably at Penelope's gift-soliciting and decision for the test, Homer simply tells rather than explains.

So also about the axes. Telemachus has dug a trench in the dirt floor of the hall and aligned them, but just how is disputed. There

---

4. "Die Leistung eines Kreophylos."

are four main views: (1) Stanford's, that the axe-heads, without handles, face forward so aligned that the empty sockets form an interrupted tube; (2) Pages's, that they are sacral metal-handled Minoan axes with holes at the base for hanging on walls, therefore that they are set head-down; (3) the older view followed by Monro, that they are two-bladed axes with the curved upper parts of the blades bending backward to make nearly complete holes above the handles; (4) Burkert's parallel of the pharaoh Ameno-phis II, which suggests simply a traditional motif.[5] Germain's wide parallels unite only in the bow as test of the true bridegroom. Four points argue for (3). The axe with which on Ogygia Odysseus felled trees for his raft is called "sharpened on both sides" (5.235); it is a double axe. Penelope likened the axes to oaken ship-props (19.574); to her mind they include wooden handles. At the funeral games for Patroclus, the first prize for archery, which, as here, needs prayer to Apollo, is ten double axes (*Il.*23.851). And at his first shot Odysseus "did not miss all the axes, at the first handle" (21.422): that is, at the end of the handle, conceivably either the base or the top, but since the axes are being described, must mean the end at the head. Two-bladed curved axes standing on their handles may have been no easier to plant in the floor than upside-down sacral Minoan axes, but better fit practical Odysseus, the tree-feller and bed-builder, in wooded Ithaca. Even so the feat is described in a legendary, not a literal spirit. Details chiefly lend viv-idness, as at the first shot "clear through them out the door went the bronze-heavy arrow" (21.422–423). The poet's mind is on the feat and its sequel.

Telemachus on failing leans the bow with an arrow across it against the door jamb, and Antinous bids the suitors try in turn, starting from the back of the hall to the right of the mixing bowl where the gentle and soft-handed Leodes son of Wine-eyes aptly sits. Like Amphinomus and Agelaus, he disapproves the others' violence, yet has stayed with them. He feels the shame of failure; better for him and many to have died, he says, yet amiably suggests courting some other lady (21.152–162), a pliant smiling man. The others' efforts are omitted, but Antinous has Melanthius fetch a wheel of tallow, not unlike the wheel of wax used on Odysseus' Siren-passing crew, with which to soften the bow at the fire. Eu-

5. Stanford and Monro at 19.572 of their respective editions. Page, *Folktales in Homer's Odyssey* 95–113. Burkert above, p. 72, n. 25.

maeus and Philoitius opportunely leave, and the beggar follows them into the court. Shall he tell them, he ponders; would they support Odysseus if a god brought him? To their vow that this is their heart's prayer, "here I even myself," he proclaims in his former words to Telemachus, "after many sufferings in the twentieth year reach my fatherland." He draws back his rags to show the scar; they embrace weeping, but he collects himself to bid Eumaeus soon bring him the bow however violently the suitors may object, then have the servant women lock the inner door of the hall. Philoitius is to lock the court; they avoid suspicion by returning separately. It is Eurymachus' turn with the bow. Failing, he less laments his loss of Penelope than the disgrace, which he describes in Nestor's words of *Iliad* 2, of the Achaeans' disgrace if they should fail of Troy (21.255, *Il*.2.119). Antinous, who has not yet tried, invokes the holiday. The axes, he says, can stay in place; let them join the public offering to Apollo; Melanthius will tomorrow bring more goats for sacrifice, and they will try again (21.257–268). But that would be to miss Apollo's day.

This is the moment when the beggar asks to try, "to test among you my arms and strength, whether the power in my curved limbs is as it was or wandering and neglect have destroyed it." They are wildly outraged; Antinous calls him as drunk as the centaur Eurytion at the Lapith Peirithous' banquet who was dragged out and had his ears and nose cut off, as will Melanthius; be quiet, do not infuriate younger men. But Penelope crucially intervenes. It is not for them, she says, to command Telemachus' guest; do they fancy that the beggar would take her home and make her his wife? That would be "not at all, not at all fitting" (21.319). Not that, replies Eurymachus, but the shame of failure if the beggar should succeed. How speak of shame, she rejoins, when you dishonor a great man's house? The beggar is strong and claims good origin; if he succeeds, I will give him cloak, chiton, spear, sword, and shoes and send him where he wishes. But Telemachus dismisses her with his early words and those of Hector to Andromache, the bow "shall be men's business."

Does she come nearer recognizing the beggar? Her words, like her response to her dreams, say not. Told later of the slaying and on sight of the blood-stained beggar, even on sight of him transformed, she still doubts. Her demand that the beggar be given the bow less supports him than rebukes the suitors; she resents the disorder and wants Telemachus in control. Yet the beggar's last night's prophecy that Odysseus would come at the new month chiefly inspired her idea of the test; it crowned yesterday's other signs. The test has been going on. When does she expect Odysseus to come?—if he will come, which she doubts. Except the beggar, no one has yet appeared. Her unawareness resembles that of Oedipus after his initial proclamation when Teiresias names him the murderer (O.T.413–428). The astounding reality cannot yet penetrate, and, in the nature of Homer's art, naturally so. He was not concerned to say when Penelope might have had her dream of the geese and eagle that expressed her yesterday's dilemma. The climax alone now matters. Her fixed scepticism sufficiently opened to admit the idea of the test; the thin crack does not extend to the beggar's identity. This is one more example of the poet's nearly total absorption with scenes; fixed in myth though they are, their presentness dominates. Penelope and the beggar have moved a step closer but remain apart. Her marvel as a character, poised between past and future, between her as agent of the myth and her as person, grows. Eumaeus, though commanded to bring the bow, falters at the outcry, and Telemachus with threats against him that more express his own agitation himself gives it to the beggar. But Eumaeus bids Eurycleia lock the inner door and stay away whatever she may hear; Philoitius locks the court.

The expedition to Troy was to retrieve a wife; a Minoan theme of the loss of the year-goddess, the loss of Persephone whom Hades carried off, has been thought a remote original.[6] The beggar's comparison of Penelope to a righteous king under whom earth and people flourish carries that suggestion; she has been beleaguered. Odysseus returns because he wished Helius' cattle to keep what should have been their immortality; Teiresias prophesied that Ithaca will flower. Whatever its origin, the theme of restored order guides both poems. The *Iliad* shows the magnitude of the first loss and of the effort to right it; the consequence carried to lengths that none foresaw. Only Zeus grasps their mortal blindness to the demand; his at once admiring and lamenting gaze is the poet's. As captors, the suitors reproduce Paris; they are as blinded by pleasure as were the warriors by effort; they show peace's

6. H. W. Clarke, *The Art of the Odyssey* 70.

slacker ignorance. It was said at the start that the suitor-slaying is not a moralistic but a mental act. The returner's wide sight of the world stretched beyond Troy, much farther beyond Ithaca, which is yet necessary to him as a man. Even Eumaeus and Philoitius, confined as is their life as slaves, have overseas memories from childhood or work, and Telemachus has gained these. Penelope as beleaguered wife is different; her travel is interior, through years rather than on land and sea. There is a sense in which any place resembles any other; as someone's own, it is unique simply to him. She is its guardian spirit, a kind of locally imprisoned and released Persephone. The slaying thus in spirit returns the Trojan cycle to its start; the summary of the Second Nekyia marks the end. A kind of circle has been drawn, from loss of a prospering place, to Troy, to the wide world, to recovery. Too young to have gone to Troy, the suitors, like the not too young Aegisthus, as greatly dim the joy of place as did wife-stealing Paris. The poem then traces the two ways by which a place may exist: as dimmed and hedged or as the flowering token of all possible places. As traveler, Odysseus is also the slayer, not alone for wife, place, and property but for all these as necessary to one who has seen and understood what a man's life offers. He and Achilles, the one old, the other young, the one with the fame of attained knowledge and wife, the other with the Muses' fame, show the two stages of the effort.

As his bardlike tale announced him to the Phaeacians, the bow that he strings as a bard strings a lyre proclaims him at home (21.406–409). The clear-flying arrow convinces more direly than did the song. He leaps to the threshold and with a second shot strikes Antinous still ignorantly drinking. His place-bound life is in his death. Dogs, Odysseus cries, you said that I should never return; you have looted my house, lain with servant women, courted a living man's wife, feared neither gods nor men's opinion; now die. In Agamemnon's manner toward Achilles and with like words (22.55–59, *Il*.9.112, 523), the more kingly and perhaps older Eurymachus proposes amends. Antinous, he says, was to blame; he thought to displace Telemachus as king. But Odysseus is implacable; all that you have and could get from elsewhere would not make up (22.62, *Il*.9.380). When Eurymachus manfully rallies the others to take the tables as shields and together advance with their swords, he too falls. Telemachus kills the once pleasant Amphinomus; here and later, Odysseus is spared the harsher killings. At the swineherd's hut Telemachus was told to leave out two sets of armor when putting away the rest, but failed to do so when he cleared the walls beneath Athene's radiant lamp. The bow has changed former plans; the addition of Eumaeus and Philoitius demands four sets of arms, but the first mistake looks to a second. Telemachus gets the arms leaving by a door at the back of the hall near the mixing bowl, but in his haste leaves the storechamber unlocked (22.155-156). The door from the hall gives not only toward the chamber but on a passage leading outside the hall into the court; the details of the architecture are as contested as the line of axes and the shape of the raft. Odysseus' arrows give out, and the four don the armor that Telemachus has brought; Eumaeus is sent to guard the narrow passage toward the court. The suitor Agelaus' hope of escaping by it to rouse help in the town is thus vain; the prospect of help looks to the final scene. But Melanthius imitates Telemachus by bringing from the unlocked storeroom twelve sets of shields, spears, and horse-plumed helmets (22.144–145), no small load. The turn is frightening; Telemachus acknowledges his error and is sent to seize Melanthius when he returns. He is to leap on him from the chamber, Eumaeus from the door to the passage; they are to tie his arms and legs behind him, throw rope over a beam, and hoist him on a pillar—all of which they do.

At this dangerous moment when twelve suitors are armed, Athene enters as Mentor. Odysseus hails his old Ithacan friend; Agelaus threatens him and his family with death if he opposes them; the spirited goddess again retorts to taunts. You are not, she tells Odysseus, what you were at Troy for nine years and on the tenth when it fell by your device; stand beside me and watch what Mentor can do. But she in fact flies to the ceiling in the form of a swallow; she is present but still testingly (22.226–240). The divine access of strength resembles many in the *Iliad,* as does the consequence that the suitors' spears miss their mark, whereas the four at the threshold strike home. Lists of slayers and slain also show the Iliadic manner, in a few cases with analogous names (22.243, cf. *Il.*11.59, 122), but the names chiefly evoke wealth, importance or self-importance, traits of otherwise undescribed suitors. They show the local opposition to Odysseus which Athene at the end will peacefully resolve as, lifting her deadly aegis, she now resolves the fight. The survivors run like gadfly-driven cattle, and the four pursue like taloned vultures; similes, rare in this varied poem, mount as in Trojan battles. Three remain when the rest are dead, the soft-handed sacrificial priest Leodes, the bard Phemius, and the herald Medon. Proteus described to Menelaus three illustrative men; the Second Nekyia rises to the three paragons of the cycle. If Leodes sacrificed, Odysseus darkly tells him, it was that he might have Penelope. But he spares Phemius who sang unwillingly before the suitors and who pleads his self-taught various song, one fit, he begs, to sing before him as for a god (22.347–349). He claims the position of bard to king that Hesiod asserts at the start of the *Theogony* (94–97). And at Telemachus' further plea Odysseus spares the reluctant herald who told Penelope the suitors' plans. Dispatched into the court, the two sit by the altar glancing about them, like Thersites in *Iliad* 2, from shock (22.380, *Il*.2.269).

Rhetorical poetry can substitute by bravura what it lacks in suggestion; intensity saves Homer, but this scene comes near. Plato in the *Ion* (535b) cites it as a rhapsode's moment of virtuosity. Echoes of Trojan battles do not obscure the difference of this fight; heroes fought there; a worn sea-farer, a youth, and two working-men are now the warriors. Philoitius' cry on killing the rich, ox-hoof-throwing Ctesippus tells among much else a cowherd's umbrage (22.287–291). Yet the climax is hardly that of *Iliad* 22. Like the adventure with the Cyclops, the suitor-slaying is basic to the plot; the former scene explains the travels, this the return; both are required and in their way obvious. Neither scene at least much shows Odysseus the searcher and finder. To survive he is of course effective; that is part, yet not the chief part of him. It is true that Achilles has a distance to go after killing Hector; the *Iliad* ends with praise of Hector, and the poet's regard for his devotion to city, parents, wife, and child is very clear; lone Achilles himself must verge toward it. Odysseus' carnage is the next-to-last, not the last step, as he becomes aware even in his heroic exultation. The mocking goddess has not finished. Unlike Achilles who in triumph briefly forgets Patroclus (*Il*.22.378–394), he spares the bard and herald and on summoning Eurycleia forbids her to exult: "Be glad of heart, old woman; check yourself, do not whoop. No piety is in boasting over dead men. The gods' fate and their harsh acts destroyed them. They respected no human being, low or high, who came among them, therefore got by their recklessness an unlovely end" (22.411–416). He repeats the judgment of the prologue of his cattle-killing followers and Zeus's judgment of Aegisthus. As at the start of the *Iliad* and throughout it, mortal error and divine will merge. The tone is that of gods who walk the earth observing men's acts; Athene at the end will in this spirit force peace on him. The suitors' disregard of strangers evokes his many past arrivals; his judgment of them is more than civic justice; it affirms the human ties that they neglected. In the same spirit he orders that the unfaithful women servants, twelve out of fifty, first carry out the dead and clean the hall, then be killed, but Telemachus who hates them and the two workingmen exact the more disgraceful death of hanging. Melanthius gets a still worse fate than the centaur Eurytion's; in bitterness they cut off his ears, nose, feet, and hands, and throw his genitals to the dogs. Telemachus, then in the court, is not said to take part, and the bitterness may be that of fellow slaves. Odysseus, still indoors, purifies the hall with sulphur; the celestial bolts that off Thrinacia drowned the cattle-eaters and in his Cretan story struck the lying Phoenician performed the same function. The sequence of killing and purification is in the spirit of the Iliadic simile of Zeus's punitive flash (*Il.*16.386–388) and of Solon's vision (fr.1.17–24) of the god's avenging storm that first lays waste the works of men, then gives shining day. Odysseus' gratulation in the massacre subsides, fully to die only at the end. Athene attends both stages; her mockery during the fight, like that before recognitions, gave support but with a forward look.

The end follows in two steps, first personal, then social, which reverse the final steps of the *Iliad*. Patroclus' pyre and the funeral games restore Achilles to the army; he is finally alone with Priam. But if the claims of the bright world show in comedy, so do society's; peace must extend to it. Odysseus' acceptance by Penelope follows from the bed, the secret of which only they and her girlhood servant Actoris knew. Their account together of the years repeats Achilles' and Priam's shared memory. The reunion differs from that with his father, obviously in intimacy but also because Laertes is the former king. As Aeneas' meeting with Anchises in the Elysian Fields gives vision of future Rome, the triad of grandfather, father, and son promises restoration. In the nature of things Laertes is not to Odysseus what Penelope is; he marks his inherited and political, she his inward recovery. Odysseus' recognition by his father necessarily precedes peace in Ithaca. But the local peace is also the general peace. It is clearly such to the poet not only in the foregoing accounts of heroes living and dead but in his final view of the three chief figures, Agamemnon, Achilles, and Odysseus, each together with a female figure, the first and last with their wives, Achilles with his immortal mother. Hence follows the reversed sequence from that of the *Iliad*. It is there one man's restoration to humanity, here that of the man who has seen the world and who brings general restoration. It is true that, since only Odysseus has seen the totality of things, others may less value peace. His suffering differs only in proportion and cost from that of Achilles. Tragic and comic revelation are not largely distinct. The peace passes into poetry.

Penelope has feared divine intrusion into her life; she assumed that for her as for Helen it might be dire. Thus when trembling Eurycleia announces the victory, she first leaps up to kiss her, then doubts. She does not doubt that the suitors are dead—they got what they deserved—only that it was Odysseus who killed them. Told of the scar, she says that gods can deceive. "Let us go to my son," she yet concedes, "that I may see the dead suitors and whoever it was that killed them" (23.81–84). Fire in the *Iliad* was divine but ruinous; Odysseus on Scheria found refuge beneath the double-natured olive as a lone farmer hides a brand beneath ashes, saving the seed of fire. His rekindled life shows in the hearth fire by which Penelope takes her place. The old Trojan councilor Antenor recalls in *Iliad* 3 (216–224) Odysseus' quiet before the snowstorm of his words; the blood-stained beggar quietly stands by a pillar watching her. She and Nausicaa have stood by pillars, tokens of the house; it is now his place. How she at one glance seemed to recognize him, at another failed, Telemachus' young impatience with her, and Odysseus' gentle command that he give his mother time—they have their secret signs, she said—has been told. But it may bear repeating that he quickly reminds Telemachus of the suitors' kinsmen: "One who in a town kills a single man, even a man lacking after-watchers, flees leaving kin and fatherland, but we have killed the city's stay, the noblest young in Ithaca" (23.118–122). On the previous night he brooded of these avengers (20.41–43). Lone Laertes and the suitors' high connections have been repeatedly mentioned; the poem is inconceivable without the meeting at the farm and the final pacification. But his regaining Penelope outweighs even his epithets Ithacan and son of Laertes;

his personal search outweighs his social goal. Only the splendid summary of the Second Nekyia rivals in feeling the reunion of husband and wife.

The half-arrivals of the travels, Circe, Calypso, Nausicaa, Aeolus' festive family, were delays; Penelope is the arrival. His age and foul clothes obscure him to her, and though Athene is not said to have noted that, she gives his last transformation; as with Irus, he needed no transformation in the fight. Penelope's secret token is the bed—with her weaving and his bow the third deeply implanted theme—and when to test him she bids Eurycleia make his bed outside her room, he at last angrily rouses to declare how he long ago built it from a living olive leaving one leg rooted in earth (23.183–204). The simile of her flying to him like a shipwrecked sailor thankfully reaching shore reproduces in changed sex those of her as just king under whom land and people flourish and of him as captive woman who has lost her husband in war. Their fates and natures are near-images, not only or chiefly in a subjective sense but in the myth. She has tested him, and their equal survival of tests is the poem. She pleads that he forgive her obduracy. She had feared strangers as Helen did not sufficiently fear; a divine will worked in Paris, but Penelope shunned such an irruption into her life. Gods exact the unforeseen, as from themselves who lost the joy of companionship from youth to age's threshold, but if gods will, they can guide to a glad end those who fulfill their imperfect yet perfectible lot. They sleep together in the rooted bed after both have recounted their years.

The statements of the Alexandrian librarians Aristarchus and Aristophanes that 23.296 is the end, *peras* or *telos*, of the poem probably means end in the sense of goal;[7] the particle *men* in the line in any case demands continuation. Odysseus has just told of Teiresias' command that he leave again to build an altar to Poseidon and of his prophecy of a shining age among a prospering people. Over and above the many references to Laertes and the suitors' kinsmen, only that return will bring full peace in Ithaca. The reunited pair's review of their past and the greater review of the Second Nekyia repeat the recapitulation of the games for Patroclus. But the poet's concern to unify the poem, visible in Book 4 and

7. Erbse convincingly argues for this meaning, in *Beiträge zum Verständnis der Odyssee* 171–177.

prominent in 15 and after, carries greater demands than those of
the linear *Iliad,* and these recur at the end. More broadly, we do
not know how these traditional poems became written. A. B.
Lord's insistence that orality and writing are incompatible carries
weight; it is hard at least to imagine a mastery got from years of
singing suddenly taking on writing. Dictation, in a fast-changing
age, seems the answer. But if so, steady dictation from start to end
can only have been novel; generations reared on writing will
hardly conceive its strangeness. There may have been interrup-
tions; the scribe may have changed or fallen ill or, if young, have
left for a girl or friends, or the poet may have had after-thoughts;
the flow in any case need not have been steady. We know nothing
of this process, strange to the poet not only in length but in the
slow pace of dictation relatively to singing. Such reflections more
apply to *Iliad* 10 than to *Odyssey* 24, which on the whole follows
smoothly from previous scenes and in language. The poet is bind-
ing together the many strands of the poem and cycle. The only
other possibility, once much favored and still accepted by some
even since Parry, is to assume a later redactor—which raises immense problems. The redactor must have had several written texts,
must have merged his diction with Homer's, though Hesiod and
the *Homeric Hymns* shows singers naturally and unconsciously
changing the diction, and must have kept inserting preparatory
passages. Yet he must at the same time have been a singer of some
gifts thus to interweave his art with the earlier and not in brief but
extended scenes. Nothing in the early history of Greek verse or
prose attests to such literal imitation or the impulse toward it.
Continuing singers, *aoidoi,* would have changed the diction; the
later rhapsodes, like actors, were performers. The end of the poem
is of a piece with the rest, as the previous action and Iliadic parallels declare.

Hermes with his golden wand charms men's eyes and wakes
sleepers (24.3–4, 5.47–48). As he roused Odysseus on Ogygia, he
now guides the suitors' shades to the asphodel meadow.[8] As nearly
dead Odysseus clung like a bat to the fig tree above Charybdis, the
shades follow squeaking like bats that in a cave drop from the clus-
ter. Hermes remains, as to Priam at night on the Trojan plain and
to Odysseus on Circe's island, the divine guide, not of the dead

8. The Second Nekyia is further discussed in Appendix I.

only. The shades pass Oceanus' streams, the White Cliff, Helius'
gates, and the deme of dreams. The Laestrygonians dwelt near the
threshold of day and night, and Circe's island whence Odysseus
crossed Oceanus to Hades lay beyond. In the *Theogony* (211–
212) Night bears as first issue Doom, black Fate, Death, Sleep, and
the tribe of Dreams. The White Cliff, if conceivably connected
with Leukas, seems closer to the White Isle where dead Achilles
was later said to dwell (Proclus' summary of the *Aethiopis,* 15) and
to the deathly Leukadian Cliff from which love-sick Anacreon
leapt (metaphorically, fr. 17). Nagy expounds the antiquity of the
theme.[9] Death in Ithaca revives in fresh form Odysseus' journey to
the dead.

As the shades are about to arrive, Agamemnon and Achilles, the
latter still among the friends with whom Odysseus saw him, Patroclus, Antilochus, and Ajax, are talking of Troy. You were the supreme king, says Achilles forgetful of their old quarrel; you had
better have died and had your grave in Troyland (as Odysseus
wished in his black moment on the raft). As it was, yours was the
most pitiful of deaths (24.24–34). Not like yours, Agamemnon replies, when many Trojans and Achaeans fell beside you. We carried you to the shore, and a marvel followed; your mother and her
sister Nereids rose from the sea with a terrifying cry that only Nestor understood. They and the nine Muses put imperishable clothing on you; for seventeen days none was tearless at the Muses'
song. On the eighteenth day we laid you on the pyre, and armed
horsemen and footmen marched about it; your grave is with Patroclus, near your next friend Antilochus. We have known many bur-
ials, but none equals yours and the games with which your mother
honored it. Your fame is immortal, but Zeus gave me a grim end at
the hands of Aegisthus and my cruel wife (24.36–97). In the conversation, death cancels Agamemnon's kingly fame; only Achilles
was peerless in life and death. At this moment they spy the suitors'
shades.

Ghostly Amphimedon, who twenty or more years ago in Ithaca
entertained Agamemnon and Menelaus when they came to enlist
Odysseus—evidently by exception an older suitor—explains their
death repeating for a third time the tale of the web. Penelope, he
says, secretly planned it for them all. When at the start of the

9. "Phaethon, Sappho's Phaon, and the White Rock of Leukas."

fourth year she was made to finish Laertes' shroud and had shown it newly washed shining like the sun or moon, Odysseus reached the swineherd's hut and Telemachus returned from Sparta. Man and wife, he goes on, devised the killing; even elders did not recognize the beggar. He had her produce the bow and axes; when we failed, Telemachus brought him the bow (24.121–190). Antinous who first told of the web likewise thought that he understood Penelope. She gave each man hope, he said, and sent messages; he admitted "her mind intends other things" (2.92, her inveterate delay) but was confident that one of them would win her. Amphimedon now as mistakenly attributes her supreme inspiration to Odysseus. Nothing in the poem posits another version by which husband and wife jointly plan the suitors' deaths.[10] "So, Agamemnon, we died, and our bodies lie untended in Odysseus' hall. Not yet in each man's house do kindred know, who would wash the black blood from our wounds and lay us out and make lament, which is the right of the dead."

"Happy son of Laertes, much-devising Odysseus," exclaims the king, "truly you gained a wife dowered with great virtue. For right was blameless Penelope's mind, Icarius' daughter; well she remembered Odysseus her wedded husband. Therefore the fame of her virtue will never die, but immortals will make for earthly creatures entrancing song of wise Penelope. Not how Tyndareus' daughter devised evil deeds in killing her wedded husband, will bitter song go out to men and bring ill fame to women, even to one whose works are fair" (24.192–202). In the night scene Penelope offered the beggar bath and bed; how otherwise, she said, would he learn her surpassing kindness; good fame alone carries beyond death (19.325–334). The Muses' seventeen-days song at Troy proclaims Achilles. Agamemnon's fame sinks with his wife's; their distinct but similar passions are indivisible; high position did not finally serve them. The Trojan story culminates in two examples, that of Achilles and the paired example of Odysseus and Penelope. Thetis' sea-nature persists in her son; neither long kept the habitable land. Odysseus came to know the placeless sea but in Calypso and Nausicaa rejected it for Penelope by the hearth fire. Ajax in the other Nekyia, though second only to Achilles at Troy, remains incomplete, lacking either immortal or mortal fulfillment. Patroclus'

10. See above, p. 14, n. 6.

shade of *Iliad* 23 recurs in both sights of the Underworld; he is the
obverse of Achilles' greatness, its early parting. Ajax Oileus, whom
Proteus described, showed the egregiousness that Telemachus was
to shun as has Odysseus by mind and experience. Nestor's golden
piety, though wide, chiefly exhibits the calm of age, and in spite of
promised Elysium Helen and Menelaus are melancholy. Only
paired Odysseus and Penelope emerge with Achilles. The contrasting fates, similar in acknowledged mortality, differ as does early
loss from longer keeping. The difference is not in kind but in the
nature of the fulfillment. Troy for Homer expresses mortal engage-
ment; the two poems show the highest possibilities.

As this Nekyia completes and summarizes the earlier, the last
Ithacan meeting reverts to the first at Eumaeus' hut.[11] Though
Laertes' simple house is fittingly larger—it has a shed and sleeps
more people—both men built their places by work. Swinepens and
pastures surround the hut; here an orchard of pears, apples, and
figs with a farther vineyard in the manner of Alcinous' paradise.
Like Eumaeus, Laertes is alone; the swineherd was indoors cutting
himself shoes from a hide; Laertes is spading his vines. He wears a
foul patched chiton, patched rawhide leggings and gauntlets to
protect him from thorns, and a goatskin cap (24.226–231). His
itemized low appearance resembles his son's as beggar. Odysseus
nearly yielded at sight of Penelope's tears, yet continued the test
that the goddess and his nature dictated and that distinguished him
from Agamemnon. So he does now and with Athene's raillery. If
mortal blindness can look absurd, irritability also marks old men.
Priam's scorn in *Iliad* 24 (253–264) of his surviving sons, old Oedipus' vituperation of Polyneices (O.C. 1354–1396), in Sophocles'
Ajax (462–472, 1017–1018) the hero's fear of his father Tela-
mon's bitter tongue, and Aristophanes' waspish old jurymen commend Odysseus' precaution. Laertes does not bother to look up as
the stranger approaches. Both men need time; mockery makes the
emotion tolerable.

Your trees and vines, Odysseus begins, show no lack of care; not
so your ragged clothes and parched look. Your master evidently
does not neglect you for your idleness; yet you do not look a slave
but a king. At your age you deserve a soft bed. Tell me whose
bondsman you are and whether this is Ithaca. A wayfarer refused

11. The meeting at the farm is further discussed in Appendix II.

my questions about my former friend Odysseus, Laertes' son. I once entertained him—no more welcome guest ever came to me—and gave him lavish gifts: talents of gold, a silver bowl, cloaks, cloths, robes, chitons, and skilled working-women (24.244–279). The smiling speech and exaggerated gifts draw widely from the poem. Laertes' low state was the beggar's, his garden and the alleged gifts are nearly Phaeacian, the man who refused questions contrasts to the talkative wayfarer of Teiresias' prophecy of the oar, Odysseus' good impression as guest repeats the beggar's to Penelope. The speech achieves its purpose; with tears Laertes recounts the suitors' usurpation. You have lost, he says, what would have been the sure return for your gifts. But how long is it, he goes on, since you entertained my son, if indeed he ever was? He died far from home; parents did not array him in death nor wife draw down his eyelids and make lament, as is the right of the dead. Who and whence are you, where are your ship and crew, or are you a trader from someone else's ship? (24.279–301) The tearful reply also harks back. The wondering and poetic "if he ever was" repeats Helen's (*Il.*3.180) and Penelope's (19.315) memory of lost happiness. Clytemnestra stonily refused to draw down dead Agamemnon's lids. The suitors lie in the house without the rites of death. The question about the ship repeats those of Telemachus to Mentes, Polyphemus to Odysseus, and Eumaeus to the beggar.

Odysseus forsakes his Cretan tale and with fictitious names conveying opulence and knowledge tells how the guest was entertained five years ago and left with good omen. The old man breaks down, like Achilles at the news of Patroclus' death pouring dust on his head (24.315–317, *Il.*18.22–24). Odysseus is as shaken; emotion presses at his nostrils. He seizes and kisses the old man: "I here, father, whom you seek have reached in the twentieth year my fatherland. Stop weeping and lamenting. I tell you we must act. I killed the suitors in the house." But the old man is nearly as sceptical as Penelope. He wants a sign, and as Odysseus early yesterday morning got two signs, he now gives two, the scar and the fruit trees and vines that Laertes gave him as a child (24.331–344).

The orchard and vineyard affirm the return; the farm is its necessary setting. Circe's glade, Helius' cattle, Calypso's meadow, and the endless cycles of Alcinous' fruits are now remote. Saving trees helped bridge the interval: the fig tree above Charybdis, the poplars and firs from which he made his raft, the double-natured olive on Scheria, the olive at the Bay of Phorkys. The rooted bed was one arrival; these vines and fruit trees are the other. Together they signify the intact family on rocky Ithaca. Laertes kept the garden; the start of the poem described him trudging its slope (1.189– 193); of summers and autumns, Anticleia said (11.187–196), he slept there on fallen leaves. If Odysseus may be about fifty, he may be about eighty.[12] His toilsome life contrasts to the Phaeacian ease almost as did old Argus on the dungheap to the golden dogs outside Alcinous' palace. If this is diminution, it is what Odysseus has sought for twenty years. To his eyes it is no falling-away, nor should this narrow scene appear such in the poem. In the Myth of Er, Plato has all the other dead choose a brilliant second life; only Odysseus chooses an eventless life at home (*Rep.*10, 620c). Scope and origin equally describe the hero; for Homer and in both poems, the two sides are reciprocal. The width of the world does not diminish but clarifies identity. Conversely, the world opens only to one who quite certainly knows who he is; he would otherwise have stopped at some deceptive byway. Hector, though admired by Homer, misjudged the centrality of city and family, as if these comprised the whole. Odysseus regains the kind of ties that Hector lost, but by long diminution, which in obverse is enhancement. This reciprocity between space and self is to Homer, for men at least, the essential human fact. The trees and vines, not magical like the Phaeacian but rooted in Ithaca, contrast to Achilles' withered scepter.

Laertes faints for joy, then cries to Zeus that gods exist if the suitors have paid (24.351–352), yet in his emotion is still more mindful of their kinsmen than was Odysseus. Messages, he thinks, will have brought avengers from all the Kephallenian cities. Achilles' meeting with Priam, though sealed in their joint tears, brings no union of father with son; the tears acknowledge their opposite loss: Achilles' of Peleus and Patroclus, Priam's of Hector.

12. The young Antilochus says of Odysseus at the games for Patroclus (*Il.*23.790–791), "he is of an earlier breed and earlier men; they call him in green age." Antilochus is hardly literal; he is marveling at Odysseus' victory in the footrace. Penelope speaks of her and Odysseus' youth together twenty years ago. One imagines him then near thirty. Solon (fr.19.7–8) thinks a man's fourth stage of seven years his fit time for marriage; Aristotle (*Pol.*4.16, 1335b 37) specifies thirty-seven. Odysseus comes from a poor island; heirs of richer land perhaps marry earlier. If Laertes too did not marry young, he will be some thirty years older than his son.

The present reunion fulfills what was denied at Troy, though still imperfectly because Anticleia is absent. In the Underworld she remembered of Odysseus the gentle-mindedness that at the end of the *Iliad* Helen remembers of Hector, but the final lament for Hector by his three kinswomen has been largely countered by Penelope's glad recognition. In that beautiful speech her confidence that Odysseus understood her delay effectually repeats Anticleia's memory of his gentleness. Because he has seen and spoken with his mother's shade, the reunion with Laertes, of whom she chiefly spoke, in some sense includes her. The poem consciously amends the loss in the *Iliad*. But Laertes is here more than a father; as the former but long passive king and as such the contrast to oaken Nestor, he affirms political continuity. In Zeus's initial condemnation of Aegisthus and in Orestes as Telemachus' model, the poem began with the theme of restoration. If the return is chiefly from Calypso's hollow caves to wife and house, it is also to land and people. Laertes ends happier than Nestor in not having lost his son, and Telemachus extends promise to the future. Father and son now fittingly rejoin Telemachus, Eumaeus, and Philoitius at the farmhouse, and Athene transfigures the ragged old man as she has Odysseus, her last such equation of outer to inner fortune. Laertes even recalls in Nestor's manner (*Il.*11.668–761) the feats of his youth; he has caught up with and in one crucial respect surpassed the Pylian king. They are about to dine when, summoned from the fields, the old Sikel woman's husband and six sons hasten back with joy and wonder. The poem is fast closing, and the recent victors have allies.

Odysseus had ordered music and singing in the palace in order that passersby might assume Penelope's wedding (23.133–136). But rumor, like that which at Troy convened the Achaeans after Agamemnon's false dream (*Il.*2.93–94), has quickly spread, and kinsmen from Ithaca and abroad—as fast as Penelope's marriage-gifts appeared and the Achaean wall rose at Troy—have borne home the dead. Antinous' father Eupeithes convenes the kinsmen; kill him, he urges as Antinous urged of Telemachus, before he gets help from the mainland (24.426–437). But the bard and herald, spared at the killing, report Athene's presence there as Mentor; it was she, Medon says, who routed the suitors. Old Haliserthes, who at the first assembly prophesied the king's return, recalls his warning of some forty days past (2.161–176); you yourselves failed, he says, to stop your sons' follies. The meeting divides; most leave, the others follow Eupeithes against the small company at the farm.

As Haliserthes reverts to the start, so does Athene. Do you decree war or peace in Ithaca, she asks her father Zeus. The supreme god understands his daughter's mind as fully as did Alcinous Nausicaa's wish for the mule-cart. As at the second divine assembly when Hermes was sent to Ogygia, he replies that she herself has planned everything (5.23–24, 24.479–480): Odysseus has been avenged and shall rule; peace shall be plighted and the deaths forgotten. She thrice in the *Iliad* descends flashing from Olympus to magnify battle; now as at the start of the poem she thus descends with peaceful purpose (1.102, 24.488). Sight of old Laertes and Dolius in arms, warriors by necessity, moves even their enemies. As Mentor, the goddess joins the twelve, and the three members of the family make their final speeches. Now you must show your breed, says Odysseus to Telemachus; father, he replies, you will see me, if you wish, bringing it no shame; dear gods, cries Laertes, what is this day to me, my son and grandson vie for virtue. Divinely strengthened, the old man strikes and kills Antinous' father; Odysseus and Telemachus attack; deaths would have followed, had not Zeus's daughter cried in a great voice, "Ithacans, hold back from hard war, that you may part without bloodshed" (24.531–532). With old impetuosity and still like an eagle, only Odysseus sweeps on, but Zeus who benignly thundered at yesterday's dawn now sends a blazing bolt in earnest. The poem opened with Athene asking her father why he was angry with Odysseus; it ends with her warning to him to shun the further wrath of the son of Kronos, wide-voiced Zeus. "So spake Athene and he obeyed and was glad of heart. And future pledges between the two sides aegis-holding Zeus's daughter Pallas Athene made, likened to Mentor in form and speech." The war-goddess at Troy has become the goddess of peace in Ithaca, and the man whom she there guided has laboriously learned her onward mind.

9. Conclusion

The foregoing detail is still inadequate to a poem in which meaning follows incident. The shifting emphasis is elusive, for several reasons: the characters live the myth, its movement posits theirs, themes and formulae set general positions which only the surrounding scenes make actual, how this version differed from others is unknown. The poet had surely heard and himself sung parts or all of it, but where he shortened or lengthened, suppressed or heightened escapes us. Penelope's gift-soliciting may serve as example. Her fixed setting in the house makes her the most consistent of the main characters, but how interpret the scene? As her protest for having been taken for granted, as her conscious step toward a remarriage that for Telemachus' sake has become necessary, as a last stratagem of delay, as a sign of how she has managed the suitors, as demonstration to Telemachus that she does not impoverish the house, as mark of likeness to her shrewd husband and (since the beggar is present and admires her skill) proof that she is unchanged, as part of her Athene-prompted awakening, an act of spiritedness matching her enhanced beauty? These and other suggestions are all present. The outcome of the poem follows from her tenacity, the cost of which shows in her troubled dreams. The gift-soliciting must somehow merge with her impressionability, her scepticism, her kindness, and her faith. It suggests the iron beneath her beauty, the self-respect beneath her tears. But her two just earlier laughs show something almost girlish in her, as if she were not at heart less ardent than Nausicaa. Her firmness nearly matches Helen's, who on disillusion at Troy welcomed the deaths that spying Odysseus caused, but in caution and kindness as in other ways, she differs radically from Helen. The problem is to unite people's many sides. Homer needed only the story, partly because he approached it with now-lost presuppositions. Let us end by considering some of them.

First, identity as fixed in origin. The assumption is in part economic, but even that part carries traditional overtones. The word *temenos* as used for property may imply that land was once apportioned kings as well as gods,[1] but the roughly contemporary *Works and Days* shows land privately owned and intensely struggled for. Dead Achilles cites servitude to a landless man as the lowest human lot; Odysseus promises Eumaeus and Philoitius wife, house, and possessions (21.214–215). According to Aristotle (*Poet.*22, 1458a18–1459a8), poetic language untouched by modernism is incomprehensible but, if wholly modern, lacks dignity, and some such compromise marks the poems, as regards property among much else. M. I. Finley sees in the *Odyssey* the mirror of post-Mycenaean Greece,[2] rightly so to the degree that auditors would hear in it what they knew. Tradition of warriors may more fully reflect the fighting settlers of the Asia Minor coast and their memory among descendants than the wealth-tabulating king who appears from the Pylos tablets. The raiding that Eumaeus mentions (14.85–88) may also better fit this local past than either the settled Mycenaean Age or Homer's present. The Phaeacians' sea-faring town, with ships and ship-gear crowding an isthmus, looks authentically recent. Yet the color of assumptions is Mycenaean. Agememnon in *Iliad* 9 (149–156) offers Achilles seven towns in Messenia, and Menelaus would here do much the same for Odysseus to have him near (4.174–178). The Trojan war was ascribed to the great age of Mycenae, L.H. IIIc starting at about 1250, and Troy VIIA shows signs of capture, but T. B. L. Webster, as was noted, infers from the siege-rhyton of the shaft graves, of M.H. III

1. L. R. Palmer, *Mycenaeans and Minoans* 92–93.
2. *The World of Odysseus* 43.

some 300 years earlier, an already existent poetry of siege. E. T. Vermeule notes the absence of great buildings contemporaneous with the shaft graves.³ The gold face-masks, the bull, the inlaid swords, the rhyton sufficiently magnified those kings. Their overseas raiding is in the spirit of the Trojan booty that Odysseus' Phaeacian treasure replaced. If, to judge by the *Works and Days,* present wealth is in land and, by the Phaeacians, partly from shipping, poetry gave it a more ancient aura. Yet the minor role of Penelope's gift-soliciting to her fidelity and of Odysseus' Phaeacian treasure to his travels and return shows where the emphasis lies. Property becomes language for something else, for place and origin which, however essential to self-expectation, must be left behind. The next step of leaving home is also partly economic. In a gift-giving society importance must be demonstrated; it demands wealth. But Achilles' renunciation of home and Odysseus' long return show a deeper human necessity. Origin and youth are insecure; they mark a person but for another end, of at once proving himself and in the process learning who he is toward the gods.

Yet to Homer origin remains fundamental. It was said earlier that his is the supreme style of human beings' position on earth, also that, unlike the Old Testament people, the Greeks lacked holy books, priestly castes, and revising prophets to declare God's will to the individual and nation. The Old Testament people looked outward from the directed self to the chaotic world; its nature is not descriptively categorized. The view is from the self outward, not as in the *Odyssey* from the world to the self. The prophets' hope is expressed in metaphors, "the rose shall bloom in the desert," "the lamb shall lie down with the lion," "the tree shall spring by the river of waters." Odysseus returns the wise man who has seen exhibited and analyzed reality—natural wonders (Scylla and Charybdis, Aeolus' winds, the bay of the Laestrygonians, the Sun's cattle), societies (the rude Cyclopes and blessed Phaeacians), and states of experience (dim Lotuseaters, alluring Circe, totally knowledgeable Sirens, the intimate and storied dead, nature-inhabiting Calypso). Sight of all these and of the lone sea beyond which they dwell is his inbreathed instruction; he has seen home's circumference. The sight transforms any origin as Odysseus is himself transformed as a beggar, by setting it within immensity. The

3. *Greece in the Bronze Age* 107–110.

fact that, in the poetry, origin carries the dignity of forsaken wealth less asserts social demand than self-demand. If people imagined that they left home for honor or duty or wealth, the length and pain of the war and, for such as got back, of their return proved otherwise. The actuality transformed self-demand into self-instruction; it changed an identity toward home into an identity toward the world. Yet origin remains firm because a man is who he is.

Second, travel. The nascent age of colonization attests a poverty that soon drove Greek settlers east and west, from the Black Sea to Sicily and beyond. They were following the example of the wealth-acquiring shaft-grave kings, of the Mycenaean attackers of Troy and Egypt and settlers of Cyprus and Ugarit, and of the post-Mycenaean colonists of Asia Minor. As poetic theme, travel is the obverse of home. Hector supremely shows the impossibility of keeping home; traveling Paris personifies its dangers. It was noted that the Heracles of Sophocles' *Trachiniae* and Creophylus' *Sack of Oechalia* is Odysseus' opposite. The waiting wives and father-seeking sons are similar, but Heracles brings back young Iole whereas Odysseus leaves Nausicaa. The one dies on Oeta in the Nessus-shirt of his passion, the other regains the hearth fire. The flame of adventure persists in the one, is tempered in the other; distance and home each have sexual analogues. In Sophocles' dark middle period the theme extends to Oedipus, who thinks home permanently left behind and the future forever open. His famous self-characterization as brother of the moons and child of fortune (*O.T.* 1080–1085) declares what he thinks his limitless path. The shock of discovered limit halts him; limit is Odysseus' conscious goal. Soaring Athenian hopes seem expressed in the one, an older temperance—older as of Greek thought and perhaps of Homer's life—in the other. The Oedipus of the *Coloneus* moves toward Odysseus in endurance, wrath, and love, but in death finds in Athens another home. The aged Sophocles prefigures Plato's vision of a renewed society, even while in reversion to his own birthplace he repeats attained Ithaca.

The common ground of these varied histories is travel which, though wide, is not random. Experience reveals stable landmarks. They are not immediately visible; only gods know them all. But a man must discover them; blind death, as at Troy or to the suitors and Aegisthus, is the alternative. The tale of the *Seven Against*

Thebes and the epic *Thebais* from the point of view of the defenders may seem to say the opposite, but the emphasis is on the violent attackers. The home-defenders are simply righteous; they are successful Hectors. The *Odyssey* is clearly not in that spirit; the travels would then be needless. Yet Odysseus does repeat Hector at a farther stage. What was benign in the life of Troy is expressed in Hector; the poet's feeling for sacred and civilized ties speaks in his scenes with wife, child, and parents. They show the other side of war and make of the *Iliad* both Achilles' tragedy and that of once-peaceful Troy. Yet to Homer such ties are not easily kept; Achilles is greater than Hector, not in responsibility but in knowledge of loneness. By the theme of travel the *Odyssey* fuses Achilles with Hector, isolation with home, but laboriously. Odysseus' and Penelope's twenty-year separation and the second milder parting that still awaits them make attainment rather a mental than an actual possession. It more confirms and validates than gives outright, even so suffices for inner security.

Third, Odysseus' travels are not in phantasy. What he meets in the course of them is as real as what he met at Troy. It is true that, as quasi-historical, the Trojan story is legendary, the travels from folktale. Yet each poem has elements of the other. Odysseus is a Mycenaean king; rocky Ithaca describes the man whom intelligence made a companion of the great; Telemachus meets some of these people. Conversely Achilles' choice between a long inglorious and a short glorious life is from folktale; it is as basic a theme as Penelope's weaving, the bow, and the rooted bed. Observant or drastic gods lift both poems into myth, and the minor divinities that Odysseus meets in his travels have a like mythical descriptiveness. The war and the travels thus express two kinds or stages of experience, within history and beyond it, and the *Iliad* does not lack both. The warring gods that frame Achilles' battle with the Scamander give widest dimension to the fight with Hector that affirms his choice of early death. He has wandered alone on a superhuman path toward near-loss of the humanity that he regains at the end. In the fifteen days between the battle with the river and the night meeting with Priam he comes near repeating Odysseus' ten-year journey. His brief but total illumination speaks his young heroism; he has no need for the older man's analytical journey; there is a sense in which he at the end becomes as old as Odysseus. Or at least he needs no further knowledge of his mortal position toward the gods. By contrast, Odysseus' idea of the wooden horse left him the clever victor; only his wandering, his sight of the dead, his seven silent years with Calypso, and his beggarly return sufficed to correct that success. There is of course a difference between instantaneous and longer sight, something like the difference (words being inadequate) between vision and reason, between the poet or saint and the philosopher. Yet to Homer the act of sight, at whatever stage and by whatever means, is compulsory and, insofar as auditors understood themselves in the poems, compulsory for all men. The difference in age and means becomes secondary; the realization unites.

As is clear from Odysseus' confidence toward the Cicones, the Lotuseaters, Polyphemus, and Aeolus (he tried to tell the tale of Troy to the Cyclops and did so to Aeolus), he only slowly grasps his position. His full wanderings follow from his blinding of Polyphemus, which may have been necessary but which he did exultingly in the spirit of his trick of the wooden horse. The Laestrygonians repeat for eleven of his twelve crews the kind of abrupt death that occurred at Troy. His trancelike delay with Circe precedes his vision of the Underworld as the less erotic, more suspended trance of his stay with Calypso follows it. He is nearly dead as he clings like a bat to the fig tree above Charybdis, and the silence of his seven years at the navel of the sea comes near another drowning. As the midpoint of the travels, the Underworld effectually amends Troy; the shades of his former friends reduce his past to theirs. Yet his return follows from just this loss. He spares the Thrinacian cattle as he did not spare Troy, by changed awareness of his family and possible future at home, of the distant and recent past of the heroines and heroes, of fabled overweeners, and of the sheer multitude of the dead. The Sirens' offer of total knowledge suggests the risk of such understanding, but their singing, a more mental invitation than that of the Lotuseaters, is not long for him. Their promised suspension as the wind drops is more dangerous than Calypso's.

Troy and travel, being equally real, transform the meaning of home. The immediate tone and prominence of small events in the latter part of the poem do not assert that home alone is actual, only that it is the irreducible actuality. It is such because it affirms a man's identity. But that self was not, as in the Old Testament, buttressed by holy books and guiding prophets. Young expectation drew from place and parentage which in turn conveyed a farther past. Telemachus' account to the beggar of the line of single sons that marked the family (16.118–120) is in the spirit of the fountain where Odysseus meets Melanthius, anciently built by Ithacus, Neritus, and Polyktor (17.207). Such stabilities mark a man; Odysseus' scar and bow, both got in youth, presage his future; Athene sees Zeus's anger in his name. When home-leaving follows, poetic themes continue to express what a man takes with him. The future will instruct; he brings only attitudes. Will to heroism is the chief of these, his main tie between past and future, his statement of faith in a discoverable farther meaning. Nothing else replaces the lack of a doctrinal religion. But since characters differ, so also do their attributes and epithets; we have rehearsed these of Odysseus. Together with the will to heroism, such mental postures show a man's equipment; the myth tells what he meets. The externality of the method draws from the poetic tradition, but that in turn from a deeper attitude: that clarification is to be drawn from the world, not brought to it. Heroism indeed imposes expectations, but outcomes change them, and the necessary revisions are truer. Myths trace the process of change, and the poet hears its reverberation in the initially fixed characters. He heeds their advancing response, in what they do and, since his feeling mounts with theirs, in their words. The difference of the two poems lies not least in the relative weight of these two elements, the myth and the response.

The tragic *Iliad* mountingly interweaves events with Achilles' reply to them; the more visual, more intellective, happier *Odyssey* more fully describes the wanderer by what he sees. Penelope is here the exception; it is her reply, not her setting, that changes. It dictates the mystery of her girl-like laughs, her impulse to appear before the suitors, her beautifying sleep, yet her wish to die, her rebuke of Telemachus, her memory of the old command that she remarry when he is bearded, her complaint at the lack of wedding gifts, her helpless grief at thought of leaving the house. Most of these themes had previously appeared; their mingled outpouring speaks her complex inwardness, which continues in the firelit scene and in her final self-explanation. As with Achilles, Homer has deeply entered into her mind. But he less often does so with Odysseus—this in spite of his farewells to Calypso and Nausicaa, his Underworld meeting with his mother, his speech to Amphinomus, and his gentleness in Penelope's delay—because what Odysseus sees goes far toward implying his response. Inflexible, single-minded Ajax is his opposite; the capacity to understand many things asks many traits of mind. If posterity (chiefly Sophocles and Euripides) could judge him merely flexible, Homer did not. For the poet, the Greek need to grasp the nature of the world speaks in him; his variety matches its, and his mingled curiosity and endurance take on heroism. But that in turn remains fixed in loyalties; the fact is as clear in Odysseus as in Hector and Achilles. It expresses the dear hope that human attachments—to wife, child, friend, parents, home, to all who touch a life (old Priam, honest Eumaeus, Andromache's father Eetion whom in death Achilles honored, Nausicaa whom Odysseus vowed to remember)—however subject to change, are valid in a huge world.

Finally, the inadequate word comedy ideally affirms this stability. Dante used it, but its elaborate future implications were hidden from Homer. These came to express a glad and grateful charity that could be thought due the world's order and beauty. Plato's high analogy that, as the sun lights the eye, the idea of the good lights the mind (*Rep.*6,507d–509a) affirms this faith, as does Socrates' serenity, like that of the aged Oedipus, in death. Vision of a beautiful order rouses even the rational Aristotle, as at *Nichomachean Ethics* 10.7, *De Anima* 2.4, and Book Lambda 7–10 of the *Metaphysics,* to something like poetry. But Homer was unaware of such future deductions, much more of such a change of heart as Prospero's at the end of *The Tempest.* Yet like Sophocles in the two Oedipus plays, he moves in the two poems from a limiting to a fulfilling view of the gods, and by much the same means, that of years and travel. As former warrior, Odysseus kills the suitors—only that could finish the story of return—yet with a final moderation not unakin to his sparing of Helius' cattle.

Yet if, as has been excessively repeated, the myth guides and the characters follow, the extreme beauty of the *Odyssey* most clearly tells the poet's purpose. His choice of the subject, his peopling it with older figures and in Nausicaa, Telemachus, and Peisistratus, with the eager young, and his unquenched, always partly repeated, never quite similar response to nature show his impulse. In what has been called the comic irony, this tone becomes in effect the poem; it surrounds the characters though they may be unconscious of it. Yet even before the end, the chief three rise to brightest feeling: Telemachus, for example, in his first night aboard the speeding ship, Penelope in her laughs, her sympathy with the beggar, and her quandary like the nightingale's changeful song, and Odysseus at many times and places, including the Underworld. It was said that, relatively to the more linear *Iliad,* the interwoven structure of the poem foreshadows a later art, and the same holds for the subject. Though portrayed by the inherited mode of theme and epithet, Odysseus, and Penelope in a different way not less, emerge to the privilege of experience and the validity of faith. The gods that act in the world do not lightly share their radiant being, yet do share it, if at times with a certain amusement. Athene's smile, like nature's, can turn stormy, yet remains the smile that Homer sees. Odysseus and Penelope see it. Their attained harbor is more than home and reunion, it is the mind's answer from the world.

Appendixes

References

Indexes

Appendix I
The Second Nekyia

The scholiast at the start of *Odyssey* 24 (Dindorf II 724–725) summarizes Aristarchus' grounds for athetizing the Second Nekyia and their rebuttal by unnamed others. Eustathius (II 317–318) echoes and somewhat expands. He ends by calling the dispute a scholastic game and by noting two chief purposes of the scene: to describe, as the *Iliad* could not, the death of Achilles and to contrast it to the outcome for the Ithacan pair. The scholiast concludes: "By brilliance of composition the poetry in still other ways declares Homer. One might reasonably have called Book Lambda the Nekyomanteia, this the Nekyia." He makes the following main points. If Hermes in uniquely here the guide of souls, so at *Il*.23.660 is Apollo uniquely the patron of boxing. But Hermes is no more a chthonic god than is Athene who at *Od*.11.626 guides Heracles to Cerberus. If Hermes' epithet Cyllenius is unique, so is his epithet *sokos,* strong, at *Il*.20.72. If it is questioned why the suitors' souls need a guide, nothing forbids one; the god's favor to Odysseus' maternal grandfather is noted at 19.397. The White Rock is at the edge of the Underworld facing daylight. Neither Agamemnon's conversation with Achilles nor Nestor's rallying of the Achaeans is out of place; the latter is elsewhere untold. Enumeration of the nine Muses is unique, but what prevents it?

The points may be merely extended. It is sobering to reflect how little later scholarship adds.

(1) As for Hermes Cyllenius, Artemis only at 6.103 haunts Taygetus and Erymanthus; Delos appears only in Odysseus' following speech, 6.162. At *Il*.15.518 Poulydamas kills the Cyllenian Otus, whose epithet stands in the same position as that of Hermes here and before a like-sounding verb.

(2) At the end of the *Iliad* Hermes meets Priam by a river and tomb; they talk of dead Hector; the old man is terrified; the mood of death is strong, *Il*.24.349–360. With Athene, he guided Heracles to Cerberus, 11.626, and he shows the way to Circe's house whence Odysseus will reach Hades, 10.275–307. His golden wand wherewith he enchants men's eyes and wakes sleepers, 24.3–4 as at 5.47–48 and *Il*.24.343–344, as naturally rouses the dead suitors as it puts to sleep the guards at Achilles' hut, *Il*.24.445.

(3) Odysseus on his raft wishes that he might have had death and burial at Troy, 5.306–312. Achilles here repeats the wish for Agamemnon, 24.31–34, echoing Odysseus' words and Nestor's memory of the toils at Troy, 3.220. Agamemnon's death has been twice related, by Proteus to Menelaus, 4.528–537, and by the dead king himself, 11.418–426. In canceling his royal greatness, it leaves as summary of the poems Achilles' young fate and that of the reunited Odysseus and Penelope. That summary in turn completes previous exhibits of three fates: to Telemachus, those of dead Ajax Oileus, dead Agamemnon, and still alive Odysseus, a partly moral exhibit fitting the youth's education, 4.496–560; and to Odysseus in the Underworld, the shades of Agamemnon, Achilles, and Telamonian Ajax, an exhibit of Troy while his return awaits, 11.385–564. Of the three feminine figures here, Clytemnestra shares her husband's canceled eminence; Thetis and Penelope contrast Achilles' half-divine to Odysseus' mortal destiny.

(4) The Muses, only here stated to be nine, are six times plural in the *Iliad*. As they sing antiphonally of Achilles, 24.60, so do they on Olympus, *Il*.1.604. The inspiration of one Muse differs from the inspiration or singing of them all. A single Muse inspires both poems, 1.10, *Il*.1.1, evidently the same goddess who loved and inspired Demodocus and taught him his paths of song, 8.63, 73, 481, 488. But Homer invokes the several Muses when many per-

sons or themes crowd his mind, as before the Catalogue of Ships, *Il.*2.484–492, and in Iliadic lists of slayers and slain, *Il.*11.218, 14.508, and 16.112. Like the Sirens, the Muses know everything, but such powers are beyond men. "Tell me, ye Muses who have dwellings on Olympus, for you are goddesses and attend and know all things, but we hear only the fame and know naught," *Il.*2.484–486. Thus Odysseus praises Demodocus' singing of the Achaeans' toils at Troy, "as were you yourself somewhere present or heard from another," 8.491. Hearing the Sirens was his most divine moment, but it was dangerous and brief, 12.39–46, 189–191. The Muses maimed Thamyris, ended his singing, and made him forget his lyre because he boasted to surpass them, *Il.*2.594–600. They fittingly sing on Olympus, and their seventeen-day song of Achilles—antiphonal, as from themes innumerably added—proclaims his half-divinity.

(5) Sudden novelties of Homeric usage are a boundless subject, which Norman Austin well expounds (*Archery at the Dark of the Moon*, esp. 66–80). Merely for example, Heos has a chariot and named horses only at 23.244–246. We cannot know the poet's range of association, as regards persons also. At 4.285–289 Aristarchus excised Anticlus' attempted reply from inside the Trojan horse to Helen's voice from outside in the tones of each man's wife, on the ground that the otherwise unmentioned hero appeared in Lesches' *Little Iliad*. Anticlus' absence from the *Iliad* may be suspicious, but did Aristarchus or do we know that Homer did not know of him? Other characters appear as they are wanted: for example, Odysseus' once-mentioned sister Ctimene with whom Eumaeus played as a child, 15.363–365, and Penelope's sister Iphthime, wife of Eumelus of Pherae, who speaks to her in a dream, 4.797–798. Eumelus himself, mentioned in the Iliadic Catalogue for his horses, reappears only in the chariot-race at the games, *Il.*2.763–767, 23.287–565. Characters and descriptive themes and epithets emerge as they occur to the poet. Granted that occasional lines were added or missing in the manuscripts that reached Alexandria, whole episodes were not missing. Ancient or modern appraisal of their authenticity is, in effect, appraisal of what fits the poems, therefore of the poet's intention and success. He had surely heard or himself sung versions of the whole tale.

Appendix II
The Reunion at the Farm

As D. L. Page says (*The Homeric Odyssey* 104, 109), the central episode of Book 24, Odysseus' meeting with Laertes, 205–412, shows more verbal oddities than do the start and close of the Book, the Second Nekyia and the fight with the suitors' kinsmen. H. Erbse (*Beiträge zum Verständnis der Odyssee* 166–244) treats a number of the points that will be made here. It will be useful to start with the episode as a whole.

(1) The poem and the example of the *Iliad* posit a unifying close. The events of Books 22 and 23 restore Odysseus to the household but neither to his father nor as king of a peaceful Ithaca. Much has been said of Laertes; his lorn old age has contrasted to Nestor's. Anticleia in the Underworld described his rural melancholy without her or Odysseus, 11.187–196; Eumaeus called him sunk in gloom after Telemachus left, 15.352–357, 16.138–145. He wanted to bring him the good news of the youth's return but was told not to, evidently because the action then looked to the palace, 16.147–153. Telemachus similarly urged his father to delay inspecting his country properties, 16.313–315. But thought of the suitors' kinsmen disturbs Odysseus on the night before the slaying, 20.41–43, and interrupts the reunion of husband and wife,

23.133–140. The suitor Agelaos during the fight expresses hope of outside support, 22.133. The poet has remained mindful of the Ithaca beyond the palace. On the morning after the suitor-slaying, Athene conceals the four victors' departure from the town as she did Odysseus' approach to the town and palace at Scheria, 7.14–15, 23.371–372. Further, the question of kingship in Ithaca, prominent from the start and bearing on Antinous' ambitions, 1.368–398, 22.48–53, extends to Laertes as the former king and link in the line of single sons descending from Arcesius, 4.750–757, 16.117–120. The patronymic describes Laertes at the end, 24.270, 517. Chiefly, the line of ongoing recognitions must include Laertes.

(2) The travels and the return differ in scope, the width of earlier scenes narrowing in the later. But from the landing in Ithaca in Book 13 to the reunion at the palace in 23, the narrowness is variously enlarged: by the beggar's and swineherd's stories, Telemachus' return, Penelope's partly retrospective actions and the mounting excitement. The scope of the narrative, with its attendant language, survives, to persist to the Second Nekyia and to the close, which reverts to Books 1, 2, and 5. The homely scene at the farm is here the exception. If, as was noted above (pp. 167–168), it has much in common with the meeting at the swineherd's hut, it lacks the forward purpose of that informative, preparatory scene, and if it finishes the line of recognitions, it somewhat repeats. Erbse (p. 246) with some reason judges it the prototype of the earlier recognitions. It is barer, less enlarged by competing events. Beyond the detail of humble clothes and doings, it carries forward the scheme whereby previous actions, described in the imperfect tense, are interrupted by an arrival described in the aorist. At Scheria Odysseus was approaching the city when Athene as a young girl met him, 7.18–20; the diners in the hall were about to leave when the magic mist fell from him, 7.136–143. In Ithaca Eumaeus was cutting himself shoes when his dogs announced the stranger, 14.22–29; he was mixing wine when Telemachus arrived, 16.13–14. Thus at the farm Laertes continues spading vines when Odysseus approaches, 24.242–243. The next arrival brings what has been thought the oddity of 24.385–389:

ἐξείης ἕζοντο κατὰ κλισμούς τε θρόνους τε.
ἔνθ' οἱ μὲν δείπνῳ ἐπεχείρεον· ἀγχίμολον δὲ

ἦλθ' ὁ γέρων Δολίος, σὺν δ' υἱεῖς τοῖο γέροντος,
ἐξ ἔργων μογέοντες, ἐπεὶ προμολοῦσα κάλεσσε
μήτηρ, γρηῦς Σικελή.

Those already at the farm were sitting down and about to eat when
Dolius and his six sons came in. As Odysseus says at 396, they
were waiting for them. The common line for dining (e.g. 1.149,
*Il.*9.91) does not fit the delay. The arrival is explained; the old
Sikel woman had summoned her husband and sons who returned
thunderstruck. Line 388 can only mean "pressing (hastening,
straining) from the fields," not as taken by Page and in *LSJ*, "tired
from work." The present participle marks continuing action. In
the description of Nestor's cup, *Il.*11.636–637, any other man, it
is said, would straining, μογέων, move it from the table when it
was full, but he lifted it effortlessly, ἀμογητί. At the destruction of
the Achaean wall, *Il.*12.29, the swollen Trojan rivers carried away
logs and timbers that the Achaeans straining, μογέοντες, set in
place. As commonly (6.259, *Il.* 16.392) ἔργα means fields. The arrivals of the poem continue to this nearly last scene, and the unique
phrases describe the astonished moment.

(3) The detail of emotion matches that of dress, occupation, and
scene. In prospect or retrospect the suitor-slaying overhung the
firelit meeting and later recognition at the palace. Meeting and recognition now stand alone. A more visionary close is preempted by
the climax at the palace, the review of the Second Nekyia, and the
familiar but necessary theme of test. Odysseus' first speech of the
poem, his reply to Calypso's offer to help him on his way, 5.173–
179, showed his sceptical desire for proof; he would not believe
her until she swore by the Styx. As Athene directed, 13.336, and as
he told Telemachus, 19.45–46, he roused Penelope's feelings in
order that for grief she might tell everything. He must act likewise
toward Laertes. Achilles, for all his humanity to Priam, is formidable to the end, *Il.*24.560–570; he remains capable of huge anger,
as is Oedipus in the *Coloneus*. Odysseus too remains himself; detail of emotion, both his and Laertes', crowns the detail of scene.

Several necessities—to end yet to bind together, to be vivid yet
in a small scene, to finish the line of recognitions yet (the great recognition being past) with the mixture of raillery and love of which
the goddess was Odysseus' model—help explain the language. If
battle, travel, assembly, and such wide themes are most traditional

to the poetry, this rural scene may be least traditional. Mycenaean overtones are now remote; the world of Hesiod's *Works and Days* is nearer. Yet the story demands this close; Odysseus is at once the ultimate traveler and his place-fixed father's son. The Second Nekyia summarizes much previous recollection of Troy, at Pylos and Sparta, in Demodocus' songs, and in the First Nekyia. The final encounter with the suitors' kinsmen reverts to Haliserthes' warning of Book 2 and the divine decisions of Books 1 and 5. The intervening scene at the farm likewise reverts and completes but more isolatedly.

To turn to specific points, on approaching his father Odysseus ponders whether he should embrace him and announce his return or test him, 24.235–238:

> μερμήριξε δ' ἔπειτα κατὰ φρένα καὶ κατὰ θυμὸν
> κύσσαι καὶ περιφῦναι ἑὸν πατέρ', ἠδὲ ἕκαστα
> εἰπεῖν, ὡς ἔλθοι καὶ ἵκοιτ' ἐς πατρίδα γαῖαν,
> ἦ πρῶτ' ἐξερέοιτο ἕκαστά τε πειρήσαιτο.

Verbs of dubitation may be followed wholly by optatives (6.141–144, *Il.* 1.189–192), wholly by infinitives (*Il.* 8.168) or as here and at 20.10–12 by both (*Il.*16.647–651 combine infinitives and subjunctives). Most such optatives look to the future, but at 4.789–790 Penelope ponders whether Telemachus has escaped death or perished by the suitors (D. B. Monro, *Homeric Grammar* 303). This past usage recurs here. It has been called Attic indirect discourse, but εἰπεῖν often takes object clauses (8.577, 11.480, 14.447); it takes ὡς at 15.158 and 22.351. The optatives of 237–238 evidently follow in a sequence of dubitation, not by indirect discourse. H. Ebeling (*Lexicon Homericum* II 498, col. 1) remarks of the passage, *ubi non est se venisse, sed quomodo venisset;* the just cited passages with ὡς are similar. Odysseus ponders whether he should tell how he returned and reached his fatherland, not that he had returned. The often repeated line following the quoted passage (e.g. 4.120) shows him reaching a decision.

His speech to his father begins, 24.244–249:

> ὦ γέρον, οὐκ ἀδαημονίη σ' ἔχει ἀμφιπολεύειν
> ὄρχατον, ἀλλ' εὖ τοι κομιδὴ ἔχει, οὐδέ τι πάμπαν,
> οὐ φυτόν, οὐ συκέη, οὐκ ἄμπελος, οὐ μὲν ἐλαίη,

οὐκ ὄγχνη, οὐ πρασιή τοι ἄνευ κομιδῆς κατὰ κῆπον.
ἄλλο δέ τοι ἐρέω, σὺ δὲ μὴ χόλον ἔνθεο θυμῷ,
αὐτόν σ᾽ οὐκ ἀγαθὴ κομιδὴ ἔχει.

There are two antitheses: the first between ignorance of gardening and care of plants, the second between Laertes' care of his plants and his care of himself. The verb ἔχω often has abstract subjects (e.g. 9.95, *Il.*21.542–543); in Ebeling's words (*Lexicon* I 518, col. 1) *saepe status sive affectus quem nobis videntur homines habere, dicuntur occupare et quasi habere hominem.* By further Homeric usage (e.g. 12.232, 14.239), ὄρχατον at 245 continues as the implied object of κομιδὴ ἔχει. εὖ does not, as has been claimed, stand with ἔχει as in the later Attic construction; strengthened by τοι it enhances the contrast to the previous line (as Ebeling further remarks, II 237, col. 2, it is a function of τοι, *ut enuntiatis addet vim affirmationis*). Thus at 245 not inexperience of tending a garden possesses Laertes; his tendance keeps the garden well indeed. But, Odysseus concludes, his care of the garden does not extend to himself. The usage is Homeric, and its slight complication expresses Odysseus' smiling, partly precautionary overture.

In his comment on the garden, the second syllable of ὄγχνη 247, is elided in a rare but familiar way (Page lists the parallels). Odysseus makes his effect by listing, and the pear tree keeps an attested place in the line (7.115, 120, 11.589). Metrical variety marked the earlier description of Alcinous' garden: the two-syllabled συκέαι of 7.116 after the just preceding three-syllabled μηλέαι; the genitive θέρευς, 7.118, of which the ending matches in the same position that of ᾽Οδυσεῦς, 24.398; ἀφιεῖσαι, 7.126, of which the long iota of the stem is often short. Gardening is a rare Homeric theme. The pretended stranger's tale of having once entertained Odysseus shares two lines with the pretended Cretan's similar tale to Penelope, 24.271–272 = 19.194–195. A third repetition, 24.268 = 19.351, ξείνων τηλεδαπῶν φιλίων ἐμὸν ἵκετο δῶμα, is preceded here by οὔ πώ τις βροτὸς ἄλλος and in Penelope's previous speech by οὐ γάρ πώ τις ἀνὴρ πεπνυμένος ὧδε. The comparative φιλίων, taken as such by the scholiast and Eustathius, is nearly echoed by Eumaeus at another arrival, οὐδ᾽ εἰ κακίων σέθεν ἔλθοι, 14.56. Two of the four Iliadic uses of γλυκίων, 2.453 = 11.13, repeat the metrical position of φιλίων. As Stanford notes at

4.684–685, Penelope in her emotion tends to run ideas together: there the ideas, would that the suitors had never courted me, not met away from home, were eating their last meal; at 19.351, no stranger so wise as ever come more welcome. Rushing words describe her. But if 19.351 is genuine, its repetition here further unites the moments before recognitions. Two lines about the gifts that the pretended stranger gave Odysseus—cloaks, cloths, robes, chitons, 24.276–277—recur in the loading of Priam's cart, *Il.*24.230–231, and in order and structure repeat Eumaeus' enumeration of Odysseus' herds and flocks, 14.100–101. The poet's compositional habit is evident.

Not a line of Laertes' feeling reply, 280–301, lacks known formulae or words in attested positions, yet its novel burden—namely, the welcome that the pretended stranger would have had in Ithaca were Odysseus alive—prompts a few novelties of phrase. ξενίη as an abstract noun, 286 repeated at 314, in both places enlarges the idea of δῶρα. Such a paired intrusion of rare words shows again, for example, in ὀλιγηπελέων and ὀλιγηπελίη, 5.457, 468; a situation momentarily grips the vocabulary. In καὶ ξενίη ἀγαθῇ· ἡ γὰρ θέμις ὅστις ὑπάρξῃ, 286, the compound verb in the sense of "initiate, first provide" merely varies the simple verb and noun familiar in that position. *Il.*9.102 is structurally and metrically close; θέμις accompanies the idea of gifts at 9.268, 14.56, and *Il.*11.779. The unique ordinal πόστον, 288, follows many such: the twentieth year since Odysseus left, 19.222, the tenth when Troy fell, 5.107, the eighth when Odysseus left Calypso, 7.261, the third and soon the fourth that Penelope has charmed the suitors, 2.89, and in Odysseus' present reply the fifth since he visited the alleged stranger, 24.309. Except for the repeated ξενίη, 314, and for descriptive names like those of the Phaeacian athletes and of some suitors and others, Odysseus' twelve-line reply shows expected words and positions.

The start of the recognition, 315–320, shares two and a half lines with the intense scene when Achilles learns of Patroclus' death, *Il.* 18.22–24; the end of 317 recurs in the mourning for Patroclus, *Il.*23.225. If Laertes' transient sorrow suffers by comparison, use of the same language for differently weighted events is not uncommon; Hector's last words to Andromache, *Il.*6.490–493, twice recur with minor change in Telemachus' dismissal of his mother, 1.356–359, 21.350–353. The next lines on Odysseus' response to his father's sorrow uniquely describe what seems the sudden onset of tears, 318–319:

τοῦ δ'ὠρίνετο θυμός, ἀνὰ ῥῖνας δέ οἱ ἤδη
δριμὺ μένος προύτυψε φιλον πατέρ' εἰσορόωντι.

Every element except ἀνὰ ῥῖνας is parallelled in the same position, and *Il.*16.349 gives an analogue to that phrase. δριμύ used at *Il.* 11.270 of the pang of childbirth evidently signifies a seizure. A. S. Gow on Theocritus I 18 cites the somewhat vague Anacreontic 29.7, which may mean tears. He in any case seems right in understanding, with Eustathius and one scholiast, the words to mean an onset of tears, as against Stanford and the other scholiast who understand anger. The blinding of the Cyclops, 9.388–390, and itemization of wounds in the *Iliad* show a like almost clinical interest.

If one wanted to make a case against the authenticity of the episode, the lines to fix on might be those in which Odysseus goes on to list his tokens of recognition. Not that the scar is unfamiliar. A few parts of lines recur from the long narrative of the boar-hunt: 24.332—19.393, 24.333—19.462, and from other previous passages, 24.331—19.391, 24.335—21.13 and 4.6. But the shorter scale of this account on the whole finds new phrases. The trees and vines that Laertes gave Odysseus as a boy are a fresh subject that has only scattered parallels: 24.336—*Il.*20.496, 24.337–13.306 and 1.67, 24.338—21.21 and 16.426. At 24.340 the trees are in an order similar to 7.120; at 24.341–342 the numerals are in attested places; the start and end of 24.344 are familiar. But one of these phrases, παιδνὸς ἐών 24.338, is striking because it recurs from the nearer of the two other accounts of Odysseus' youth, when he met Iphitus in Messenia and got the bow, 20.21. Laertes' emotion on being convinced brings back other recoveries. 24.345–346 nearly repeat Penelope's glad recognition, 23.205–206; the old man embraces his son as she did Telemachus on his return, 24.347—17.38. The unique word for Laertes' fainting, ἀποψύχ-οντα 348, echoes in the same position the term for drying off sweat, *Il.*22.2. In πίονι δήμῳ, πίονι δημῷ, M. L. Nagler discusses the use of such like-sounding words ("Towards a Generative View of the Oral Formula" 269–311; *Spontaneity and Tradition* 6–9). To the departure of father and son to join the others at the farmhouse the only novelty is Laertes' exclamation that there are indeed gods on Olympus, 351. Not a word even of that joyous line lacks parallels in the same position; the sole change is in syntax.

By Athene's magical hand the old man, after a bath and in clothes quite different from his former sad attire, receives such a rejuvenation, 367–371, as Odysseus had at 6.229–235, 8.18–20, 16.172–176, and 23.156–163 and Penelope at 18.187–196; usages recur. Like Nestor at *Il.*11.670–762, he wishes that he might have shown against the suitors the power that he had in the battles of his youth. The company now including Telemachus, Eumaeus, and Philoitius is about to begin eating when the astounded Dolius and his six sons rush back from the fields in the manner described in (2) above. For the name Dolius, Stanford cites the argument of M. Lambertz ("Zur Etymologie von δοῦλος") that the short vowel of the stem reflects non-Greek names that to Greek ears could convey both slavery and cunning. It is clearly one of the many so-called speaking names of the poem, used of three people: of Penelope's now old gardener, 4.735–736, who like her bed-keeper Actoris, 23.228, on her marriage accompanied her to Ithaca; of the father of Melanthius and Melantho, 17.212, 18.322; and of Laertes' present slave, husband of the Sikel woman and father of the six sons. The poet does not connect the three, and it seems idle to pursue the possibility. The word δοῦλος is notably absent from Homer, though it shows in a feminine, an adjective, and an abstract noun. The two connotations of servitude and cunning variously mark the three uses of the name.

Dolius' approach and first words follow, 397–402:

Ὣς ἄρ'ἔφη, Δολίος δ'ἰθὺς κίε χεῖρε πετάσσας
ἀμφοτέρας, 'Οδυσεὺς δὲ λαβὼν κύσε χεῖρ'ἐπὶ
   καρπῷ,
καί μιν φωνήσας ἔπεα πτερόεντα προσηύδα.
"ὦ φίλ', ἐπεὶ νόστησας ἐελδομένοισι μάλ'ἡμῖν
οὐδ'ἔτ'ὀϊομένοισι, θεοὶ δέ σε ἤγαγον αὐτοί,
οὐλέ τε καὶ μάλα χαῖρε, θεοὶ δέ τοι ὄλβια δοῖεν.

The start of 402 is parallelled only at *H. H. Apoll.* 466; the end occurs in Odysseus' acceptance of Euryalus' apology after the games at Scheria, 8.413. He has just bidden Dolius cease from amazement, θάμβευς 394. The contracted genitive appeared in the previously noted θέρευς 7.118 (so θάρσευς *Il.*17.573) and may contribute to one of the two chief oddities of the whole episode, the unique such genitive of the name Odysseus at 398. The rest of the line, notably including the name in the nominative (some twenty other times in the poem), shows familiar positions. As J. B. Hainsworth says (*The Flexibility of the Homeric Formula* 30), "It is too readily assumed within the terms of Parry's theory that because a formula is supposed to be called to mind when it is required so it comes to mind *only* when required. . . . I assume that from time to time formulae force themselves upon his attention which he can only deploy in the verse by bending them out of their normal shape." Chantraine (*Grammaire Homérique* I 36–38) notes uncontracted short syllables replacing a long at theseis: e.g. νέα 9.283, πλέων 1.183, Μηκιστέος υἱός *Il.*2.566, Πηλέος υἱός *Il.*16.21 (the latter two in most manuscripts). Those genitives can appear as -ηος if the first syllable of υἱός is treated as short, but -ηος is impossible at 398. The line contains elements of the famous *Il.* 24.478, χερσὶν 'Αχιλλῆος λάβε γούνατα καί κύσε χεῖρας. The uncontracted genitive 'Οδυσσέος, though with two sigmas in the stem and the short final syllables in the arsis of the foot, appears at *Il.*4.491. The accusative 'Οδυσσέα is unique at 17.301. The other words of 398 take common places, usages collide, and as elsewhere the poet adjusts. The genitive of the name Odysseus must be contracted here; it resembles in the same position the genitives θέρευς and θάμβευς noted above. The lines fit the vivid scene.

What may seem the other main oddity is metrical; it occurs near the start of the episode when Odysseus ponders how he should address his father, 239–240:

ὧδε δέ οἱ φρονέοντι δοάσσετο κέρδιον εἶναι
πρῶτον κερτομίοις ἐπέεσσιν πειρηθῆναι.

Page rightly calls unique the use of nu-movable to lengthen the arsis of the fourth foot, but Wernicke's law which he cites is shown by Thea Stiffler to be unknown to Homer, though operative for Alexandrian and later writers ("Die Wernickesche Gesetz und die bukolische Dihärese"). She lists, p. 330, other instances (*Il.* 2.522, 813, 5.734, 7.436, 19.384, 21.494) where the lengthened short might have been avoided by a shift of order, as it might have been here by πειρηθῆναι ἐπέεσσι, and she cites, p. 346, three trochees remaining in the position (*Il.* 11.36, 10.292 = *Od.* 3.382). They resemble, she thinks, the shorts that exceptionally appear in theseis. The obvious reason why the order is not shifted here is the quantitatively similar uses of πειράομαι and πειρητίζω: sixteen other times in the *Odyssey*, including the just previous πειρήσαιτο 238, fourteen times in the *Iliad*. Usage evidently dictates, but whereas other occurrences commonly involve contest—e.g. στίχας ἀνδρῶν πειρητίζων, τόξου πειρησαίμην—Odysseus now makes his trial by words, not of them. Thea Stiffler explains the comparative rarity of lengthened final syllables in the fourth foot by the convenience of trochaic endings before one of the earlier cesurae but their inconvenience soon thereafter. T. L. Agar ("The Lengthening of Final Syllables by Position before the Fifth Foot in the Homeric Hexameter") adduces early forms that he thinks were changed to conform to Alexandrian practice.

If these two last usages—the genitive 'Οδυσεῦς at 398 and the nu-movable making position at the end of the fourth foot of 240— are the chief irregularities of the episode, they hardly suffice to mark it un-Homeric. An average of verbal and metrical irregularities in any two hundred lines of the poems obviously cannot be had. The nature of the episodes and, still more undeterminable, the poet's state of attention will always have varied. People's response to the episode at the farm doubtless also varies, but a few points are firm: the poem demands it, it verges toward the close, in combining the themes of test, recognition, and return it shows some but not all sides of Odysseus, and it is narrow in scope. Those who think it a decline from the rest of the poem may imagine the poet hastening to finish; all must grant its exceptional confinement to homely intimacy. These considerations affirm its genuineness, and the language does not conflict.

References

A. W. H. Adkins, *Merit and Responsibility*, Oxford 1960.

T. L. Agar, "The Lengthening of Final Syllables before the Fifth Foot of the Homeric Hexameter," *Class. Rev.* 11 (1897) 29–31.

Lydia Allione, *Telemaco e Penelope nell' Odissea*, Universita di Torino Publicazioni della Faculta di Littere e Filosofia 14, Fascicolo 3, 1963.

Erich Auerbach, *Mimesis*, transl. by W. Trask, Princeton 1953.

Norman Austin, *Archery at the Dark of the Moon*, Berkeley 1975.

Sylvia Benton, "The Cave of Polis," *Annual of the British School at Athens* 35 (1934–35) 35–130.

Victor Bérard, *Dans le sillage d'Ulysse*, Paris 1933; *Les navigations d'Ulysse*, Paris 1927–1929.

Siegfried Besslich, *Schweigen-Verschweigen-Übergehen*, Heidelberg 1966.

Alan Blakeway, "Greek Commerce with the West, 800–600 B.C.," *Annual of the British School at Athens* 33 (1932–33) 170–208.

E. D. S. Bradford, *Ulysses Found*, London 1963.

Walter Burkert, *Homo Necans*, Berlin 1972; "Von Amenophis II. Zur Bogenprobe des Odysseus," *Grazer Beiträge* 1 (1973) 69–78; "Die Leistung eines Kreophylus," *Mus. Helv.* 29 (1972) 74–85.

D. E. Bynum, "Themes of the Young Hero in Serbocroatian Oral Epic Tradition," *PMLA* 83 (1968) 1293–1303.

Rhys Carpenter, *Folk Tale, Fiction, and Saga in the Homeric Epics*, Berkeley 1946.

Pierre Chantraine, *Grammaire homèrique*[2], Paris 1948–1953.

H. W. Clarke, *The Art of the Odyssey*, Prentice-Hall, Englewood Cliffs, N.Y. 1967.

Marcel Detienne, *Les maîtres de vérité dans la Grèce archaique*, Paris 1967.

George Devereux, "Penelope's Character," *Psychoanalytic Quarterly* 26 (1957) 378–386.

G. E. Dimock, Jr., "The Name of Odysseus," *Hudson Review* 9 (1956) 52–70.

E. R. Dodds, *The Greeks and the Irrational*, Berkeley 1951.

T. J. Dunbabin, *The Greeks and their Eastern Neighbors*, The Society for the Promotion of Hellenic Studies, London 1957; "The Early History of Corinth," *J.H.S.* 68 (1948) 59–69.

Heinrich Ebeling, *Lexicon Homericum*, Leipzig 1885.

Hartmut Erbse, *Beiträge zum Verständnis der Odyssee*, Berlin 1972.

Eustathii Commentarii ad Homeri Odysseam, Hildesheim 1960.

M. I. Finley, *The World of Odysseus*, New York 1954.

Friedrich Focke, *Die Odyssee*, Tubinger Beiträge 37, 1943.

D. G. Frame, *The Myth of Return*, New Haven 1978.

Gabriel Germain, *Genèse de l'Odyssée*, Paris 1954.

Oskar Hackman, *Die Polyphemsage in der Volksüberlieferung*, Helsinki 1904.

J. B. Hainsworth, *The Flexibility of the Homeric Formula*, Oxford 1968.

Albert Hartman, *Untersuchungen über die Sagen vom Tod des Odysseus*, Munich 1917.

Hesiod, *Hesiodi Opera*, ed. Friedrich Solmsen, Oxford 1970; *Theogony*, M. L. West, Oxford 1966; *Fragmenta Hesiodea*, ed. Reinhold Merkelbach and M. L. West, Oxford 1967.

Alfred Heubeck, *Der Odyssee-Dichter und die Ilias*, Erlangen 1954.

Homer, *Homeri Opera, Ilias*[3], ed. D. B. Monro and T. W. Allen, Oxford 1919; *Odysseia*[2], ed. T. W. Allen, Oxford 1917. Vol. V, 1911; *Homer's Odyssey* I–XII[2], ed. W. W. Merry and James Riddell, Oxford 1886; *Homer's Odyssey* XIII–XXIV, ed. D. B. Monro, Oxford 1901; *The Odyssey of Homer*, ed. W. B. Stanford, London 1955; *Scholia Graeca in Homeri Odysseam*, Wilhelm Dindorf, Oxford 1855.

G. L. Huxley, *Greek Epic Poetry, from Eumelus to Panyassis*, London 1969; "Odysseus and the Thesprotian Oracle of the Dead," *La Parola del Passato* 61 (1958) 245–248.

Felix Jacoby, "Die geistige Physiognomie der Odyssee," *Die Antike* 9 (1933) 159–194 = *Kleine philologische Schriften* I 107–138, Berlin 1961.

Werner Jaeger, "Solons Eunomie," *Sitzungsber. der Preuss. Akad. der Wissensch.,* Phil.-Hist. Kl. 11 (1926) 69–85 = *Scripta Minora* I 314–337, Rome 1960.

Adolf Kirchhoff, *Die Homerische Odyssee²*, Berlin 1879.

G. S. Kirk, *Myth: Its Meaning and Function in Ancient and other Cultures,* Berkeley 1970.

M. Lambertz, "Zur Etymologie von δοῦλος," *Glotta* 6 (1914) 1–18.

Albin Lesky, "Göttliche und menschliche Motivation in Homerischen Epos," *Sitzungsber. der Heidelberger Akad. der Wissensch.,* Phil.-Hist. Kl. (1961) 1–52.

Claude Lévi-Strauss, *La pensée sauvage,* Paris 1962; *Le cru et le cuit,* Paris 1964; "The Structural Study of Myth," *Journ. of American Folklore* 68 (1965) 428–444.

Hugh Lloyd-Jones, *The Justice of Zeus,* Berkeley 1973.

A. B. Lord, *The Singer of Tales,* Cambridge, Mass., 1960.

H. L. Lorimer, *Homer and the Monuments,* London 1950.

Bronislaw Malinowski, *Argonauts of the Western Pacific,* London 1922; *Myth in Primitive Psychology,* New York 1926.

Wilhelm Mattes, *Odysseus bei den Phaaken,* Wurzburg 1958.

Reinhold Merkelbach, *Untersuchungen zur Odyssee,* Zetemata 2, Munich 1969.

Karl Meuli, *Odyssee und Argonautika,* Berlin 1929.

D. B. Monro, *A Grammar of the Homeric Dialect²*, Oxford 1891.

Louis Moulinier, *Quelques hypothèses relatives a la géographie d'Homère dans l'Odyssée,* Annales de la Faculté des Lettres, N.S.23, Aix-en-Provence 1958.

Marion Müller, *Athene als göttliche Helferin in der Odyssee,* Heidelberg 1966.

Gilbert Murray, *The Rise of the Greek Epic²*, Oxford 1911.

M. N. Nagler, *Spontaneity and Tradition,* Berkeley 1974; "Towards a Generative View of the Oral Formula," *T.A.P.A.* 98 (1967) 269–311.

Gregory Nagy, *Comparative Studies in Greek and Indic Meter,* Cambridge, Mass., 1974; "Phaethon, Sappho's Phaon, and the White Rock of Leukas," *H.S.C.P.* 77 (1973) 137–177.

M. P. Nilsson, *The Minoan-Mycenaean Religion and its Survival in Greek Religion²*, Lund 1950.

Mauricio Obregón, *Ulysses Airborne,* New York 1971.

D. L. Page, *The Homeric Odyssey,* Oxford 1955; *Folktales in Homer's Odyssey,* Cambridge, Mass., 1973.

L. R. Palmer, *Mycenaeans and Minoans,* New York 1962.

Gilbert Pillot, *Le code secret de l'Odyssée,* Paris 1969; transl. by F. E. Albert, New York 1972.

J. B. Pritchard, *Ancient Near Eastern Texts*[3], Princeton 1969.

Karl Reinhardt, *Tradition und Geist,* Göttingen 1960.

Lord Rennell of Rodd, "The Ithaca of the Odyssey," *Annual of the British School at Athens* 33 (1932) 1–21.

P. W. Rose, "Class Ambivalence in the *Odyssey,*" *Historia* 24 (1975) 129–149.

Auguste Rousseau-Liessens, *Géographie de l'Odyssée,* Brussels 1961–1964.

Klaus Rüter, *Odysseeinterpretationen,* ed. by Kjeld Matthiessen, Hypomnemata 19, Göttingen 1969.

Wolfgang Schadewaldt, "Die beiden Dichter der Odyssee," in *Homer. Die Odyssee Übersetzt,* Hamburg 1958; *Von Homers Welt und Werk,* Stuttgart 1965.

Eduard Schwartz, *Die Odyssee,* Munich 1924.

Charles Segal, "Transition and Ritual in Odysseus' Return," *La Parola del Passato* 116 (1967) 321–342.

Bruno Snell, *Die Entdeckung des Geistes,* Hamburg 1948, transl. by T. G. Rosenmeyer, *The Discovery of the Mind,* Cambridge, Mass., 1953; "Die Welt der Götter bei Hesiod," *Fondation Hardt, Entretiens* 1, Geneva 1952.

Theodore Spencer, *Shakespeare and the Nature of Man,* New York 1942.

Thea Stiffler, "Die Wernickesche Gesetz und die bukolische Dihärase," *Philologus* 79 (1924) 323–354.

Agathe Thornton, *People and Themes in Homer's Odyssey,* London and Dunedin 1976.

E. T. Vermeule, *Greece in the Bronze Age,* Chicago 1964.

Paolo Vivante, *The Homeric Imagination,* Bloomington 1970.

P. Von der Mühll, "Odyssee," *R.E.* Suppl. 7 (1940) 696–768.

T. B. L. Webster, *From Mycenae to Homer,* London 1955.

C. H. Whitman, *Homer and the Heroic Tradition,* Cambridge, Mass., 1958.

Ulrich von Wilamowitz-Moellendorff, *Homerische Untersuchungen,* Berlin 1884; *Die Heimkehr des Odysseus,* Berlin 1927.

W. J. Woodhouse, *The Composition of Homer's Odyssey,* Oxford 1930.

Index of Passages

Index of Subjects